Advance Praise for *Finnish Lessons*

"The story of Finland's extraordinary educational reforms is one that should inform policymakers and educators around the world. No one tells this story more clearly and engagingly than Pasi Sahlberg, who has lived and studied these reforms for decades. This book is a must read."

—**Linda Darling-Hammond,** Charles E. Ducommun Professor of Education and Co-Director of the Stanford Center for Opportunity Policy in Education, Stanford University

"A terrific synthesis by a native Finn, a teacher, a researcher and a policy analyst all rolled up into one excellent writer. Pasi Sahlberg teaches us a great deal about what we need to know before engaging in national educational reforms."

—**David C. Berliner,** Regents' Professor of Education, Arizona State University

"Pasi Sahlberg is the best education policy expert to share the Finnish experience with the international community. I have known him for decades and this book confirms that he is not only a practitioner but also a visionary that we Finns need when searching for the solutions to our educational challenges."

—**Erkki Aho,** Director General (1973–1991), Finnish National Board of Education

"This book is a wake-up call for the United States. Finland went from mediocre academic results to one of the top performers in the world. And they did it with teacher unions, minimal testing, national collaboration, and elevating teaching to a high-status calling. This is the antidote to the NCLB paralysis."

—**Henry M. Levin,** William Heard Kilpatrick Professor of Economics and Education, Teachers College, Columbia University and David Jacks Professor of Education and Economics, Emeritus, Stanford University

"It is essential also for us Finns to get a balanced analysis of what really is behind the success of the Finnish educational system. Pasi Sahlberg, as an insider, knows what has happened and, as a researcher, has an objective perspective on cause and effect relationships. This story makes sense to me."

—**Olli-Pekka Heinonen,** Director, Finnish Broadcasting Company, and former Minister of Education (1994–1999)

"Finland's remarkable educational story, so well told in this book by Pasi Sahlberg, is both informative and inspiring for others because it shows that with appropriate effort sustained over time, a country can make huge improvements for its young people, something that all countries aspire to do."

—**Ben Levin,** Canada Research Chair, Ontario Institute for Studies in Education, University of Toronto

WITHDRAWN

the series on school reform

Patricia A. Wasley
University
of Washington

Ann Lieberman
Senior Scholar,
Stanford University

Joseph P. McDonald
New York
University

SERIES EDITORS

Finnish Lessons: What Can the World Learn
from Educational Change in Finland?
PASI SAHLBERG

The Networked Teacher: How New Teachers Build
Social Networks for Professional Support
KIRA J. BAKER-DOYLE

How Teachers Become Leaders:
Learning from Practice and Research
ANN LIEBERMAN & LINDA D. FRIEDRICH

Peer Review and Teacher Leadership:
Linking Professionalism and Accountability
JENNIFER GOLDSTEIN

Improving the Odds: Developing Powerful Teaching
Practice and a Culture of Learning in Urban High Schools
THOMAS DEL PRETE

The Mindful Teacher
ELIZABETH MACDONALD & DENNIS SHIRLEY

Going to Scale with New School Designs:
Reinventing High School
JOSEPH P. MCDONALD, EMILY J. KLEIN, & MEG RIORDAN

Managing to Change: How Schools Can Survive
(and Sometimes Thrive) in Turbulent Times
THOMAS HATCH

Teacher Practice Online: Sharing Wisdom, Opening Doors
DÉSIRÉE H. POINTER MACE

Teaching the Way Children Learn
BEVERLY FALK

Teachers in Professional Communities:
Improving Teaching and Learning
ANN LIEBERMAN & LYNNE MILLER, EDS.

Looking Together at Student Work, 2nd Ed.
TINA BLYTHE, DAVID ALLEN, &
BARBARA SCHIEFFELIN POWELL

The Power of Protocols:
An Educator's Guide to Better Practice, 2nd Ed.
JOSEPH P. MCDONALD, NANCY MOHR, ALAN DICHTER, &
ELIZABETH C. MCDONALD

Schools-within-Schools:
Possibilities and Pitfalls of High School Reform
VALERIE E. LEE & DOUGLAS D. READY

Seeing Through Teachers' Eyes:
Professional Ideals and Classroom Practices
KAREN HAMMERNESS

Building School-Based Teacher Learning Communities:
Professional Strategies to Improve Student Achievement
MILBREY MCLAUGHLIN & JOAN TALBERT

Mentors in the Making:
Developing New Leaders for New Teachers
BETTY ACHINSTEIN & STEVEN Z. ATHANASES, EDS.

Community in the Making: Lincoln Center Institute, the
Arts, and Teacher Education
MADELEINE FUCHS HOLZER & SCOTT NOPPE-BRANDON, EDS.

Holding Accountability Accountable:
What Ought to Matter in Public Education
KENNETH A. SIROTNIK, ED.

Mobilizing Citizens for Better Schools
ROBERT F. SEXTON

The Comprehensive High School Today
FLOYD M. HAMMACK, ED.

The Teaching Career
JOHN I. GOODLAD & TIMOTHY J. MCMANNON, EDS.

Beating the Odds:
High Schools as Communities of Commitment
JACQUELINE ANCESS

At the Heart of Teaching: A Guide to Reflective Practice
GRACE HALL MCENTEE, JON APPLEBY, JOANNE DOWD,
JAN GRANT, SIMON HOLE, & PEGGY SILVA, WITH
JOSEPH W. CHECK

Teaching Youth Media: A Critical Guide to Literacy,
Video Production, and Social Change
STEVEN GOODMAN

Inside the National Writing Project:
Connecting Network Learning and Classroom Teaching
ANN LIEBERMAN & DIANE WOOD

Standards Reform in High-Poverty Schools:
Managing Conflict and Building Capacity
CAROL A. BARNES

Standards of Mind and Heart:
Creating the Good High School
PEGGY SILVA & ROBERT A. MACKIN

Upstart Startup:
Creating and Sustaining a Public Charter School
JAMES NEHRING

One Kid at a Time:
Big Lessons from a Small School
ELIOT LEVINE

Guiding School Change:
The Role and Work of Change Agents
FRANCES O'CONNELL RUST & HELEN FREIDUS, EDS.

Teachers Caught in the Action:
Professional Development That Matters
ANN LIEBERMAN & LYNNE MILLER, EDS.

(Continued)

the series on school reform, *continued*

The Competent Classroom:
Aligning High School Curriculum, Standards, and
Assessment—A Creative Teaching Guide
ALLISON ZMUDA & MARY TOMAINO

Central Park East and Its Graduates: "Learning by Heart"
DAVID BENSMAN

Taking Charge of Curriculum:
Teacher Networks and Curriculum Implementation
JACOB E. ADAMS, JR.

Teaching With Power:
Shared Decision-Making and Classroom Practice
CAROL REED

Good Schools/Real Schools:
Why School Reform Doesn't Last
DEAN FINK

Beyond Formulas in Mathematics and Teaching:
Dynamics of the High School Algebra Classroom
DANIEL CHAZAN

School Reform Behind the Scenes
JOSEPH P. MCDONALD, THOMAS HATCH, EDWARD KIRBY,
NANCY AMES, NORRIS M. HAYNES, & EDWARD T. JOYNER

Looking Together at Student Work: A Companion Guide
to Assessing Student Learning
TINA BLYTHE, DAVID ALLEN, & BARBARA SHIEFFELIN POWELL

Looking at Student Work:
A Window into the Classroom (Video)
ANNENBERG INSTITUTE FOR SCHOOL REFORM

Teachers—Transforming Their World and Their Work
ANN LIEBERMAN & LYNNE MILLER

Teaching in Common:
Challenges to Joint Work in Classrooms and Schools
ANNE DIPARDO

Charter Schools: Another Flawed Educational Reform?
SEYMOUR B. SARASON

Assessing Student Learning:
From Grading to Understanding
DAVID ALLEN, ED.

Racing with the Clock: Making Time for Teaching and
Learning in School Reform
NANCY E. ADELMAN, KAREN PANTON WALKING EAGLE, &
ANDY HARGREAVES, EDS.

The Role of State Departments of Education in Complex
School Reform
SUSAN FOLLETT LUSI

Making Professional Development Schools Work:
Politics, Practice, and Policy
MARSHA LEVINE & ROBERTA TRACHTMAN, EDS.

How It Works—Inside a School–College Collaboration
SIDNEY TRUBOWITZ & PAUL LONGO

Surviving School Reform: A Year in the Life of One School
LARAINE K. HONG

Eyes on the Child: Three Portfolio Stories
KATHE JERVIS

Revisiting "The Culture of the School and the Problem
of Change"
SEYMOUR B. SARASON

Teacher Learning: New Policies, New Practices
MILBREY W. MCLAUGHLIN & IDA OBERMAN, EDS.

What's Happening in Math Class? Envisioning New
Practices Through Teacher Narratives (Vol. 1)
DEBORAH SCHIFTER, ED.

What's Happening in Math Class? Reconstructing
Professional Identities (Vol. 2)
DEBORAH SCHIFTER, ED.

The Subjects in Question:
Departmental Organization and the High School
LESLIE SANTEE SISKIN & JUDITH WARREN LITTLE, EDS.

Authentic Assessment in Action:
Studies of Schools and Students at Work
LINDA DARLING-HAMMOND, JACQUELINE ANCESS, &
BEVERLY FALK

School Work:
Gender and the Cultural Construction of Teaching
SARI KNOPP BIKLEN

School Change: The Personal Development of a Point of View
SEYMOUR B. SARASON

The Work of Restructuring Schools: Building from the
Ground Up
ANN LIEBERMAN, ED.

Stirring the Chalkdust: Tales of Teachers Changing
Classroom Practice
PATRICIA A. WASLEY

Finnish Lessons

What Can the World Learn

from Educational Change in Finland?

Pasi Sahlberg

Foreword by Andy Hargreaves

Teachers College, Columbia University
New York and London

Excerpt from *Rumblin'* on p. ix: Words and music by Neil Young.
Copyright © 2010 by Silver Fiddle Music. All rights reserved. Used with permission.
Reprinted by permission of Hal Leonard Corporation.

Published by Teachers College Press, 1234 Amsterdam Avenue, New York, NY 10027

Library of Congress Cataloging-in-Publication Data

Sahlberg, Pasi.
    Finnish lessons : what can the world learn from educational change in Finland /
        Pasi Sahlberg ; foreword by Andy Hargreaves.
            p. cm.
    ISBN 978-0-8077-5257-9
        1. Educational change—Finland. 2. Education—Finland. I. Title.
    LA1013.7.S34 2011
    370.94897—dc23   2011033428

ISBN 978-0-8077-5257-9 (paper)

Printed on acid-free paper
Manufactured in the United States of America

18   17   16   15   14   13   12   8   7   6   5

For Einar Frithiof Sahlberg (1895–1977)

I can feel the weather changing
I can see it all around
Can't you feel that new wind blowing?
Don't you recognize that sound that sound?
And the earth is slowly spinning
Spinning slowly, slowly changing.

— *Neil Young: Rumblin' (2010)*

Contents

Series Foreword *by Ann Lieberman*   **xiii**

Foreword: UnFinnished Business *by Andy Hargreaves* **xv**

Acknowledgments   **xxi**

Introduction: Yes, We Can (Learn from One Another) **1**

Northern Exposure   2

Finland as an Example   4

Learning from One Another   7

The Plan of This Book   10

1. The Finnish Dream: Equal Educational Opportunities **13**

Post-War Finland   14

Toward Universal Basic Education   16

The New School Is Born   21

Expanding Upper-Secondary Education   25

Improving Educational Attainment   27

A Generation of Educational Change   32

The Finnish Education System in 2011   39

2. The Finnish Paradox: Less Is More **41**

From Periphery to Limelight   41

Level of Educational Attainment   43

Equity of Outcomes   45

Student Learning   49

Cost of Education   57

Finnish Paradoxes of Education   60

3. The Finnish Advantage: The Teachers   **70**

The Culture of Teaching   70

Becoming a Teacher   73

Academic Teacher Education   78

Teachers as Researchers   83

Professional Development   86

Time for Pedagogical Reflection   88

Leaders Are Teachers   92

Good Teachers, Great Schools   93

4. The Finnish Way: Competitive Welfare State   **96**

The Power of Globalization   97

The Global Educational Reform Movement   99

A Knowledge-Based Economy   106

Welfare, Equality, and Competitiveness   112

Two Finnish Icons: Nokia and *Peruskoulu*   116

The Finnish Dream Challenged   121

5. Is the Future Finnish?   **124**

Excellence by Being Different   125

Successful Educational Reform   127

The Transfer of Change Knowledge   131

The Future of Finnish Education   135

Notes   **147**

References   **149**

Index   **157**

About the Author   **167**

Series Foreword

It is most fitting to have *Finnish Lessons* by Pasi Sahlberg as a part of the School Reform Series. Finland, as we learn from this fine book, has transformed teaching and teacher education over the course of 30 or so years. We learn not only the history of this school reform effort, but the details of this important example of what it means to provide equal educational opportunity for all.

In the following chapters we learn what it means to have a teacher preparation program that is "research-based" and its effects on student learning. Finland is number one in international comparisons, and this book shows us not only *why* but *how* they got there.

The focus of this reform effort is on the teacher education program, which provides a comprehensive framework for all who teach—from primary to secondary school teachers. All of them are required to get a master's degree, giving time enough to study pedagogy as well as practice and to learn how to do research. Students learn that inquiry into teaching is part of what it means to teach. Teaching is an intellectual enterprise enhanced by the teacher's own research questions and subsequent findings.

In the Finnish context, teaching is a high-status profession, akin to being a doctor. Those who enter not only stay in teaching, but many continue their studies, not to leave, but to learn more and contribute more to their profession. This heightened sense of professionalism makes teaching a sought-after position and one obtained only by those who are fortunate enough to be chosen for candidacy.

We have much to learn from the examples that are written about in this book: few standardized tests; autonomy in each school; research as an important focus for learning to teach; and leadership emanating from the teachers themselves. These are lessons to be learned and studied. Such a unique example gives us much food for thought and provides us with an important primer for school reform.

—Ann Lieberman

Foreword:
UnFinnished Business

In the 1960s, the Russian launch of Sputnik propelled a massive drive to develop science and mathematics innovation in U.S. schools. In the 1980s and 1990s, the rising sun of Japan and other Asian tiger economies prompted calls to copy Japanese educational methods—making schoolwork more rigorous, extending the impact of standardized testing, and increasing the number of hours of schooling over the school year. In the past decade, the burgeoning economies of India and China have provoked United States commissions and initiatives to advocate the teaching of 21st-century skills, tougher curriculum requirements, common national standards, yet more testing, increased competition between teachers and schools, and harder work for everybody. Nevertheless, over the past quarter century, the standards and performance of American teachers and schools have steadily declined in relation to international benchmarks. In spite of this, across more than 2 decades of educational reform, the United States, like many other Anglo-American nations, has epitomized Einstein's definition of madness: keep doing the same thing while expecting to get a different result. Force, pressure, shame, top-down intervention, markets, competition, standardization, testing, and easier and quicker passages into teaching, closure of failing schools, the firing of ineffective teachers and principals, and fresh starts with young teachers and newly established schools—the very reform strategies that have failed dismally over 2 decades in many Anglo-Saxon nations—are being reinvented and re-imposed and with even greater force and determination.

THE LEMMING RACE TO THE TOP

The critics are already out in force. International change adviser Michael Fullan predicts that President Obama's Race to the Top strategy, with its intention to turn around the nation's 5,000 worst performing schools, lift limits on establishing charter schools, and introduce measures such as performance-related pay to raise the teacher quality—will end in failure (Fullan, 2010). The strategy, Fullan says, pays little or no attention to developing the capacity of leaders and teachers to improve together or as a system; it is based on a failed theory that teacher quality can be increased by a system of competitive rewards, and it rests on a badly flawed model of management where everyone manages their own unit, is accountable for results, and competes with their peers—creating fiefdoms, silos, and lack of capacity or incentives for professionals to help each other.

Former Assistant Secretary of Education Diane Ravitch also condemns Barack Obama's "awful education plan," which she regards as even worse than its much derided predecessor, No Child Left Behind (Ravitch, 2010a). The plan promotes charter schools even though the evidence indicates that they do not consistently or even on average outperform their public school district alternatives, and that they simply "skim the best students in poor communities," leaving the rest to flounder (Ravitch, 2010a). Meanwhile performance-based pay ties teacher rewards to results on appallingly designed tests of dubious validity and "destroys teamwork" among professionals who instead "need to share what they know." The reform, she concludes, is "mean-spirited, punitive, and deeply indifferent to the real problems that teachers face."

Professor Yong Zhao, the leading American expert on educational reform in China and Southeast Asia, points out that China, the leading economic competitor of the United States, is actually decentralizing its curriculum, diversifying assessment, and encouraging local autonomy and innovation. Meanwhile, Zhao concludes, while China is decentralizing and Singapore is promoting a creative environment characterized by the principle of "Teach Less, Learn More," U.S. education has been stubbornly "moving toward authoritarianism, letting the government dictate what and how students should learn and what schools should teach" (Zhao, 2009, p. 40).

In culture, politics, and business—as well as in educational reform—too many Anglo-American cultures and societies have developed an unhealthy obsession with all that is bigger, harder, tougher, faster, and stronger. Companies that sacrifice customer safety to short-term shareholder value; businesses that wreak ecological havoc with excessively bold and risky efforts to increase profitability; financial collapses that result from astronomical levels of unrepayable debt; turnaround specialists who create arbitrary disruption by setting unrealistic targets for growth and equally arbitrary quotas for staff dismissals—these are the consequences of the impatience, hubris, arrogance, and greed that characterize the worst kinds of business. Failure, firings, competition, and closures are the educational equivalent of unsustainable change in business. What they offer is oversized, pumped-up, artificially enhanced school reform on steroids.

Even in business, these larger-than-life strategies of turnaround and improvement do not produce sustainable improvement. Companies may be broken up, assets sold off, and employees fired with impunity, and all this might increase short-term shareholder returns, but few strategies of these sorts survive in the long-term and many turnaround companies eventually become casualties of their leaders' reckless behavior. Indeed, management expert Manfred Kets de Vries explains how many so-called turnaround specialists are little more than psychiatrically disturbed narcissists, sociopaths, and control freaks (Ket De Vries, 2006).

THIRD AND FOURTH WAYS AHEAD

The worst of the steroidal school reform movement has been tempered by lighter, less punitive alternatives in other Anglo-American contexts. Here, the political targets and goals for test-driven improvement in the fundamentals of literacy, mathematics, and science are still imposed with insistent inflexibility, but they are now moderated by a less harsh improvement discourse and by higher levels of professional support in the form of improved materials, increased resources, and better training.

About a decade ago in England, and more recently (and somewhat differently) in Ontario, Canada, and Australia, a model has been advanced and advocated that stands between and beyond the complete professional autonomy of the 1970s, and the mean-spirited, miserly, market-driven, and standardized reforms that characterized England in the early 1990s, and other places after that.

The "Third Way" of educational change reflected in the models offers a double twist on more blatantly steroidal reform efforts:

- a clear emphasis on the moral purpose of education
- a commitment to capacity building

These components sound more professionally plausible and inspiring than their reform counterparts that hounded and hectored the teaching profession into submission. Yet in reality, they are still highly problematic.

First, the admirable advancement of moral purpose in Third Way reforms repeatedly turns out, in practice, to be *the same* moral purpose irrespective of culture, country or context—*Raise the bar and narrow the gap* to improve tested achievement scores in literacy and mathematics (linked to imposed system-wide achievement targets). Whether it is Ontario, Australia, Bermuda, or Greater Manchester in England, the goal or moral purpose is almost identical. The countries and cultures may differ but the consultants' PowerPoint slides remain pretty much the same. In the Third Way, people aren't defining or developing their own shared visions or moral purposes. They don't *own* their visions. They *rent* them from other people.

Second, while the Third Way has an admirable commitment to capacity-building, it has often distorted the meaning of "capacity people" and diverted people from the noble purposes that underpinned its origins. The idea of capacity-building first emerged in the context of developing countries. Much like the concept and strategy of community organizing, capacity-building meant helping a community help itself. It was a humanistic and empowering concept directed toward assisting people to fulfill their own personally compelling purpose. In Third Way policies, though, capacity-building has often turned into something else—training people in prescribed strategies to deliver accountability goals and targets imposed by others.

In the Third Way, capacity-building is about training for policy delivery. In the Fourth Way of inspiration, innovation, and collective responsibility, as set out by Dennis Shirley and myself as a result of our direct work in high-performing jurisdictions like Finland and Alberta, Canada, capacity-building is more about self-directed growth and development (Hargreaves & Shirley, 2009). In short, and to be very clear: The Third Way is about renting and delivering the policies of others, while the Fourth Way is about shared ownership and development of a community's own compelling purposes.

THE NORTHERN LIGHT APPROACH

Into all this policy mix has come the unlikeliest exemplar of educational success—Finland. With its unexpectedly and consistently superlative performance on international tests of student achievement, its possession of the narrowest achievement gaps in the world, and its equally high rankings on ratings of economic competitiveness, corporate transparency, and general well-being and quality of life, this little Nordic country of barely 5.5 million people has illuminated a different path to educational and economic goals than those being forged by the Anglo-American groups of nations.

Curious about and intrigued by Finland's unusual example, educators and policy makers from all over the world have visited this Scandinavian country to try and discover the secrets of its success. I have been fortunate enough to be among them. In 2007, I had the rare opportunity to take a small team from the Organization for Economic Cooperation and Development (OECD) to Finland to examine the relationship between the country's achievement record and its strategies of school improvement and leadership development (Hargreaves, Halasz, & Pont, 2008).

Unlike many other commentators on the Finnish experience, we did not rely solely on secondary sources, or on a few interviews with senior policy makers, or on the available educational research literature. We observed and interviewed students, teachers, school and district administrators, university research experts, and Ministry of Education staff up to the very highest level. We read material on the history and organization of Finland as a society and of its dynamic leading company, Nokia. We wanted to understand the country and its history as well as its schools, and to grasp what explained its dramatic economic and educational turnaround after the fall of the Berlin Wall and the collapse of Finland's protected

Soviet markets in 1990. In all this research, it quickly became evident to us that the leading authority on Finland's distinctive educational reform strategy was and still is Pasi Sahlberg.

Sahlberg grew up in a Finnish educational family. He taught in the Finnish school system and then at the university level. From there, he went on to oversee the professional development strategy for the Ministry of Education. Like all the best researchers and commentators, Sahlberg was and remains both an insider and outsider. As a loyal and trusted insider who now heads up one of Finland's leading organizations in the field of innovation, Sahlberg possesses a rich and authentic grounding in and understanding of the inner workings of the country's educational and societal system that are often so mysterious to outside visitors.

Leaving Finland for a significant position with the World Bank, Pasi Sahlberg quickly developed the capacity to understand, interpret, and provide systemic support for countries in Eastern Europe, Central Asia, North Africa, and the Middle East. In addition to publishing a range of key scholarly articles on Finland, he also wrote the definitive country report on Finland for the World Bank.

Pasi Sahlberg's insider status here is critical. He is not only interested in systemic educational reform in a cerebral sense. He cares passionately about and remains deeply connected to the students, teachers, and communities that reforms ultimately serve. One of the distinguishing features of his character is that upon entering a new country anywhere in the world to provide systemic evaluation and support, one of his first professional acts is always to teach a mathematics lesson and converse with the students in one of the country's everyday secondary schools.

Pasi Sahlberg helped our OECD team to understand, as he will help readers of this book understand, what makes Finnish reform distinctively successful, and why it has proved inconvenient to the Anglo-American group of nations as an exemplar of educational change. Finland, he shows,

- has developed and owned its own vision of educational and social change connected to inclusiveness and creativity, rather than renting a standardized vision that has been developed elsewhere;
- relies on high-quality, well-trained teachers, with strong academic qualifications and master's degrees, who are drawn to the profession by its compelling societal mission and its conditions of autonomy and support—compared with the rapid entry strategies of short-term training and high teacher turnover advanced in countries like England and the United States;
- has an inclusive special educational strategy where nearly half of the country's students will have received some special education support at some time before completing 9-year basic school, rather than the special education strategy of legal identification, placement, and labeling of individuals favored by Anglo-American nations;

- has developed teachers' capacity to be collectively responsible for developing curriculum and diagnostic assessments together rather than delivering prescribed curricula and preparing for the standardized tests designed by central governments; and
- has linked educational reform to the creative development of economic competitiveness and also the development of social cohesion, inclusiveness, and shared community within the wider society.

Pasi Sahlberg urges us not to follow the educational reform strategies (which he calls GERM) advanced by Anglo-American political leaders and their educational advisors who dismiss the potential lessons of Finnish educational reform because of their ideological inconvenience. Nations that have become committed to and stuck with high rates of economic inequality respond only to public impatience for tough talk and short-term gain. He shows how those who dismiss Finland (in favor of their own preferred models, of course) on the grounds of its modest size as a nation overlook how its population of 5.5 million is close to the average of most U.S. states, where the bulk of educational policy decisions are made. Against the argument that Finland is just too different from America, England, or Canada (as if India, China, and Japan are not!), Sahlberg reveals how Finland has dramatically changed its identity and orientation as a nation, and how other countries can and must also do so as well.

There are unresolved questions in Anglo-American educational reform that pumped-up steroidal reform strategies and the "lemming" Race to the Top will never be able to answer but that Sahlberg's work profoundly can. This is not just because Pasi Sahlberg is the most credible indigenous expert on his own country's exemplary reforms. It is also because, as a world-ranking scholar, and former World Bank expert on a host of countries and their educational systems, Sahlberg has developed an international perspective on educational reform in general as well as the outsider's advantage in being able to make all that is familiar in Finland fresh to others.

One of the ways that teachers improve is by learning from other teachers. Schools improve when they learn from other schools. Isolation is the enemy of all improvement. We have spent decades breaking down the isolation of teachers within and between our schools. It is now time to break down the ideology of exceptionalism in the United States and other Anglo-American nations if we are to develop reforms that will truly inspire our teachers to improve learning for all our students—especially those who struggle the most. In that essential quest, Pasi Sahlberg is undoubtedly one of the very best teachers of all.

—Andy Hargreaves

Acknowledgments

Before writing this page, I went to my neighborhood bookstore and read the acknowledgments in several other authors' books. Many of them include lengthy lists of names—colleagues, friends, students, and sometimes opponents—who are given credit in the book. Some texts made me wonder if all those mentioned really deserved to be thanked. With this book, I can assure you that everyone named below has had a role to play in developing or writing this book. Some contributions were smaller than others but they were all important.

Writing a book about a topic so close to your own life and work is difficult without occasionally soliciting an outsider's perspective. For the writing of this book, I have depended on the knowledge, wisdom, and experience of some close colleagues and friends. Their confidence that the story of Finland is worth sharing with others was an important kick off to write this book. But to listen to only those who agree with you won't make a good story. This is when I remember my grandmother's wisdom: If we all think the same way, none of us probably thinks very much. In this regard, I am particularly thankful to those trusted ones who have dared to disagree with me or raise their concerns, but always in eloquent and respectful terms.

Special thanks go to Erkki Aho, Lisa Belzberg, David Berliner, Jean-Claude Couture, Linda Darling-Hammond, Carrie Fuller, Slavko Gaber, Kauko Hämäläinen, Andy Hargreaves, Tom Hatch, Jarkko Hautamäki, Hannah Hayman, Henry Heikkinen, Olli-Pekka Heinonen, Martti Hellström, Stephen Heyneman, Peter Johnson, Ben Levin, Henry Levin, Stephen Murgatroyd, Cera Murtagh, Hannele Niemi, David Oldroyd, Lyda Peters, Kari Pitkänen, Veera Salonen, Laura Servage, Robert Schwartz, Dennis Shirley, and Win Wiencke. I want to thank Sam Abrams for his critical friendship and his assistance in the editing of this book.

An important source of inspiration to write this book has been the tens of thousands of people around the world that I have met at hundreds of conferences, seminars, and symposia. They have taught me to understand better and respect more deeply the complexity of educational change. As a consequence, I am humble before the question of why some nations do better in educating their people than others. It is easy to overlook contextual differences and give simple explanations to such questions as to why Finnish students do better in international tests than most others. Questions, discussions, and critical concerns in this light have been essential for me in giving shape to the story of educational development in Finland.

My international students at the University of Helsinki have also been a source of inspiration when we have explored the secrets of the Finnish education system from perspectives that often include very different experiences and expectations from those of Finnish students. I am grateful to all my audiences and students who have made writing this book an exciting journey and a process of personal growth for me.

This book has been developed from earlier versions of various parts of my analyses, research and arguments that can be found in the works listed in the reference section of this book. Reviewers and editors of the journals and edited volumes in which my previous works have appeared have also had a significant role in enhancing my own argumentation and clarity in telling the story of Finland.

I am eternally grateful to Petra for her enduring support and wisdom to show me the way forward when my own power and will have been low.

Finnish Lessons

Introduction: Yes, We Can
(Learn from One Another)

During the next 10 years about 1.2 billion young 15-to-30-year-olds will be entering the job market and with the means now at our disposal about 300 million will get a job. What will we offer these young, about a billion of them? I think this is one of the greatest challenges if we want to achieve peaceful development and hope for these young.

—Martti Ahtisaari
(former President of Finland, 1994–2000,
and Nobel Peace Prize Laureate)

It has become clear everywhere that the schools we have today will not be able to provide opportunities to learn what is necessary in the future. The demand for better quality teaching and learning, and more equitable and efficient education is universal. Indeed, educational systems are facing a twin challenge: how to change schools so that students may learn new types of knowledge and skills required in a unpredictably changing knowledge world, and how to make that new learning possible for all young people regardless of their socioeconomic conditions. To be successful with these challenges is both a moral and economic imperative for our societies and their leaders. It is a moral obligation because each person's well-being and ultimately happiness arises from knowledge, skills, and worldviews that good education provides. It is also an economic imperative because the wealth of nations depends as never before on know-how. The aftermath of the recent global economic crisis is showing how unemployed young people are becoming hopeless to the extent that is bringing governments down. Many of these young people lack relevant education and training that would help them to help themselves.

This book is about Finland and how the Finns transformed their educational system from mediocre in the 1980s to one of the models of excellence today. International indicators show that Finland has one of the most educated citizenries in the world, provides educational opportunities in an egalitarian manner, and makes efficient use of resources. Finnish education has recently attracted attention from many international scholars. Linda Darling-Hammond (2010) writes extensively about it in her book, *The Flat World and Education*. Andy Hargreaves and Dennis Shirley (2009) chose Finland as an example of a nation that has successfully transformed its education system in their book, *The Fourth Way*. A chapter on Finnish education has become an integral part of any international handbook or volume that reports contemporary thinking and practice in the field. International development agencies, consulting firms, and media houses refer to Finland as a good model and "a witness" of successful transformation of public education.[1] Monographs on Finnish school and teachers have been published in China, Korea, Japan, France, Slovenia, and Germany, just to mention a few countries. This book is a comprehensive description of educational change in Finland written by a native Finn from an international perspective.

In leading the way toward educational reform in Finland in the early 1990s, Dr. Vilho Hirvi, then Director General of the National Board of Education, said that "an educated nation cannot be created by force." He acknowledged that teachers and students must be heard, and that the way forward called for active collaboration. In Finland, teachers and students were insisting on more flexibility and freedom in deciding how to design instruction, what to study, and when. "We are creating a new culture of education and there is no way back," Hirvi said to his staff at the National Board of Education. Basic to this new culture has been the cultivation of trust between education authorities and schools. Such trust, as we have witnessed, makes reform that is not only sustainable but also owned by the teachers who implement it.

NORTHERN EXPOSURE

At the beginning of the 1990s, education in Finland was nothing special in international terms. All young Finns attended school regularly, the school network was wide and dense, secondary education was accessible for all Finns, and higher education was an option for an increasing number of upper secondary school graduates. However, the performance of Finnish students on international assessments was close to overall averages, except in reading, where Finnish students did better than most of their peers in other countries. The unexpected and jarring recession of that time period brought Finland to the edge of a financial breakdown. Bold and immediate measures were necessary to fix national fiscal imbalances and revive the foreign trade that disappeared with the collapse of the Soviet Union in 1990. Nokia, the main global industrial brand of Finland, became a critical engine in boosting Finland from the country's biggest economic dip since World War II. Another Finnish brand, *peruskoulu*, or the 9-year comprehensive basic school, was the other key player in this turnaround of the Finnish economy and society. Interestingly, both Nokia and the Finnish public educational system have their origins in the same time period in Finnish history: the golden years of building the Finnish national identity in the mid-19th century, as will be described in Chapter 4 of this book.

There are countries around the world where education leaders find their own educational systems in a situation very similar to that of Finland in 1990. The global economic downturn is hitting many schools, universities, and entire education systems hard. Take Ireland, Greece, England, or the United States—student achievement is not anywhere close to what it should be in knowledge-based economies where productivity and innovation are necessary conditions for competitiveness. Students seem to find teaching offered in schools and universities increasingly boring and irrelevant to their needs in a rapidly changing world. The story of educational change in Finland in this book brings hope to all those worried about whether improving their educational systems is at all possible. It also provides food for thought to those who look for ways to adjust education policies to the realities of economic recovery. The lessons from Finland should be refreshing because they depart from the ideas commonly presented in books or journals on educational development. Moreover, these lessons show that systemic improvement is indeed possible if only policies and strategies are designed in smart and sustainable ways.

While these lessons hold great promise, they call for patience. In this age of immediate results, education requires a different mindset. Reforming schools is a complex and slow process. To rush this process is to ruin it. The story of Finland's educational transformation makes this clear. Steps must be grounded in research and implemented in collaboration by academics, policy makers, principals, and teachers.

This book is about how such a process evolved in Finland since World War II. It is the first book written for international readers that tells the story of how Finland created a system praised as much for its equity as for its high quality. Many of the world's great newspapers and broadcast services—the *New York Times, Washington Post, Times of London, Le Monde, El Pais, National Public Radio, NBC, Deutsche Welle,* and *BBC*—have covered this Finnish educational miracle. Thousands of official delegations have visited Finnish authorities, schools, and communities to learn about what drives excellence in education. This story, however, has till now not received the book-length treatment necessary for enumerating, linking, and explaining the many players, institutions, and impersonal forces involved.

My approach in this book is both personal and academic. It is personal because of my intimate relationship with education in Finland. I was born in northern Finland and raised in a village primary school, as both of my parents were teachers at that school. Most of my childhood memories are in one way or another linked to school. I had the privilege of looking beyond the secrets of the classroom after everybody else was gone and I found that world rich. It was my home and an enchanted one. It is perhaps no surprise then that I went on to become a teacher. My first position was at a junior high school in Helsinki. I taught mathematics and physics there for 7 years. Later I spent enough time in educational administration and in university teacher education to understand the difference between education in school and out. As a policy analyst for the Organisation for Economic Cooperation and Development (OECD), an education specialist for the World Bank, and an expert of the European Commission, I gained the global perspective necessary for a deeper appreciation of Finland's distinct place in education.

As a representative of Finland in these different capacities, I have also been forced to develop a keener understanding of what distinguishes Finnish methods by answering questions from audiences and media around the world. Since the beginning of 2000, I have given more than 250 keynote addresses and 100 interviews about the Finnish educational system around the world. My estimate is that this means talking to some 50,000 people directly and many more through published stories and news. Numerous conversations with people who are interested in education, as I am, have greatly advanced the writing of this book. The following are some of the questions that have been asked over and over again: "What is the secret of Finnish educational success?" "How do you get the best young people into teaching in Finland?" "How much does lack of ethnic diversity have to do with good educational performance there?" "How do you know that all schools are doing what they should when you don't test students or inspect teachers?" "How did Finland save its education system during the economic downturn in the 1990s?" For such questions and also critical remarks related to my thinking, I am grateful. But for them, I would never have been able to hone my assessment of Finnish differences.

This book also has an academic orientation because it stems from research that I have been part of over the last 2 decades as an author, co-author, or critic. This book is thus not a typical monograph written as a result of a research project or an event. It is a synthesis of a decade of policy analysis, experience as a teacher and administrator, and dialogue with thousands of educators around the world. I have been privileged to spend enough time outside of Finland and work with a number of foreign governments to better understand the true nature and peculiarity of Finnish education and life in Finnish schools.

FINLAND AS AN EXAMPLE

Public education systems are in crisis in many parts of the world. The United States, England, Sweden, Norway, and France, just to mention a few nations, are among those where public education is increasingly challenged because of endemic failure to provide adequate learning opportunities to all children. Tough solutions are not uncommon in these countries: Tightening control over schools, stronger accountability for student performance, firing bad teachers, and closing down troubled schools are part of the recipe to fix failing education systems. This book does not suggest that tougher competition, more data, abolishing teacher unions, opening more charter schools, or employing corporate-world management models in education systems would bring about a resolution to these crises—quite the opposite. The main message of this book is that there is another way to improve education systems. This includes improving the teaching force, limiting student testing to a necessary minimum, placing responsibility and trust before accountability, and handing over school- and district-level leadership to education professionals. These are common education policy themes in some of the high performing countries—Finland among them—in the 2009 International Programme for Student Assessment (PISA) of the OECD (2010b, 2010c). The chapters of this book offer five reasons why Finland is an interesting and relevant source of ideas for other nations that are looking for ways to improve their education systems.

One, Finland has a unique educational system because it has progressed from mediocrity to being a model contemporary educational system and "strong performer" over the past 3 decades. Finland is special also because it has been able to create an educational system where students learn well and where equitable education has translated into small variation in student performance between schools in different parts of country at the same time. This internationally rare status has been achieved using reasonable financial resources and less effort than other nations have expended on reform efforts.

Two, because of this proven steady progress, Finland demonstrates that there is another way to build a well-performing educational system using solutions that differ from the market-driven education policies. The Finnish way of change, as described by Andy Hargreaves and Dennis Shirley in *The Fourth Way*, is one of trust, professionalism, and shared responsibility (Hargreaves & Shirley, 2009). Indeed, Finland is an example of a nation that lacks school inspection, standardized curriculum, high-stakes student assessments, test-based accountability, and a race-to-the-top mentality with regard to educational change.

Three, as a consequence of its success, Finland can offer some alternative ways to think about solutions to existing chronic educational problems in the United States, Canada, and England (such as high school drop-out rates, early teacher attrition and inadequate special education) and emerging needs to reform educational systems elsewhere (such as engaging students in learning, attracting young talents into teaching, and establishing holistic public sector policies). The Finnish approach to reducing early school leavers, enhancing teacher professionalism, implementing intelligent accountability and student assessment in schools, and improving learning in mathematics, science, and literacy can offer inspiration to other school systems looking for a path to success.

Four, Finland is also an international high performer in commerce, technology, sustainable development, good governance, and prosperity and thus raises interesting questions concerning interdependencies between education and other sectors in society. It appears that other public policy sectors, such as health and employment, seem to play a role also in long-term educational development and change. In Finland, this holds true as well regarding income parity, social mobility, and trust within Finnish society, as the chapters that follow will show. This book also explains how there are interesting parallel evolutions between the Finnish schooling and the iconic Finnish telecommunication giant Nokia.

Finally, we should listen to the story of Finland because it gives hope to those who are losing their faith in public education and whether it can be changed. This book reveals that the transformation of educational systems is possible, but that it takes time, patience, and determination. The Finnish story is particularly interesting because some of the key policies and changes were introduced during the worst economic crisis that Finland has experienced since World War II. It suggests that a crisis can spark the survival spirit that leads to better solutions to acute problems than a "normal situation" would. This book speaks against those who believe that the best way to solve chronic problems in many education systems is to take control away from school boards and give it to those who might run them more effectively, by charters or other means of privatization. Although there are limits to the ideas that can be transferred from Finland to other nations, certain basic lessons may have general value for other educational systems, such as the practices of building on teacher strengths, securing relaxed and fear-free learning for students, and gradually enhancing trust within educational systems.

As this book illustrates, there is no single reason why any educational system succeeds or fails. Instead, there is a network of interrelated factors—educational, political and cultural—that function differently in different situations. I would, however, like to cite three important elements of Finnish educational policies since the early 1970s that appear to transcend culture. The first one is an inspiring vision of what good public education should be: Finland has been particularly committed to building a good publicly financed and locally governed basic school for every child. This common educational goal became so deeply rooted in politics and public services in Finland that it survived opposing political governments and ministries unharmed and intact. Since the introduction of *peruskoulu* in early 1970s, there have been 20 governments and nearly 30 different ministers of education in charge of educational reforms in Finland. So strong has this commitment to having common basic school for all been that some call it the Finnish Dream. This hints to other nations intent on educational transformation that it is better to have a dream of your own than rent one from others.

The second aspect of educational change that deserves attention when reading this book is the way Finland has treated advice offered externally vis-á-vis its own educational heritage in educational reforms. Much of the inspiration in building independent Finland since 1917 has come from its neighbors, especially from Sweden. The welfare state model, health care system, and basic education are good examples of borrowed ideas from our western neighbor. Later, Finnish education policies were also influenced by guidance from supranational institutions, especially the OECD (which Finland joined in 1969) and the European Union (which Finland joined in 1995). In this book, I launch an argument that, despite international influence and borrowing educational ideas from others, Finland has in the end created its own way to build the educational system that exists today. I call this the *Finnish Way* because it is different from the global educational reform movement that has dominated educational policies in most parts of the world during the last 2 decades. The Finnish Way of change preserves the best of traditions and present good practices, and combines it with innovations found from others. Cultivating trust, enhancing autonomy, and tolerating diversity are just some of the examples of the change ideas that are found in Finnish schools today. Many pedagogical ideas and educational innovations are initially imported from other countries, often from North America or the United Kingdom. These include curriculum models from England, California, and Ontario; cooperative learning from the United States and Israel; portfolio assessment from the United States; teaching of science and mathematics from England, the United States, and Australia; and peer-assisted leadership from Canada, to mention a few. At the same time, the Finnish Dream of education is "made in Finland" and therefore also owned by Finns rather than rented.

The third aspect of change is a systematic development of respectful and interesting working conditions for teachers and leaders in Finnish schools. This book raises an important question that is repeated in almost any situation when whole-system educational reforms are discussed: How do we get the best young people into teaching? Experience from Finland, as illustrated in Chapter 3, suggests that it is not enough to establish world-class teacher education programs or pay teachers well. Finland has built world-class teacher education programs. And Finland pays its teachers well. But the true Finnish difference is that teachers in Finland may exercise their professional knowledge and judgment both widely and freely in their schools. They control curriculum, student assessment, school improvement, and community involvement. Much as teachers around the world enter the profession with a mission to build community and transmit culture, Finnish teachers, in contrast to their peers in so many countries, have the latitude and power to follow through.

LEARNING FROM ONE ANOTHER

Can Finland be a model for educational change in other countries? Many are fascinated by the fact that Finland has been able to transform its educational system from something elitist, unknown, and inefficient into a paragon of equity and efficiency (Schleicher, 2006). Finland is also one of the few nations among the 34 OECD countries that have been able to improve educational performance as measured by international indicators and student achievement tests. Furthermore, many foreign visitors have been particularly surprised to find out that teaching has become the number one

profession among young Finns—above medicine and law—and that primary teacher
education in Finnish universities is one of the most competitive choices of study. All
these aspects of the educational system are explored further in this book.

There are, however, those who doubt that Finland has much relevance to other
educational systems because of its special characteristics. The most commonly presented argument is that since Finland is so exceptional, it hardly provides anything
meaningful to the United States, England, Australia, France, or other much larger
nations, or that it is "too different to serve as models for whole-system reform for
North America as a whole," as Michael Fullan writes (2010, p. xiv). Two points are
often emphasized when the relevance of Finland as a model for educational change
is considered.

First, Finland is culturally and ethnically rather homogeneous and thus too
unlike the United States, for example. Fair enough, but the same holds true for
Japan, Shanghai, or Korea. The proportion of foreign-born citizens in Finland was
4.7% in 2010 and the number of non-Finnish speaking citizens about 10% (Statistics Finland, 2011). It is noteworthy that Finland is a trilingual country, where
Finnish, Swedish, and Sami are all official languages. The largest language and ethnic minorities are Russian, Estonian, and Somali. The diversification of Finnish
society since the mid-1990s has been the fastest in Europe. When I began my teaching career in Helsinki in the mid-1980s, it was rare to have anybody in my classroom that looked or sounded different than others. The number of foreign-born
citizens in Finland has nearly tripled during the first decade of the 21st century.
Finland is not that homogeneous anymore, but, of course, it doesn't compare to
the United States or Canada as a multicultural nation as far as the ethnic diversities
are concerned.

Second, Finland is considered to be too small to be a good model for system-
wide reform for North America. This is a more tricky argument to defend. When
the size factor in educational reforms is considered, it is necessary to note that in
many federal nations, states, provinces, or regions are to a large extent autonomous in terms of educational management and running of their schools. This
is the case in the United States, Canada, Australia, and Germany, for example.
Population in Finland is today 5.5 million. It is about the population of Minnesota in the United States or Victoria in Australia, and just slightly more than
the size of Alberta in Canada or Nord-Pas de Calais in France. Indeed, about 30
states of the United States have a population close to or less than Finland. These
include the states of Maryland, Colorado, Oregon, and Connecticut. The states of
Washington, Indiana, and Massachusetts are also smallish and close to Finland in
size. In Australia, only New South Wales has a slightly larger population than Finland; all other Australian states are smaller. In France, Île-de-France is the only
region that surpasses Finland in size. In Canada, only Ontario is significantly
larger in population (and land area) than Finland; all other provinces are similar
in size. If these jurisdictions have freedom to set their own educational policies
and conduct reforms as they think best, then experiences from an educational

system of the size of Finland should be particularly interesting and relevant to them. France is the only country mentioned above that employs centralized educational management, and therefore the French education policy makers could argue irrelevance of smaller education systems as models for their reforms.

Finally, there are those who doubt that international comparisons are relevant or reliable in what they claim to show. One point of view is that academic achievement tests, such as the Programme for International Student Assessment (PISA), Trends in International Mathematics and Science Study (TIMSS), and Progress in International Reading Literacy Study (PIRLS) focus on areas too narrow to capture the whole spectrum of school education, and thus ignore social skills, moral development, creativity, or digital literacy as important outcomes of public education for all (See Chapter 2 for references to this argument). There is also a growing concern that these comparisons are influencing educational policies and endorsing the culture of "governing by numbers" (Grek, 2009). Another skeptical group simply argues that chosen measurement methodologies in current international tests favor Finland because they match better with the culture of teaching in Finland; this group includes both Finnish and foreign scientists and experts.[2] Recently, Harvard professor Howard Gardner warned his audience in Finland to treat these current student assessment studies with caution,[3] contending that results in studies like these always depend on the subject-area knowledge tested and the respective methodologies of the studies used. In addition, these studies do not measure interpersonal, spatial, or creative skills, and these skill sets are increasingly important in our contemporary world.

Although Finland has persistently outperformed other nations, its achievements have been downplayed in numerous accounts of recommended policy. In a recent report by McKinsey and Company (Mourshed, Chijioke & Barber, 2010), for example, Finland is not even listed as a "sustained improver" in terms of education. The consequence is that policy makers in many contexts will not consider Finnish strategies as they develop their repertoire of school improvement practices. Recent national education strategies and policy guidelines, such as the 2010 Schools White Paper in England (Department for Education, 2010), Lessons from PISA for the United States (OECD, 2010c), and the World Bank Education Strategy 2020 (World Bank, 2011), often refer to common features of high-performing education systems as desired criteria for improvement. Focus on teacher effectiveness, school autonomy, accountability, and data are all central elements of education systems in Korea, Singapore, Alberta, and Finland, but in very different ways. As this book will show again and again, Finland is unique in terms of how these aspects of education policy are employed. The Finnish experience shows that consistent focus on equity and cooperation—not choice and competition—can lead to an education system where all children learn well. Paying teachers based on students' test scores or converting public schools into private ones (through charters or other means) are ideas that have no place in the Finnish repertoire for educational improvement.

The size of Finland's population and relative homogeneity of its society obviously make many aspects of setting education policies and implementing reforms easier than in larger, more diverse jurisdictions. But these factors alone don't explain all the progress and achievements in education that are described in this book, and they should not stop us from learning from one another as we strive to improve education for all students. Finland is, however, very unique among nations in terms of its values, cultural determinants, and social cohesion within society. Fairness, honesty, and social justice are deeply rooted in the Finnish way of life. People have a strong sense of shared responsibility, not only for their own lives, but also for those of others. Fostering the well-being of children starts before they are born and continues until they reach adulthood. Day care is a right of all children before they start school at age 7, and public health service is easily accessible to all during childhood. Education in Finland is widely seen as a public good and is therefore protected as a basic human right to all in the Constitution. Adages such as "small is beautiful," "don't talk unless you have something to say," and "less is more" are typical descriptors of good life and everyday culture in Finland.

In this book I describe how Finns have built a functional, sustainable, and just country with an equitable public education system by doing things in their own way. The Country Brand Delegation that was chaired by ex-CEO of Nokia, Jorma Ollila, wrote in 2010 that "in Finland, people do not aspire to do everything the same way as the others, to dress or to live like others. Rather than the 'done thing,' Finns do what they think is the rational thing to do" (Ministry of Foreign Affairs, 2010, p. 59). The intense individuality of Finns blended with low hierarchy and traditional willingness to work with others has opened pathways to endless creative potential. Inspiration and vision to create a society with an education system that is good and accessible to all was drawn from this pool of creative potential.

Data for this book are not from only one source, nor does this book claim that educational excellence could be justified by any one international study. Evidence is drawn from available international databases, such as PISA and TIMSS, global education indicators, and versatile official statistics in Finland.

THE PLAN OF THIS BOOK

This book draws from the following ten notions that are explained in detail on the pages of this volume:

1. Finland has an education system in which young people learn well and performance differences among schools are small—and all with reasonable cost and human effort.
2. This has not always been so.

3. In Finland, teaching is a prestigious profession, and many students aspire to be teachers.
4. Therefore, the Finns have probably the most competitive teacher-education system in the world.
5. As a consequence, teachers in Finland have a great deal of professional autonomy and access to purposeful professional development throughout their careers.
6. Those who are lucky enough to become teachers normally are teachers for life.
7. Almost half of the 16-year-olds, when they leave comprehensive school, have been engaged in some sort of special education, personalized help, or individual guidance.
8. In Finland, teachers teach less and students spend less time studying both in and out of school than their peers in other countries.
9. Finnish schools lack the standardized testing, test-preparation, and private tutoring of the United States and much of the world.
10. All of the factors that are behind the Finnish success seem to be the opposite of what is taking place in the United States and much of the rest of the world, where competition, test-based accountability, standardization, and privatization seem to dominate.

After this Introduction, the book has five chapters. Chapter 1 explains both the political and historical realities after World War II and how they shaped the move toward common basic school for all by the end of the 1960s. When telling the story of educational change in Finland to scores of foreign visitors, I have learned that it is important to go back further in time than the birth of *peruskoulu* in 1970. This chapter illustrates the process of reforming the old school system, which divided pupils into two tracks and relied heavily on privately governed and co-financed grammar schools, into a comprehensive, publicly managed and funded system. It also outlines the main features of post-compulsory education that emerged soon after implementing the *peruskoulu* reform in late 1970s. The main characteristics of the iconic Finnish Matriculation Examination as a school-leaving test for general upper secondary education in Finland are described in this chapter.

Chapter 2 tackles a fundamental question: Was Finland also a high-performer in education in the past? The answer provided in this chapter is as expected: no. It immediately invites a corollary: What constitutes a good educational system and which educational reforms have made such impressive progress possible in Finland? The core of this chapter is an insight that the Finnish educational success in international comparisons can, at least to some extent, be understood by paradoxes. This can be crystallized by a simple principle in educational reform: Less is more. Chapter 2 provides evidence-based examples of how this paradoxical idea appears in the Finnish educational system today.

Chapter 3 is about teachers and teacher education in Finland. It examines the crucial role that teachers play in Finland and describes the main features of the teaching profession, teacher education, and teacher responsibilities in Finland. By relying on the Finnish experience, this chapter suggests that whereas high-quality university-based teacher education and continuous professional development are necessary conditions for attracting the most talented and committed young people into teaching, they are not sufficient alone. Teachers have to be provided with a professional working environment so that they feel dignified and are able to fulfill their moral purposes in schools. This chapter also looks at some of the future prospects of teaching and teacher education in Finland.

Since Finland's amazing recovery from a grave economic recession in the early 1990s—and more recently from the global financial crisis of 2008—many have spoken about the Finnish model of building an inclusive information society and competitive knowledge economy (Castells & Himanen, 2002; Routti & Ylä-Anttila, 2006; Saari, 2006). What is significant in the process of economic recovery is that at the same time when Finnish economy and especially the public sector have adjusted to tougher competition and better productivity, performance of the education system has been steadily improving. Chapter 4 illustrates some interdependencies between Finnish educational policy and other public sector policies that are at the heart of the economic comeback. Furthermore, it suggests that progress in the educational sector has happened in tandem with changes in government that have improved economic competitiveness, transparency, and welfare policy. For a concrete example of this interplay between education and business development in Finland, this chapter traces the parallel evolution of Nokia and Finnish schooling.

Finally, Chapter 5 asks a question that is, surprisingly, not often asked of Finns by their visitors: What is the future of Finnish schooling? Being in the global limelight takes its toll. While Finns have hosted thousands of foreign education pilgrims since late 2001, they have had only a little time and energy to think about what their own education system should look like in the future. This chapter summarizes the main elements of successful educational change but concludes that being at the center has prevented Finns from thinking about what kind of education is needed in the future. It closes with a discussion of the necessity to change, although the system is praised for its excellence and seems to be working well.

To follow the latest developments in Finnish education and to hear news about events related to this book, be sure to visit http://www.finnishlessons.com.

CHAPTER 1

The Finnish Dream:
Equal Educational Opportunities

God mend us! The fact is that we don't even know the first letter of the alphabet, and that knowing how to read is the first duty of every Christian citizen. The power of law, of church law, may force us to it. And you know what kind of contraption the State has watching, eager to snap us up in its jaws if we don't obediently learn to read. The stocks are waiting for us, my brothers, the black stocks; their cruel jaws gaping wide like those of a black bear. The provost has threatened us with those hell his pincers, and he is bound to carry out his threat unless he sees us eagerly studying every day.

—Aleksis Kivi, *Seven Brothers* (1870/2005)

The story of Finland is a story of survival. It is eloquently captured by Aleksis Kivi in the first Finnish novel, *Seven Brothers,* which was first published in 1870. It is a story of orphan brothers who realize that becoming literate is the key to happiness and a good life. Since those days, reading has been an integral part of Finnish culture. Education has served as the main strategy for building a literate society and a nation that is today known by the world for its cultural and technological achievements. Therefore, *Seven Brothers* belongs to the list of core texts in most Finnish schools today.

Being a relatively small nation situated between much larger powers of the East and the West has taught Finns to accept existing realities and take chances with available opportunities. Diplomacy, cooperation, problem-solving, and seeking consensus have thus become hallmarks of contemporary Finnish culture. These traits all play an important part also in building an educational system that has enjoyed global attention due to its equitable distribution of good teaching and learning throughout the nation.

This chapter describes how Finland has progressed from being a poor, agrarian, and only modestly educated nation to a modern knowledge-based society with a high-performing education system and world-class innovation environment. Expanding education according to the principle that good education should be accessible to all Finnish children, from early childhood education all the way to the highest academic degrees, has been a long-term ideal in Finnish society. This chapter first provides a historic and political context for realization of this Finnish Dream. It then describes the evolution of the unified comprehensive basic school, or *peruskoulu* as it is called in Finnish, and some principles of upper secondary education that are an important part of Finnish educational success.[1] Present structures and policies of the Finnish education system are briefly outlined at the end of the chapter.

POST-WAR FINLAND

War poses among the most serious of imaginable crises for any democratic nation. Except for a short period of cease-fire, Finland was at war from December 1939 to spring 1945. The cost of war for that young, independent democracy with a population of less than 4 million was enormous: 90,000 dead and 60,000 permanently injured. In addition, 25,000 were widowed, and 50,000 children were orphaned. A peace treaty with the Soviet Union was signed in Moscow on September 19, 1944, but military campaigns to remove German troops from Finland continued until April 1945. The conditions accepted by the Finns were severe. Finland had to hand over 12% of its territory to the Soviets and to relocate 450,000 people—11% of Finland's total population. The Finnish concessions to the Soviets were estimated to reach 7% of its Gross Domestic Product (GDP). A peninsula near Helsinki had to be rented to the Soviet army as a military base, political prisoners had to be released, and wartime leaders were judged in war tribunals. Several political associations were prohibited, and the communist party was established as a legal Finnish political entity. These concessions led to such fundamental political, cultural, and economic changes in Finland that some have identified the post-war era as the emergence of a "Second Republic."[2]

Most important, Finland had fought for its freedom and survived. External threats experienced during and after World War II united Finns, who still felt the wounds of the previous 1918 civil war. The post-World War II era was one of political instability and economic transformation, but it also gave rise to new social ideas and social policies—in particular the idea of equal educational opportunities. It is difficult to understand why education has become one of the trademarks of Finland without examining these post-World War II political and social developments. Even among Finns there are those who argue that the search for key success factors in the Finnish educational system has to extend much earlier than 1970, a year often recognized as an historical milestone in Finnish education for reasons explained later in this chapter.

History is often easier to understand when it is segmented into periods or phases of development, and the recent history of Finland is no exception to this strategy. Although there are many ways to recount Finland's history depending on the purposes and perspectives of its authors, in this case it is helpful to illustrate congruencies between the development of Finland's education system, and three stages of economic development following World War II:

- enhancing equal opportunities for education by way of transition from a northern agricultural nation to an industrialized society (1945–1970)
- creating a public comprehensive school system by way of a Nordic welfare society with a growing service sector and increasing levels of technology and technological innovation (1965–1990)
- improving the quality of basic education and expanding higher education in keeping with Finland's new identity as a high-tech knowledge-based economy (1985–present) (Sahlberg, 2010a).

The 1950s were already a time of rapid changes to Finland's economic structure, but the 1960s have been characterized as phenomenal by international standards (Routti & Ylä-Anttila, 2006; Aho, Pitkänen, & Sahlberg, 2006). The decade of the 1960s saw Finnish society, in more general terms, relinquish many of its old values, and traditional Finnish institutions began to transform. Public services—especially basic education—were among the most visible sites of change. When the time for decisive change arrived, its speed and thoroughness took many Finns by surprise.

The end of World War II prompted such radical changes to Finnish political, social, and economic structures that immediate changes to education and other social institutions were required. Indeed, education soon became the main vehicle of social and economic transformation in the post-war era. In 1950, educational opportunities in Finland were unequal in the sense that only those living in towns or larger municipalities had access to grammar or middle schools. Most young people left school after 6 or 7 years of formal basic education. Where private grammar schools were available, pupils could apply to enroll in them after 4, 5, or 6 years of state-run basic school, but such opportunities were limited. In 1950, for example, just 27% of 11-year-old Finns enrolled in grammar schools consisting of 5-year middle school and 3-year high-school. An alternative educational path after the compulsory 7 years of basic education was 2 or 3 years of study in one of the so-called *civic schools*, offered by most Finnish municipalities. This basic education could be followed by vocational training and technical education, but only in larger municipalities and towns that housed these institutions.

In 1950, there were 338 grammar schools offering further educational opportunities after the 6-year basic school in Finland (Kiuasmaa, 1982). The Finnish state operated 103 of these schools, and municipalities ran 18. The remaining 217 grammar schools, about two-thirds of the total, were governed by private citizens or associations. The major burden of the rapid expansion of education following basic schooling was absorbed by these private schools. A significant social innovation in 1950 was issuance of legislation that guaranteed state subsidies to private schools, and simultaneously extended the government's control over these schools.

This change made it possible to respond to the public's growing interest in education by opening new private schools, as their financial risks were diminished through state funding.

In the early years after Finland's independence, teaching in primary schools was formal, teacher-centered, and more focused on moral than on cognitive development. Although pedagogical ideas aimed at social gains and more holistic interpersonal development were known in Finland as early as the 1930s, school education was not greatly influenced by them (Koskenniemi, 1944). Three dominant themes in Finnish national education policy between 1945 and 1970 would come to change this traditional model:

- The structure of the education system would provide access to better and more education for all.
- The form and content of curricula would focus on development of individual, holistic personalities of children.
- Teacher education would be modernized to respond to needs arising from these developments. The future dream of Finland was built on knowledge and skills; thus, education was seen as a foundation for establishing the future (Aho et al., 2006).

Finland's economic structure in 1950, comparable to Sweden's economy in 1910, was in transition. Key industries were shifting from farming and small business to industrial and technological production. The new political environment in the post-war era had also activated working-class families, who insisted that their children should have opportunities to benefit from extended public education. Consequently, a model for comprehensive schools offering universal access and a unified curriculum, first proposed in the 1920s, was revived and entered education policy discussions soon after the end of World War II. It was clear that to become a recognized member of the community of Western democracies and market economies, Finland needed a better-educated population. This was a vision for the entire nation.

TOWARD UNIVERSAL BASIC EDUCATION

The first 2 decades after World War II were politically turbulent in Finland. The Communist Party returned to the main stage of daily politics in the first post-war elections in 1944, and identified education as one of its primary strategies for building a Finnish socialist society. In the 1948 elections, three political parties received nearly equal seats in the Finnish national Parliament: the Social Democratic Party (50 seats), the Agrarian Centre Party (49 seats), and the Communist Party (49 seats). The rebuilding of Finland began; political consensus was a precondition for reforms, including renewing the Finnish educational system. The

Conservative Party increased its popularity in the 1950s and became a fourth political force to be reckoned with in Finnish parliamentary negotiations. The political education committees played particularly important roles as the groundwork for comprehensive basic schooling for all Finnish students was laid, and the vision finally realized in 1970.

Three politically oriented education committees are particularly worth mentioning. First, in June 1945, the government established the Primary School Curriculum Committee. The secretary of that committee was Professor Matti Koskenniemi (1908–2001) who had, a few years earlier, written a seminal book on primary school didactics (Koskenniemi, 1944). Through his contributions, perspectives on curriculum in Finland shifted from focusing on syllabi (the German term *lehrplan*) to describing educational objectives, process of education, and evaluation. These reforms were the first to modernize Finnish curriculum by international standards, and still resonate in contemporary curriculum thinking.

There are several reasons why this committee has a central place in the history of Finnish education. First, the members devoted special attention to formulating new objectives for education, thereby deviating from German tradition in Finnish education. The committee put forth the idea that school should aim at educating young people to realize themselves as holistic individuals, possessing intrinsic motivation for further education. The content of education that would lead to this general aim was grouped into five thematic, cross-curricular areas, which later became a model for the Comprehensive School Curriculum Committee in 1970.

Second, curriculum reform was grounded in empirical studies conducted in 300 field schools involving 1,000 teachers. In this way, research became part of education policy making. Third, and a corollary of the previous two reasons, the quality of the committee's work was regarded as exceptionally high. The Final Memorandum of the committee, published in 1952, has merit in its systematic formulation of educational objectives, broad child-centered perspective, modernized presentation and richness of educational content, and emphasis on the primacy of social cohesion as one important goal in education. Significant milestones in the post-war history of Finland were realized in 1952: hosting the Summer Olympics in Helsinki, the coronation of Miss Finland Armi Kuusela as the first-ever Miss Universe, and completion of heavy reparations to the Soviet Union. It is appropriate, also, to append to Finland's 1952 milestones the new internationally comparable curriculum for Finland's primary school system that paved the way to educational success some half a century later.

A second committee of significance, the Education System Committee, launched its work in 1946 to establish regulations for compulsory education and a common framework of principles for determining how different parts of the education system should be interlinked. The committee included representatives of all of the leading political parties of that time and was chaired by the National Board of Education's Director General Yrjö Ruutu, ally of the Finnish Communist

Party. Less than 2 years after commencing its work, this committee proposed that the foundation of the Finnish educational system should be an 8-year compulsory basic school that would be common to all children regardless of their socioeconomic situation. The committee advised that this school system ought to avoid tracking to "academic" subjects for more able students and "vocational" studies for those preferring to learn manual skills, as existed in the then-current parallel education system.

However, the committee retained the standard that only those students who had learned foreign languages during basic school would be allowed to enter upper secondary school or *gymnasium*—which represented the only pathway to higher education. Although the idea of comprehensive school was clearly formulated, it was not acted upon due to bitter criticism by universities and the Grammar School Teachers' Union. However, the committee's proposal stimulated further debate within Finnish society about social justice and equal educational opportunities—tenets which, 2 decades later, would be realized and entrenched as foundations of Finnish education policy.

Development of different sectors of education continued in the 1950s. The baby boom after World War II led to rapid expansion in the number of schools. New laws stipulated that compulsory education was to consist of 6 years of primary school and 2 years of civic school for those who didn't advance further to grammar schools. The new curriculum launched in 1952 began to change work and life in schools. Vocational education became part of the education sector. Finland's dream of common schooling for all was alive, but, in practice, parallel-schooling structures remained. Consequently, a third committee of key significance, the School Program Committee, was established in 1956 to unify the Finnish education system and bring coherence to changes in various subsectors of education. The establishment of this committee under the leadership of Reino Henrik Oittinen, Director General of the National Board of Education and a Social Democrat, was one further step toward the big dream of Finnish education.

The work of this committee was built on an unprecedented analysis of international education policies. Particularly significant was the committee's observation that Nordic countries shared much in common regarding their education policies at that time. Increasing equality of educational opportunities—a priority at the time in England and the United States—became a central theme in the committee's strategic thinking. The period of 1956 to 1959, during which this politically broad-based committee conducted almost 200 meetings, was particularly turbulent: Global economic recession, tough political conflicts both domestically and with the Soviet Union, and the launch of the Sputnik soon impacted educational reforms around the world. Nevertheless, the committee persevered, and its work became a cornerstone in the history of educational reforms in Finland.

The School Program Committee published its recommendations in the summer of 1959. The committee suggested that future compulsory education in Finland should be based on a 9-year municipal comprehensive school with the following structure:

- The first four grades would be common to all pupils.
- Grades 5 and 6 would constitute a middle school where pupils could choose to focus on either practical subjects or foreign languages.
- Grades 7 through 9 would have three streams: vocational and practical orientation, an "average" track with one foreign language, or an advanced stream with two foreign languages.

The committee was unable to unify political will around this structure of comprehensive school; indeed, strong disagreement arose even within the committee about main policy principles. The proposed system would, however, gradually merge private grammar and public civic schools into a new municipal structure, and diminish the role of private schools. Overall, the work of this committee initiated deep and significant debate about core values in education in Finnish society. The key question was: Is it possible, in principle, that all children can be educated and attain similar learning goals? Answers to this question created divided opinions, even within families. Primary school teachers believed all students could learn equally well, universities typically doubted the proposition, and politicians remained divided. At that time, given its need to advance both politically and economically on the world stage, Finland had no choice but to accept the proposition that anyone—if given adequate opportunities and support—could learn foreign languages and advance to higher levels of education than had previously been believed. It was more difficult for many politicians at that time to accept that the educational architecture of the day, which maintained and actually more deeply entrenched inequality in Finnish society, would be unable in the long run to ensure that Finland would achieve its goal of becoming a knowledge society. Figure 1.1 illustrates the characteristics of the parallel educational system until the early 1970s, which divided pupils at the age of 11 or 12 into one of two separated streams. There was practically no possibility to move between these streams once students had decided which pathway to follow.

The original 1959 proposal of the School Program Committee was further elaborated by the National Board of General Education in the early 1960s, and then finally taken to Parliament on November 22, 1963. The ensuing debate was harsh. Some predicted a gloomy future for Finland if the new ideas related to common unified public school for all were approved: declining level of knowledge, waste of existing national talent, and Finland, as a nation, being left behind in the international economic race. In the final vote, the proposal for the new educational system in Finland was supported, with 123 voting in favor and 68 against. The celebration of the birth of the new school in Finland was disturbed by an announcement by the speaker of the Parliament: President John F. Kennedy had been assassinated in Dallas, Texas just minutes prior.

Figure 1.1. Structure of the Education System in Finland before 1970

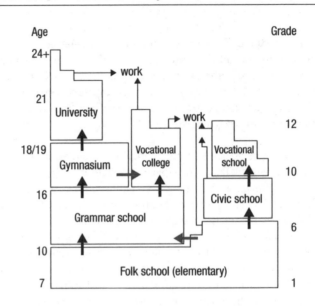

It would be inappropriate to claim that the birth of the new Finnish comprehensive school or *peruskoulu* system, which is frequently identified as a structural foundation for Finland's educational fame today, was created by politicians and authorities alone. Many others, including both school practitioners and academia, contributed to the process of defining Finland's new school system. Particularly significant was the role played by some of Finland's civil society organizations. It is beyond the scope of this chapter to conduct deeper analysis of the influence that many of these groups exerted on Finnish educational reform. However, a good example of civil society involvement in education policy development is the role played by the Finnish Primary School Teachers' Association (FPSTA). As early as 1946, FPSTA had expressed its support for the idea of a unified basic school system. In the mid-1950s, the association published its own education development program accompanied by a detailed, well-argued proposal for a unified, comprehensive school system. What was unusual about this proposed program was that, unlike appeals of union-based teacher associations, it was progressive and future-oriented. It was widely supported by the FPSTA, representing nearly 90% of all Finnish primary school teachers. The FPSTA's proposal took 5 years to complete and stimulated a national discussion that was clearly focused on the need to enhance equality and social justice in Finnish society through a more equitable education system. Perhaps most importantly, the publication of the FPSTA's program proposal was a clear sign that schools and teachers were ready for radical change.

In 1955–1956, the nation's grammar schools enrolled approximately 34,000 pupils. Five years later, enrollment had swelled to 215,000, and continued to soar, rising to 270,000 in 1965 and 324,000 in 1970 (Aho et al., 2006). Finland's old system could barely hold together as parents demanded an improved and more comprehensive basic education for their children in the hope of securing better lives for them. Such social pressure introduced a new theme in the education policy debate: the individual's potential for growth. Researchers then argued that an individual's abilities and intelligence always rose to the level required by society, and that education systems merely reflected these limits or needs.

THE NEW SCHOOL IS BORN

New legislation (1966) and a national curriculum (1970) were prepared in the second half of the 1960s. The social policy climate at the time had consolidated the values of equality and social justice across the social classes of Finnish society. The expenditures incurred by the ideal of a welfare state were seen, as argued by a prominent Finnish political scientist, Professor Pekka Kuusi, an investment in increasing productivity rather than a necessary social cost of maintaining an industrial society (Kuusi, 1961). The new comprehensive school system was poised for implementation in 1972. According to the plan, a wave of reform was to begin in the northern regions of Finland, and reach the southern urban areas by 1978.

A fundamental belief related to the old structure was that *everyone cannot learn everything*; in other words, that talent in society is not evenly distributed in terms of one's ability to be educated. In Finland, there were echoes of the Coleman Report, favoring the view that a young person's basic disposition and characteristics were determined in the home, and could not be substantially influenced by schooling (Coleman et al., 1966). It was important that the new *peruskoulu* shed these beliefs and thus help to build a more socially just society with higher education levels for all.

The central idea of *peruskoulu*, as shown in Figure 1.2, was to merge existing grammar schools, civic schools, and primary schools into a comprehensive 9-year municipal school. This meant that the placement of students after 4 years of primary education into grammar and civic streams would come to an end. All students, regardless of their domicile, socioeconomic background, or interests would enroll in the same 9-year basic schools governed by local education authorities. This implementation was revolutionary, although as noted previously, the idea behind it was not new. Critics of the new system maintained that it was not possible to have the same educational expectations of children coming from very different social and intellectual circumstances. Opponents argued that the entire future of Finland as a developed industrial nation was at risk because overall education attainment would have to be adjusted downward to accommodate less talented students.

Figure 1.2. Structure of the Education System in Finland Since 1970

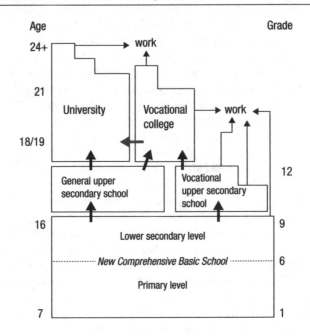

As planned, the wave of implementation began in the northern parts of Finland in 1972. The *National Curriculum for the Comprehensive School* steered the content, organization, and pace of teaching throughout the country. While the structure of the comprehensive school was similar for all students, the National Curriculum provided schools with tools to differentiate instruction for different ability groups and personalities. Foreign languages and mathematics teaching, for example, were arranged in a way that offered students options for three levels of study in grades 7 through 9: basic, middle, and advanced. The syllabus of the basic study program corresponded to what had previously been offered in civic schools, and the advanced study program was equivalent to that offered by the old grammar schools. The reasoning behind these differentiated syllabi was that if learning foreign languages was made a requirement for all, there had to be different courses of study for different kinds of students. The last of the southern municipalities shifted to the new comprehensive school system in 1979. Ability grouping was eventually abolished in all school subjects in 1985. Since then, all students have studied according to the same curricula and syllabi.

Comprehensive school reform triggered the development of three particular aspects in the Finnish education system, which would later prove to be instrumental in creating a well-performing education system. First, bringing together a wide variety of students with often very different life circumstances and aspirations to learn in the same schools and classes required a fundamentally new approach to teaching and learning. The equal opportunity principle insisted that all students be offered a fair chance to be successful and enjoy learning. From early on, it was understood that the education of pupils with special needs would only be successful if learning difficulties and other individual deficits were identified early enough and promptly treated. Special education quickly became an integral part of school curricula, and all municipalities and schools soon housed experts trained to support special needs pupils. Special education is discussed in more detail in the following chapter.

Second, career guidance and counseling became a compulsory part of the comprehensive school curricula in all schools. It was assumed at the time that if all pupils remained in the same school until the end of their compulsory education, they would need systematic counseling on their options after completing basic school. Career guidance was intended to minimize the possibilities that students would make inappropriate choices regarding their future. In principle, students had three options: continue education in upper secondary general school, go on to vocational school, or find employment. Both types of upper secondary education offered several internal options. Career guidance and counseling soon became a cornerstone of both lower- and upper-secondary education, and has been an important factor in explaining low grade repetition and drop-out rates in Finland (Välijärvi & Sahlberg, 2008). Career guidance has also served as a bridge between formal education and the world of work. As part of the overall career guidance curriculum, each student in *peruskoulu* spends 2 weeks in a selected workplace.

Third, new *peruskoulu* required that teachers who were working in very different schools, namely the academic grammar schools and work-oriented civic schools, had to begin to work in the same school with students with diverse abilities. As Professor Jouni Välijärvi explains, comprehensive school reform was not just an organizational change but a new philosophy of education for Finnish schools (Välijärvi et al., 2007; Hautamäki et al., 2008). This philosophy included the beliefs that all pupils can learn if they are given proper opportunities and support, that understanding of and learning through human diversity is an important educational goal, and that schools should function as small-scale democracies, just as John Dewey had insisted decades before. New *peruskoulu* therefore required that teachers employ alternative instructional methods, design learning environments that enable differentiated learning for different pupils, and perceive teaching as a high profession. These expectations led to wide-scale teacher education reform in 1979: a new law on teacher education, emphasizing professional development and focusing on research-based teacher education (discussed in detail in Chapter 3).

Another concrete consequence of the emergence of *peruskoulu* was a rapid expansion of upper-secondary education. Parents expected their children to study further, and young Finns themselves also hoped to reach higher in their

---

BOX 1.1: What is the Finnish Consensus?

The Finnish Parliament reached a decision-in-principle for comprehensive school reform in November 1963. The decision was not unanimous; the basis of the majority consisted of the Agrarian Party and the leftists. This decision, perhaps the most important single consensus in the history of Finnish education, would not have been possible without the support of the Agrarian Party and wider national consensus for the common good.

The Agrarian Party had for a long time resisted the idea of a comprehensive school system. The youth wing of that party understood that restructuring of the Finnish economy and related urbanization required the development of the old-fashioned education system existing at that time. It was particularly important to secure access to good education in rural parts of Finland that were suffering from rapid migration to urban centers and to Sweden. The interesting question is: Why did the Agrarian Party support education reform that was based on the idea of common comprehensive school for all? A new generation of politicians who were near to the Primary School Teachers Association became convinced that all children could have similar learning goals and that they could be taught in the same schools. The president of Finland and former Agrarian Party member, Urho Kekkonen, was one of the supporters of this reform.

The dream of a common public school for all Finnish children had existed since the birth of the Finnish Folk School in the 1860s. The process that led to the decision by the Parliament in 1963 was strictly a political one. It guaranteed that the political elite of Finland was strongly committed to the comprehensive school reform. Political support for the reform was important because it made it possible to proceed swiftly without being halted by the new government. The foundation for a sustainable education policy was created. This same principle of the Finnish consensus has carried throughout the decades until today.

The implementation of comprehensive school reform required several other political compromises. Professor Pauli Kettunen has said that the Nordic welfare state was constructed using three political ideals: the legacy of liberated peasants, the spirit of capitalism, and the utopia of socialism. Equality, efficiency, and solidarity, the essential principles of these three political ideals, merged into a consensus that enriched each other. I think that this is the root of the solid ground on which Finnish education policy has been established.

Erkki Aho
Director General (1973–1991)
National Board of General Education

self-development. Let us now take a look at how upper-secondary education provided pathways to improving human capital in Finland.

EXPANDING UPPER-SECONDARY EDUCATION

The general upper-secondary school had a traditional school-like organization until 1985 when the new Act on General Upper-Secondary Education abolished the old system and introduced a modular curriculum structure. Two annual semesters were replaced by five or six periods per-school year, based on how schools planned their teaching. This meant that teaching and studying was reorganized into 6- or 7-week periods during which they would complete the courses they had chosen. This change enabled schools to rearrange teaching schedules, and, in turn, affected local curriculum planning because schools had more flexibility to allocate lessons into these periods differently (Välijärvi, 2004). The next phase of development was to replace age cohort–based grouping of students with a nonclass organizational system in the mid-1990s. This new general upper-secondary school organization is not based on fixed classes or grades (previously called 10th, 11th, or 12th grades). Students thus have greater choice available to them in planning their studies in terms of both the content and the sequencing of their courses. The new curriculum framework places a stronger emphasis on understanding students' cognitive development and also invited schools to make the best use of their own and their community's strengths. Although students now have more freedom to plan and choose their studies, all students are still obliged to study the basics of the 18 compulsory subjects. Students have to successfully complete at least 75 courses of 38 lessons each. About two-thirds of these are compulsory and the rest freely chosen by students for their general upper-secondary education diploma. Normally students exceed this minimum limit and study more, typically between 80 and 90 courses.

Student assessments and school evaluations are additional important factors affecting the nature of teaching and learning in general upper-secondary school. Teachers assess the achievement of each student at the end of each period (of 6 or 7 weeks), which means students are assessed five or six times per subject per school year. The National Matriculation Examination that students take after successfully completing all required courses is a high-stakes external examination, and therefore has notable effect on curriculum and instruction. A frequently expressed criticism by teachers and school principals in Finland is that the matriculation examination causes "teaching to the test" and thus narrows curriculum and increases stress among students and teachers. As a former mathematics and science teacher, I concur.

Vocational upper-secondary education also underwent significant adaptations to better suit new economic and political situations. Structures, curricula, and methodology of vocational education were renewed to meet the expectations of a knowledge-based economy and provide required labor knowledge and skills.

One of Finland's key policy targets has been to increase the attractiveness of vocational education at the upper-secondary level (Ministry of Education, 2004). Currently, more than 40% of new upper-secondary school students start their studies in vocational schools.

The *structure* of vocational education was simplified and all initial vocational qualifications today consist of 120 credits, equivalent to 3 years of full-time study. One quarter of the study time is allocated to general or optional courses. The number of vocational qualifications was reduced from more than 600 to 52, and related programs of study to 113. In principle, vocational school students are eligible to take the matriculation examination, although very few do. Moreover, providers of upper-secondary education are required to promote transferability, ensuring that students have access to general upper-secondary schools from vocational schools, and vice versa, if they wish to include courses from other schools into their learning plans.

Curriculum and study programs in vocational schools were revised to match the changes made in upper-secondary education, especially the modular-based structure, as well as the needs of labor markets in a knowledge society. The new curriculum was designed to balance the need for more general knowledge and skills and specific professional competences required in each vocational qualification. Performance assessments of achieved professional knowledge and skills are developed via collaboration among three key stakeholders: schools, employers, and employees' representatives.

Methods of instruction and training have been gradually changing in vocational secondary schools. At least one sixth of the training has to be arranged as on-the-job learning, and this is an integral part of the curriculum. Alternative workshops, apprenticeship training, and virtual learning have become commonplace in upper-secondary education. A result-based component of the funding system for vocational schools allocates a factor of 6% on the top of the school's core funding for staff development. Vocational schools are increasingly investing these funds to upgrade their teachers' pedagogical knowledge and skills. Two key factors appear to influence the efficacy of students' choices at the critical point of transition to upper-secondary education. First, when entering upper-secondary education, Finnish students have no experience with high-stakes standardized testing in school, unlike their peers in many other countries where testing has become an integral element of school life. In a comparative study of teachers' experiences under different accountability regimes, we concluded that "the pressure of a structured instructional model of teaching and external assessment of pupils' achievement is having dramatic consequences according to some teachers" (Berry & Sahlberg, 2006). Consequences of the high-stakes testing environment include avoidance of risk taking, boredom, and fear. The study also suggested that in Finland, most lower-secondary schoolteachers teach in order to help their students to learn, not to pass tests. The PISA studies provide further evidence for this argument: Finnish students experience less anxiety in learning mathematics compared to their peers in other countries (Kupari & Välijärvi, 2005).

A second contributing factor to the successful transition to upper-secondary schooling is that students are well prepared to make decisions about postcompulsory education, because counseling and career guidance are widely available in basic school. During their 3-year lower-secondary school, all students are entitled to 2 hours a week of educational guidance and counseling. This reduces the risk that students will make ill-informed decisions regarding their further studies. It also helps students to put more effort into those areas of their studies most important to their anticipated route in upper-secondary school.

Finnish students today enter the transition point between lower- and upper-secondary education with a more effective set of knowledge, skills, and attitudes than in the past. Implemented reforms to upper-secondary education in Finland have had a fundamental impact on school organization, especially with respect to teaching and learning. Traditional school organization based on presentation-recitation models of instruction, age-grouping, fixed teaching schedules, and the dominance of classroom-based seatwork has been gradually transformed to provide more flexible, open, and interaction-rich learning environments, where an active role for students comes first. Ongoing school improvement has therefore been facilitated by the implemention of structural changes in upper-secondary school and by the enrichment of schools and classrooms with alternative instructional arrangements and teaching methods.

IMPROVING EDUCATIONAL ATTAINMENT

Comprehensive school reform has generated obvious consequences. As the number of graduates from these schools has increased, so too has the demand for upper-secondary education. Annually, about 95% of those graduating from *peruskoulu* immediately continue their studies in one of the two types of upper-secondary education settings or enroll in an additional 10th grade. Some students who do not continue their formal education immediately after *peruskoulu* enroll in nonformal educational programs, and will return later to adult educational programs. Figure 1.3 illustrates the choices made by *peruskoulu* leavers between 2000 and 2009, given the options of participating in general or vocational upper-secondary education, additional 10th grade,[3] or exiting formal education. Vocational education has become a true alternative for many students because of its more generally oriented curricula but also because there are more opportunities to continue studies in higher education after receiving a professional qualification from vocational school.

As shown in Figure 1.3, in 2009 about 94.5% of those who completed compulsory basic education immediately continued their studies at the upper-secondary level or undertook an additional 10th grade of *peruskoulu*. In 2009, the number of students enrolled in general and vocational upper-secondary education stood at 50.6% and 41.9%, respectively. In absolute numbers, the 2009–2010 school year marked the first time when more young people enrolled in vocational upper-secondary schools than in general upper-secondary schools when all students were counted (gross-enrollment rate includes those who enroll in vocational schools after the age of 16). In 2009 about 5.5%, or 3,500 basic-school leavers, opted not to continue studying in upper-secondary education or 10th grade of *peruskoulu*. Some of these students enroll in other postcompulsory educational programs, such as arts, crafts, or manual trades. Despite these overall successes, a relatively high number of youth are dropping out of education, and this is considered to be one of the most significant problems faced by the Finnish education system today.

The voluntary additional 10th grade of *peruskoulu* has proved a useful option for young Finns who opt for this route after comprehensive school, although the enrollment trend is declining: In 2003, out of 1,800 who studied 1 additional year in basic school, 83% enrolled in general or vocational upper-secondary education (35% and 48%, respectively). Fewer than 2% of pupils who enroll in the 10th grade drop out during the school year. The accepted education policy target of having only 2.5% basic-school leavers not immediately continue education in upper-secondary

Figure 1.3. Transition from *Peruskoulu* to Upper-Secondary Education as a Percentage of Age Cohorts Between 2000 and 2009

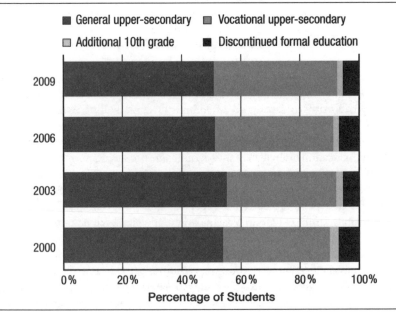

Source: Statistics Finland (n.d.a).

level is ambitious and requires systematic measures from education authorities as well as from schools. According to current education policies, the voluntary 10th grade of basic school will be made available for more pupils who may benefit from it, student guidance and career counseling will be made available for all students, and appropriate methods of teaching will continue to be developed in both basic and upper-secondary schools.

It is noteworthy that in Finland all education after the 9-year *peruskoulu* is noncompulsory. Rather than making upper-secondary education compulsory, Finnish education policies have relied on developing equal opportunities for all to participate in upper-secondary education as a matter of individual choice, while at the same time creating incentives for young people to stay on in the education system after completion of compulsory education. Since the introduction of the comprehensive school in the 1970s, the aims of education policy have been to provide a place of study for all young people in postcompulsory educational institutions. (Aho et al., 2006). Most of the general and vocational upper-secondary schools today are under municipal (and in some cases regional) administration, and municipalities therefore determine provision and accession policies for postcompulsory education. However, this does not mean that local authorities have complete freedom; curricula, teachers' professional requirements, and expectations regarding overall pedagogical environments are fairly unified throughout the country and create a common culture of schooling in Finland.

Due to the noncompulsory nature of upper-secondary education, one important indicator of both the quality and effectiveness of postcompulsory education is the completion rate. As part of the newly introduced education efficiency system in Finland, state authorities have, since 1999, collected systematic data and analyzed completion rates in upper-secondary education. If an ideal completion time of vocational or general upper-secondary studies is set at 3.5 years, then about three out of four students successfully completed their studies in that desired time. Table 1.1 shows how many students terminated upper-secondary and higher education in Finland in academic year 2007–2008. Overall graduation rates in Finland are internationally high. Only 0.2% of the age cohort will not complete compulsory education successfully. Upper-secondary education graduation rate in Finland in 2008 was 93% compared to 76% and 77% in Canada and the United States, respectively. The OECD average upper-secondary education graduation rate is 80% (OECD, 2010a).

Because personalized learning plans in upper-secondary school are not tied to age groups or classes, some students will take more time to complete their studies than others. Some others will leave the education system without a qualification or diploma. Early school-leaving rates thus provide a further measure of the quality and efficiency of secondary education. According to national statistics in Table 1.1, in recent years about 2% per annum of general upper-secondary school students terminate their studies without moving into some other form

Table 1.1. Termination of Upper-Secondary and Higher Education in Finland in Academic Year 2007–2008 as a Percentage of Total Number of Students

Type of Education	Academic Year 2007–08
General Upper Secondary	2.0
Vocational Upper Secondary	9.2
Polytechnic	6.8
University	4.8

Source: Ministry of Education (2009).

of upper-secondary education or training (Committee Report, 2005). Approximately the same number of students move from general to vocational secondary education and complete their studies there. In vocational secondary education, the situation is worse. For example, in 2008 almost 10% of vocational school students terminated their initial studies, of whom 1.5% continued their education in some other school or institution.

Dropouts from formal education and training in Finland are slowly declining, and in upper-secondary education, drop-out rates are substantially lower than those of most other countries (Välijärvi & Sahlberg, 2008). As far as all upper-secondary education is concerned, about 6% of students terminated their studies during the academic year 2008–2009 without immediately continuing studies in some other degree program. The need for preventing educational failure and drop-outs is greatest in upper-secondary and higher vocational education. Keeping students in education has become a particular incentive for schools through a results-based central-government funding scheme, which was introduced in upper-secondary vocational education in the early 2000s and will be extended to all upper-secondary education by 2015. When the results-based financing index for education and training providers is calculated, reduced dropout rates and improved completion rates have a positive effect on overall issued budget. Although the financing index concerns only a small part of overall education budgets, it has been a sufficient incentive to rapidly focus the attention of schools and teachers on measures to improve the early recognition and prevention of problems that might lead to drop out, and on improved direct supports for students' learning and overall well-being in school. Moreover, because the basic funding of schools is tied to the student numbers, success in preventing dropout has a positive impact on the school budget. Vocational schools in particular have developed innovative solutions for those students whose learning styles work best with a more practically oriented curriculum. For example, practice-oriented workshops where students can design and build concrete forms have become a popular way to increase the attractiveness and relevance of secondary education for many students who are at risk of leaving school.

Matriculation Examination

Students who have passed the required courses in upper-secondary general school are eligible to take the National Matriculation Examination. The test is organized by the Matriculation Examination Board and administered at the same time in all schools nationwide. There is no national examination for students graduating from upper-secondary vocational schools. Instead, vocational schools assess the form and content of certification examinations. Students who successfully complete either track can apply to institutions of higher education, namely polytechnics or universities. However, vocational school graduates make up a lesser share of total enrollment in higher education.

The Matriculation Examination first debuted in 1852 as an entrance test for the University of Helsinki. Students had to show sufficient evidence of general academic knowledge and be proficient in Latin. Today, the purpose of the examination is to discover whether students have assimilated the knowledge and skills required in the national core curriculum, as well as whether they have reached a level of maturity in line with the goals of upper-secondary general school. Students take tests in at least four subjects. Passing the matriculation examination, which is given only in upper-secondary general schools, entitles candidates to continue their studies at higher education institutions.

The Matriculation Examination Board is responsible for administering the examination, preparing the tests, and grading the answer sheets. The Ministry of Education nominates the chairman of the board and its members (approximately 40) after consultation and recommendations from universities and the National Board of Education. The members represent the various subjects covered on the Matriculation Examination. Approximately 330 associate members assist the Board in preparing and marking the tests. Technical arrangements, such as printing and distribution of the examinations, are taken care of by the secretariat, which has 22 employees. The total annual cost of this examination in Finland is about 10 million U.S. dollars and is entirely covered by the fees from students—a rare expenditure not covered by public sources in the Finnish education system.

Held twice a year in spring and autumn in all Finnish upper-secondary general schools, the examination is a high-stakes event for students. A candidate must complete all selected exams within three consecutive examinations, that is, within 18 months, but they can also be completed in one period. The examination consists of at least four subject areas. All candidates must take the Mother Tongue test; they then may choose three other exams from the following four domains: Second Domestic Language (Finnish or Swedish), Foreign Languages, Mathematics, and General Studies (consisting of social and natural sciences). The candidate may also include exams in one or more optional subjects. All exams are paper-and-pencil, mostly essay based and open ended, with an increasing amount of reference materials that students must refer to when answering the questions. The matriculation examination will be computer based from 2015 forward.

Some exams have two different attainment levels, and candidates may choose which to take, regardless of their course of study in upper-secondary school. Mathematics and foreign languages offer advanced and ordinary course-level exams; so does the second domestic language subject area. The candidate must pass an exam based on the advanced course in at least one elective subject. Candidates who have passed an exam may try to improve their score one time, except for the general studies test, which can be taken twice more. Students who have passed the matriculation examination can try to improve their scores once or they can take extra exams in subjects that were not included previously. A candidate receives a certificate after successfully passing all the compulsory tests.

Instead of a national examination, vocational students take a school-level assessment of learning outcomes and skills. The principle behind the assessment is to develop a positive self-image and personal growth in students with different kinds of competencies. Students are gauged according to their own self-assessments, as well as through interviews with their teachers. In addition, their on-the-job training instructors participate in workplace assessments. Performance is graded from 1 (satisfactory) to 3 (excellent). In the absence of a national vocational-education examination, the National Board of Education issues recommendations to ensure equality in school-based performance assessments.

A current topic of debate in vocational education is how to ensure the quality of certification from school to school. Parliament recently passed an act on this issue, and certification will now include both the teachers' assessment and a demonstration of skills to prove that a student has achieved the vocational proficiency set out in the curriculum. These skills demonstrations are to take place, wherever possible, at work sites, mostly in conjunction with periods of on-the-job learning. Representatives of employers and employees are to take part in assessment. Depending on the program, students can expect to undergo from 4 to 10 demonstrations of proficiency during the course of their studies.

A GENERATION OF EDUCATIONAL CHANGE

Since the terrain of educational change has not been explored much in Finland, it is safe to suggest theories-of-action and conceptual models to organize the thinking about what has happened and why. After the comprehensive school reform in the 1970s, educational change in Finland can be described in terms of three phases (Sahlberg, 2009):

- rethinking the theoretical and methodological foundations (1980s)
- improvement through networking and self-regulated change (1990s)
- enhancing efficiency of structures and administration (2000–present).

This process is illustrated in Figure 1.4. Each phase conveys a certain policy logic and theory of action. By the early 1980s, the structural reforms that led to creating *peruskoulu* were completed. After that, attention was focused on *conception of knowledge* and *conception of learning* in the school practices embedded into the philosophy of *peruskoulu*. The second phase emerged from the liberalization of Finnish education governance, a period characterized by self-directed networking of schools and collaboration among individuals. The third and ongoing phase was initiated by a need to raise productivity in the public sector, and was accelerated by publication of the initial PISA results in December 2001 and later by the 2008 economic downturn. This phase focuses on reforming the structures and administration of education and is careful to avoid disturbing the sensitive balance of a well-performing education system in the pursuit of enhanced efficiency. I will describe next each of these three phases in more detail.

Phase 1: Rethinking the Theoretical and Methodological Foundations (1980s)

Several research and development projects launched within the new comprehensive school system in the late 1970s and early 1980s led to criticism of then-current pedagogical practices, especially teacher-centered methods of teaching in Finnish schools. The new school system was launched with philosophical and educational assumptions that insisted the role of public education must be to educate critical and independent-thinking citizens. One of the main themes of school development then was the realization of a more dynamic *conception of knowledge*. As a result, renewed approaches to teaching would lead to meaningful learning and understanding, teachers believed (Aho, 1996). A significant driver of this change was emerging information and communication technologies in schools at that time. Some feared, quite correctly, that the expansion of computers in classrooms

Figure 1.4. Three Phases of Educational Change in Finland Since the 1980s

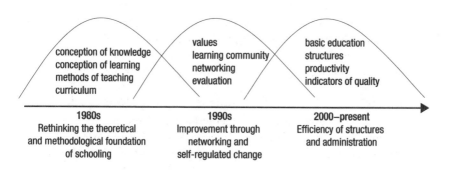

1980s	1990s	2000–present
conception of knowledge conception of learning methods of teaching curriculum	values learning community networking evaluation	basic education structures productivity indicators of quality
Rethinking the theoretical and methodological foundation of schooling	Improvement through networking and self-regulated change	Efficiency of structures and administration

would lead to problems, including isolated knowledge, unnecessary information, and technological determinism.

Technological development corresponded with the revolution in learning sciences. The dominance of cognitive psychology, along with the emergence of constructivist theories of learning and the advances in neurosciences on the horizon, attracted Finnish educational researchers to analyze existing conceptions of knowledge and learning in schools. Several influential and teacher-friendly readers were published and sent to schools. They included "Conception of Knowledge" (1989), "Conception of Learning" (1989), and "About Possibilities of School Change" (1990). Questions like "What is knowledge?," "How do pupils learn?," and "How do schools change?" were common themes for teacher in-service training and school improvement until the end of the 1990s (Lehtinen et al., 1989; Miettinen, 1990; Voutilainen, Mehtäläinen, & Niiniluoto, 1989).

From an international perspective, this first phase of educational change in Finland was exceptional. At the same time as Finnish teachers were exploring the theoretical foundations of knowledge and learning and redesigning their school curricula to be congruent with them, their peers in England, Germany, France, and the United States struggled with increased school inspection, controversial externally imposed learning standards, and competition that disturbed some teachers to the point that they decided to leave their jobs (Hargreaves & Shirley, 2009). In England and the United States, for example, deeper analysis of school knowledge and implications of new research on learning remained mainly issues among academics or reached only the most advanced teachers and leaders. Perhaps it is due to these philosophical aspects of educational change that Finland remained immune to the winds of market-driven education policy changes that arose in many other OECD countries in the 1990s.

Although the nature of educational development in Finland during this phase was genuinely Finnish work, it is important to give credit to knowledge and ideas that were brought from abroad, especially from the United States, Canada, and the United Kingdom, as well as other Nordic countries. Particularly significant was the role of teaching and student assessment methods —especially those published by the Association for Supervision and Curriculum Development (ASCD)—that were developed in the United States and then adopted into Finnish culture and educational practice. Two examples deserve to be mentioned here. First, Finland was one of the first countries to launch a large-scale implementation of cooperative learning in select Finnish universities and later in schools. Research and development work done at the University of Minnesota (David and Roger Johnson), Stanford University (Elizabeth Cohen), Johns Hopkins University (Robert Slavin), and Tel Aviv University (Shlomo Sharan and Yael Sharan) had an important role to play in the transformation of teaching and learning in schools according to the philosophical principles described in the Finnish readers mentioned above. Second, in the late 1980s, the National Board of General Education in Finland launched a national initiative to diversify teaching methods in science teaching. The Models of Teaching by Bruce Joyce and Marsha Weil (later with Beverly Showers) was the main source of inspiration and ideas for this work (Joyce & Weil, 1986). Bruce Joyce visited Finland in the late 1980s and his work has left a permanent impression on the history of Finnish school improvement that still lives today in hundreds of Finnish schools through expanded teaching methods repertoires. Work by David Berliner in educational psychology, Linda Darling-Hammond in teacher education, and Andy Hargreaves and Michael Fullan in educational change have been closely studied and implemented in developing Finnish education since the 1970s. The secret of the successful influence of these educational ideas from the United States, United Kingdom, and Canada is that there was fruitful ground in Finnish schools for such pragmatic models of change. Interestingly, the Finns themselves have developed only a little novel pedagogical practice that would have had more international significance.

There is surprisingly little reliable research on how this first phase of educational change actually affected teaching and learning in Finnish schools. Reflection by one of the key figures in Finland of that time and the author of some of the readers mentioned earlier, Professor Erno Lehtinen, was cautiously reserved about the impact:

> Discussion on conceptions of knowledge and learning has clearly affected how teachers talk about learning and teaching. Earlier discourse that was characterized by traditional values of socialization and teaching of facts and automated ideals of mastery has been replaced by understanding, critical thinking, problem solving, and learning how to learn. Expanding the conceptions of knowledge and learning was also reflected in implementation of the new curriculum in the mid-1990s at all levels of schooling, and also in the national curriculum reforms in this new decade. (2004, p. 54)

This phase of educational change in Finland has been characterized as a time that challenged conventional beliefs, searched for innovation, and increased trust in schools and their abilities to find the best ways to raise the quality of student learning. Deeper understanding of knowledge and learning strengthened schools' moral foundations. A recent evaluation of education in Finnish comprehensive schools concludes that "teachers pay conscious attention to diversifying teaching and learning environments. Teachers think that the use of versatile teaching methods is important both to planning and classroom work" (Atjonen et al., 2008, p. 197). This suggests that schools have made progress in teaching and learning, at least modestly.

Phase 2: Improvement through Networking and Self-Regulation (1990s)

The National Curriculum Reform of 1994 is often regarded as the major educational reform in Finland, along with the previous Comprehensive School Reform of the 1970s. The main vehicle of change was the active role of municipalities and schools in curriculum design and implementation of related changes. Schools were encouraged to collaborate with other schools and also to network with parents, businesses, and nongovernmental organizations. At the level of central administration, this new collaborative and self-directed movement culminated in the Aquarium Project, a national school improvement initiative enabling all Finnish schools, principals, and teachers to network with each other.[4] The aim of the Aquarium Project was to transform schools into active learning communities. According to Martti Hellström this project was "a unique self-directed school improvement network that was open to all active educators" (Hellström, 2004, p. 179). As a form of practice, this was previously unheard of in Finnish educational administration, and only rarely found elsewhere.

The Aquarium Project offered schools a new context for improvement—something that combined traditional community work and modern Facebook-type social networking. It has close links to the ideas of Alberta Initiative for School Improvement (AISI), a unique long-term government-funded school and teacher-development program in Alberta, Canada (Hargreaves et al., 2009). Research has shown that school improvement through networking and self-regulation has positively impacted the engagement level of schools in development in Finland and Alberta. Particularly important has been the notion that the majority of schools involved in these initiatives reported that during a time of economic downturn and decreasing resources, teachers believed that they had succeeded in improving their schools. Despite different educational governance systems, the Aquarium Project and AISI have stimulated local innovations and research activity among principals and teachers who pursued advanced educational studies in universities. They also have demonstrated that it is the school, not the system, that is the locus of control and capacity—a point reinforced by Hellström (2004) and Murgatroyd (2007).

At the beginning of 1997, there were more than 1,000 projects in 700 schools and 163 municipalities participating in the Aquarium Project. My best estimate is that this included about 5,000 teachers and 500 principals directly involved in this school improvement initiative. The project was in accord with new ideas of decentralization, increased school autonomy, and stronger school identity in the 1990s. As a strategy for school improvement, this project stressed shared responsibility in schools, personalization, and collaborative efforts to enhance the quality of learning. In this sense, the Aquarium Project incorporated features consistent with neoliberal education policies, and occasionally, these characteristics were seen as signals of increased competition among schools in the education sector. It is true that school choice creates a competitive environment, but the school improvement network transformed bold competition into mutual striving for better schools. The strong social aspect of the Aquarium Project valued sharing ideas and solving problems together, thus preventing schools from viewing each other as competitors. In this respect, the project relied on earlier values of equal educational opportunities and social responsibility, rather than competition and administrative accountability. Perhaps this political duality served as the Achilles' heel of the Aquarium Project. The project was terminated by a political decision in early 1999 at the dawn of the era of enhanced efficiency of administration and structural reforms.

Phase 3: Enhancing Efficiency of Structures and Administration (2000—the present)

The first PISA results published on December 4, 2001, took everyone by surprise. In all three academic domains—mathematics, science, and reading literacy—Finland was one of the highest performing nations of the OECD countries. Earlier student performance gaps with Japan, Korea, and Hong Kong were closed. Finns seemed to learn all the knowledge and skills they demonstrated on these tests without private tutoring, after-school classes, or large amounts of homework, unlike many of their peers in other countries (OECD, 2010b; Sahlberg, 2010a). Furthermore, the relative variation of educational performance between schools was exceptionally small in Finland.

Initial reactions after the first PISA results within the education community were confusing. The world media wanted to know the secret of good Finnish education. Within the first 18 months after the first PISA results were published, several hundred official foreign delegations toured around Finland to learn how schools operate and how teachers teach. Questions from the foreign visitors regarding the "Finnish miracle" of PISA were often such that Finns themselves were not prepared to respond with reliable answers. The next three PISA cycles in 2003, 2006, and 2009 advanced and consolidated Finland's reputation even further, thus elevating the interest of world media in Finnish education. The power of Finnish education is in its high quality and equitable student learning, as shown in Figure 1.5. Finland, Canada, and Korea produce more consistent learning results regardless of students' socioeconomic status. France and the United States have both below-average achievement scores and a wide performance variance.

What PISA surveys, in general, have revealed is that education policies that are based on the ideal of equal educational opportunities and that have brought teachers to the core of educational change have positively impacted the quality of learning outcomes. Further analysis of PISA data indicate that factors related to domicile and geography play significant roles in explaining variations of assessed student learning and their future career paths as well (Välijärvi, 2008). Apparently, the variations in student performance caused by geographic and social factors are increasing. There is increasing skepticism among teachers and researchers in Finland, as well, regarding limitations that international student assessments impose on their definition of student performance.

Combining PISA results with other global education indicators and national surveys of people's satisfaction with schools, it is safe to conclude that Finland's education system is in very good condition by international standards. This is obviously a challenge to Finnish education policy makers and to the school-improvement community—after all, it is difficult to renew a system that is already performing well. Perhaps this explains the rather conservative mode of developing primary and secondary schools in Finland recently. Structural reforms have focused on post-secondary education and the efficiency of the entire education administration. In the Finnish school system, multiculturalism, special education, and abolishing the administrative line between primary and lower-secondary schools are the main areas of development since year 2000. National Curriculum Frameworks for comprehensive and upper-secondary general education were revised but no significant changes were introduced. Focus on enhanced efficiency and productivity has led to shrinking school budgets in many parts of the country and the need to do more or the same as before with fewer resources. Many practitioners, among the school leaders and teacher leaders, have been waiting for new directions in school improvement as compensation for these negative developments in resourcing.

Figure 1.5. National Average PISA Score and Percentage of Variance of Student Reading Performance as a Function of Socioeconomic Status in 2009 in Selected OECD Countries

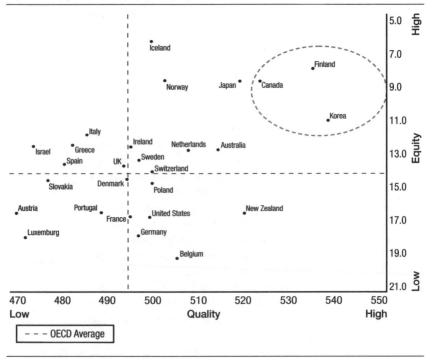

Source: OECD (2010b).

Some of the possible trends for Finnish primary and secondary education in this decade will be discussed in Chapter 5.

THE FINNISH EDUCATION SYSTEM IN 2011

One of the key messages of this book is that unlike many other contemporary systems of education, the Finnish system has not been infected by market-based competition and high-stakes testing policies. The main reason is that the education community in Finland has remained unconvinced that competition and choice with more standardized testing than students evidently require would be good for schools. The ultimate success of a high-stakes testing policy is whether it positively affects student learning, not whether it increases student scores on a particular test (Amrein & Berliner, 2002). If student learning remains unaffected, or if testing leads to biased teaching, the validity of such high-stakes tests must be questioned. Finnish education authorities and especially teachers have not been convinced that frequent external census-based testing and stronger accountability would be beneficial to students and their learning.

Education policies are necessarily intertwined with other social policies, and with the overall political culture of a nation. The key success factor in Finland's development of a well-performing knowledge economy with good governance and a respected education system has been its ability to reach broad consensus on most major issues concerning future directions for Finland as a nation. The conclusion is that Finland seems particularly successful in implementing and maintaining the policies and practices that constitute *sustainable leadership and change* (Hargreaves & Fink, 2006). Education in Finland is seen as a public good and therefore has a strong nation-building function.

Education policies designed to raise student achievement in Finland have put a strong accent on teaching and learning by encouraging schools to craft optimal learning environments and establish instructional content that will best help students to reach the general goals of schooling. It was assumed very early in Finland's reform process that instruction is the key element that makes a difference in what students learn in school, not standards, assessment, or alternative instructional programs. As the level of teacher professionalism gradually increased in schools during the 1990s, the prevalence of effective teaching methods and pedagogical classroom and school designs increased. A new flexibility within the Finnish education system enabled schools to learn from one another and thus make the best practices universal by adopting innovative approaches to organize schooling. It also encouraged teachers and schools to continue to expand their repertoires of teaching methods, and to individualize teaching in order to meet the needs of all students. The structure and the internal dynamics of the education system in Finland are illustrated in Figure 1.6.

Figure 1.6. The Education System in Finland in 2011

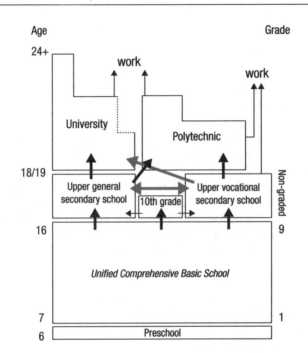

What the scheme shown in Figure 1.6 is not able to reveal are the principles of education and care that are typical to Finnish schools today. For example, schools are encouraged to maintain strong support systems for teaching and learning—nutritious, free school meals for all pupils, health services, psychological counseling, and student guidance are normal practices in every school. Another strong element of the education system in Finland is built-in networks of schools and communities of teachers in municipalities and school improvement initiatives. Andreas Schleicher, who leads the PISA team at the OECD, concluded in his analysis of Finnish education that building networks among schools that stimulate and spread innovation helps to explain Finland's success in making "strong school performance a consistent and predictable outcome throughout the education system, with less than 5% variation in student performance between schools" (Schleicher, 2006, p. 9). The question is: Has Finland always had such a well-performing education system? If the answer is no, then it is worth asking yet another question: What factors have contributed to Finland's educational improvement?

CHAPTER 2

The Finnish Paradox: Less Is More

If everybody thinks the same way, nobody thinks very much.

—My grandmother's advice to me for succeeding in life.

Today Finland is regarded as one of the world's most literate societies. As a nation of modest people, Finland never actually intended to be the best in the world in education. Finns like to compete, but collaboration is a more typical characteristic of this nation. In the early 1990s when Finnish education was known internationally as average, the Finnish minister of education visited her colleague in neighboring Sweden to hear, among other things, that by the end of that decade the Swedish education system would be the best in the world. The Finnish minister replied that the Finns' goal is much more modest than that. "For us," she said, "it's enough to be ahead of Sweden." This episode is an example of close sibling relationships and coexistence between Finland and Sweden. In fact, companionship is more common than rivalry between these neighboring Nordic nations that share many values and principles in their education systems and societies.

This chapter answers such questions as: Has the Finnish education system always been a top performer? What do we mean by a good education system? and How much does homogenous society explain good educational performance? This chapter also describes how Finland has been able to improve participation in education, creating equal educational opportunities for all, and spread a good quality of teaching in most schools and classrooms with modest overall cost. Rather than increasing time for teaching and learning, testing students more frequently, and insisting students work harder on their homework, Finland has done the opposite, as this chapter illustrates. The key lesson from Finland is: There are alternative ways to build good public education systems that differ from those commonly offered in world education policy forums.

FROM PERIPHERY TO LIMELIGHT

In the 1980s the Finnish education system had only a few features that attracted any interest among international educators. Many aspects of education policy were adopted from Finland's wealthier western neighbor, Sweden. In international comparisons, Finnish education was exceptional on only one account: The Finnish 10-year-olds were among the best readers in the world (Allerup & Medjing, 2003; Elley, 1992). Other than that, international education indicators left Finland in the shadows of traditional education superpowers, such as Sweden, England, the United States, and Germany. What is noteworthy is that Finland has been able to upgrade human capital by transforming its education system from mediocre to one of the best international performers in a relatively short period of time. This success has been achieved through education policies that differ from those in many other nations. Indeed, some of the educational reform policies appear to be paradoxes because they depart so clearly from the global educational reform thinking.

Prior to the first cycle of the PISA in 2000 many countries thought that their education systems were world class and that students in their schools were better learners than elsewhere. These countries include Germany, France, Norway, England, and naturally the Soviet Union and the United States. Educational indicators such as educational attainment, spending, and college graduation rates, as well as academic competitions such as the International Olympiads in mathematics, physics, and chemistry (and later in subjects such as computer science, biology, and philosophy) had given these nations reason to celebrate the respective performances of their school systems. In academic scholarly competitions, high school-aged students compete to demonstrate advanced-level knowledge in their fields. Naturally those education systems that have established effective selection systems to identify talents and special abilities early on and then provide gifted students with optimal learning opportunities have succeeded well in these games. Especially population-rich nations with large numbers of students, like China, the United States, and the former Soviet Union, have acquired reputations as high-performing education nations on the basis of Academic Olympiads. Interestingly, several Central and Eastern European countries, among them Hungary, Romania, and Bulgaria, are ranked high in the overall league tables of these Olympiads. Table 2.1 illustrates the position of Finland among some selected nations in Mathematics Olympiads since 1959 when Finland participated for the first time in these games.

Success in these Academic Olympiads was often used as a proxy for the quality of national educational systems. Even if Finnish students' performance in mathematics is adjusted for population size, the relative position of Finland has fluctuated between 25th and 35th in the overall global rank list. Until 2001—and in some circles quite some time after that—a common conception in Finland was that the level of mathematical and scientific knowledge and skills of Finnish students was internationally modest, at best.

As Finland attracts global attention due to its high-performing education system, it is worth asking whether there has really been any progress in the performance of its students since the 1970s. If such progress in any terms can be reliably

Table 2.1. Finnish Upper-Secondary School Students in Mathematics Olympiads Compared with their Peers in Selected Countries since 1959

Country	Medals			Number of Participations	Number of Participating Students
	Gold	Silver	Bronze		
China	101	26	5	23	134
USA	80	96	29	34	216
Soviet Union	77	67	45	29	204
Hungary	74	138	77	48	324
Romania	66	111	88	49	332
Russia	65	28	9	17	102
Bulgaria	50	89	88	49	336
Japan	23	52	30	19	114
Canada	16	37	66	28	168
Sweden	5	23	66	41	271
The Netherlands	2	21	48	38	250
Norway	2	10	24	25	142
Finland	1	5	47	35	224
Denmark	0	3	18	18	102

Source: International Mathematical Olympiad (http://www.imo-official.org/).

identified, then, consequently, the question becomes: *What factors might be behind successful education reform?* When education systems are compared internationally, it is important to have a broader perspective than just student achievement. What is significant from this analysis is the steady progress during the past 3 decades within four main domains: 1. increased levels of educational attainment of the adult population, 2. widespread equity in terms of learning outcomes and performance of schools, 3. a good level of student learning as measured by international student assessments, and 4. efficiency and moderate overall spending, almost solely from public sources. Let us next take a look at each of these domains in more detail.

LEVEL OF EDUCATIONAL ATTAINMENT

Finland remained rather poorly educated until the 1960s. Education was accessible only to those who could afford it and happened to live close to a grammar school and university. When *peruskoulu* was launched in the early 1970s, for three-quarters of adult Finns, basic school was the only completed form of education. Holding an academic degree was rare, as only 7% had some kind of university degree. Overall progress since 1970 in educational attainment by the Finnish adult population (15 years and older) is shown in Figure 2.1 (Sahlberg, 2006b). The current situation is congruent with a typical profile of the human capital pyramid in advanced knowledge economies, having about 30% higher educational attainments and about 40% upper-secondary-education degree holders.

Figure 2.1 indicates that there has been a steady growth in participation in all levels of education in Finland since 1970. The growth has been especially rapid in the upper-secondary-education sector in the 1980s and, then, within the higher and adult education sectors in the 1990s and up to the present. Education policies that have driven Finnish reform since 1970 have prioritized creating equal opportunities, raising quality, and increasing participation within all educational levels across Finnish society. As a result, more than 99% of the age cohort successfully complete compulsory *peruskoulu*, about 95% continue their education in upper-secondary schools or in the 10th grade of *peruskoulu* (3%) immediately after graduation, and 93% of those starting upper-secondary school eventually receive their school-leaving certification, providing access to higher education (Statistics Finland, n.d.a).

More than 50% of the Finnish adult population participates in adult-education programs. What is significant in this expansion of participation in education is that it has taken place without shifting the burden of costs to students or to their parents. According to recent global education indicators, only 2.5% of Finnish expenditure on educational institutions (all levels of education) is from private sources compared with an average of 17.4% of total educational expenditure (OECD, 2010a). For example, in the United States 33.9% and in Canada 25.3% of all expenditure on educational institutions is from private sources.

Figure 2.1. Level of Educational Attainment Among the Finnish Adult Population Since 1970

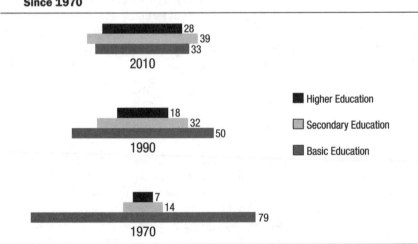

Source: Statistics Finland (n.d.a).

School life expectancy, which predicts the duration of formal education of a citizen at the age of 5, is one of the highest in the world at over 20 years in 2010. This is mainly because education is publicly financed and hence available to all. The two types of higher-education institutions offer a place of study to about two thirds of the age cohort. Since studying in Finnish universities and polytechnics is free, higher education is an equal opportunity for all those who have successfully completed upper-secondary education. The current challenge in Finnish higher education is to encourage students to complete their studies faster than before and thereby enroll in labor markets sooner. The government of Finland is introducing new conditions for student loans and carrots to those who graduate on time.

EQUITY OF OUTCOMES

Equity in education is an important feature in Nordic welfare states. It means more than just opening access to an equal education for all. Equity in education is a principle that aims at guaranteeing high quality education for all in different places and circumstances. In the Finnish context equity is about having a socially fair and inclusive education system that is based on equality of educational opportunities. As a result of the comprehensive school reform of the 1970s, education opportunities for good quality learning have spread rather evenly across Finland. There was a visible achievement gap among young adults at the start of comprehensive school in the early 1970s due to very different educational orientations associated with the old parallel system (see Figure 1.1). This knowledge gap strongly corresponded with the socioeconomic divide within Finnish society at that time. Although students' learning outcomes began to even out by the mid-1980s, the streaming of pupils according to ability grouping in mathematics and foreign languages kept the achievement gap relatively wide.

After abolishing streaming in comprehensive school in the mid-1980s and making learning expectations the same for all students, the achievement gap between low and high achievers began to decrease. This meant that all pupils, regardless of their abilities or interests, studied mathematics and foreign languages in the same classes. Earlier, these subjects had three levels of curricula that pupils were assigned to based on their prior performance in these subjects, but often also based on their parents' or peers' influence. Clear evidence of more equitable learning outcomes came from the OECD's first PISA survey in 2000. In that study, Finland had the smallest performance variations between schools in reading, mathematics, and science scales of all OECD nations. A similar trend continued in the 2003 PISA cycle and was even strengthened in the PISA surveys of 2006 and 2009 (OECD, 2001; 2004; 2007; 2010b). Figure 2.2 shows performance variance within and between schools in the OECD countries as assessed by the reading scale in 2009 (OECD, 2010b).

According to Figure 2.2, Finland has about 7% between-school variance on the PISA reading scale whereas the average between-school variance in other OECD countries is about 42%. Student achievement variation between different schools in Finland in PISA 2009 is at a similar level to the previous PISA cycles. The fact that almost all Finnish inequality is within schools, as shown in Figure 2.2, means that the remaining differences are probably mostly due to variation in students' natural talent. Accordingly, variation between schools mostly relates to social inequality. Since this is a small source of variation in Finland, it indicates that schools successfully deal with social inequality. This suggests, as Professor Norton Grubb observed in his review of equity in education in Finland, that Finnish educational reform has succeeded in building an equitable education system in a relatively short time, a main objective of Finland's education reform agenda set in the early 1970s (OECD, 2005a; Grubb, 2007).

An essential element of the Finnish comprehensive school is systematic attention to those students who have special educational needs. Special education is an important part of education and care in Finland. It refers to designed educational and psychological services within the education sector for those with special needs. The basic idea is that with early recognition of learning difficulties and social and

Figure 2.2. Variance Within and Between Schools in Student Reading Performance on the 2009 PISA Study

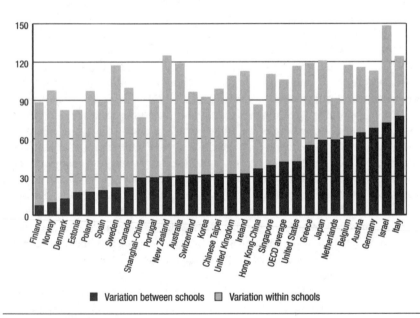

Source: OECD (2010b).

behavioral problems, appropriate professional support can be provided to individuals as early as possible.

The aim of special education is to help and support students by giving them equal opportunities to complete school in accordance with their abilities and alongside their peers. There are two main pathways in special education in the Finnish comprehensive school. The first path sees the student included in a regular class and provided with *part-time special education* in small groups. These groups are led by a special education teacher if the difficulties in learning are not serious. The student may also have an individual learning plan that adjusts the learning goals according to his or her abilities. Students with special educational needs may complete their studies following a general or an adjusted curriculum. Student assessment is then based on the individual learning plan.

The second alternative is to provide *permanent special education* in a special group or class in the student's own school or, in some cases, in a separate institution. Transfer to special education in this case requires an official decision that is based on a statement by a psychological, medical, or social welfare professional, with a mandatory parental hearing. In Finland the transfer decision to special needs education is made by the school board of the pupil's municipality of residence, and can be processed rather quickly (within a few months in most cases). In order to promote success in learning, each student in special education has a personalized learning plan that is based on the school curriculum and adjusts educational expectations individually.

In school year 2008–2009, almost one third of all students in *peruskoulu* was enrolled in one of the two alternative forms of special education described above. More than one fifth of *peruskoulu* students were in part-time special education that focuses on curing minor dysfunctions in speaking, reading, writing, or learning difficulties in mathematics or foreign languages. Respectively, 8% of students were permanently transferred to a special education group, class, or institution. The number of students in permanent special education has doubled in the last 10 years; at the same time, the number of special education institutions has declined steadily since the early 1990s. Since those students who are in part-time special education normally vary from one year to another, up to half of those students who complete their compulsory education at age of 16 have been in special education at some point in their schooling. In other words, it is nothing special anymore for students. This fact significantly reduces the negative stigma that is often brought on by special education. In vocational upper-secondary education, approximately 10% of all students were in special education during the school year 2008–2009.

At the dawn of *peruskoulu* reform, Finland adopted a strategy of early intervention and prevention in helping those individuals who have special educational needs of some kind. This means that possible learning and development deficits are diagnosed during early childhood development and care before children enter school. In the early years of primary school, intensive special support, mostly in reading, writing, and arithmetic, is offered to all children who have major or minor special needs. Therefore the proportion of students in special education in Finland in the early grades of primary school is relatively higher than in most other countries. As Figure 2.3 shows, the number of special needs students in Finland declines by the end of primary school and then slightly increases as students move to subject-based lower-secondary school. The reason for the increased need for special support in lower-secondary school in Finland is that the unified curriculum sets certain expectations for all students, regardless of their abilities or prior learning. The common strategy internationally is to repair problems in primary and lower-secondary education as they occur rather than try to prevent them from happening (Itkonen & Jahnukainen, 2007). Countries that employ the strategy of repair have an increasing relative number of special needs students throughout primary and lower-secondary education, as Figure 2.3 shows.

High-equity education in Finland is not a result of educational factors alone. Basic structures of the Finnish welfare state play a crucial role in providing all children and their families with equitable conditions for starting a successful educational path at the age of 7. Early childhood care, voluntary free preschool that is attended by some 98% of the age cohort, comprehensive health services, and preventive measures to identify possible learning and development difficulties before children start schooling are accessible to all in Finland. Finnish school also provide all pupils with free and healthy lunch everyday regardless of their home socioeconomic situation. Child poverty is at a very low level, less than 4% of the child population compared with over 20% in the United States. In order to prevent early childhood learners from being ranked according to their educational performance in schools, grade-based assessments are not normally used during the first 5 years of *peruskoulu*. It has been an important principle in developing elementary education in Finland that structural elements that cause student failure in schools should be removed. That is why grade retention and over-reliance on academic performance have gradually vanished in Finnish schools.

Figure 2.3. Estimated Relative Number of Students in Part-Time or Full-Time Special Education in Finland and Other Countries during Primary and Lower-Secondary Education

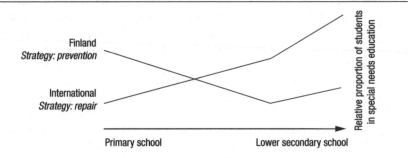

Although this book focuses first and foremost on primary and secondary education in Finland, it is noteworthy that Finnish higher education is one of the most equitable in the world. The Toronto-based Higher Education Strategy Associates compares equity- and equality-related issues in higher education in different countries. Its *Global Higher Education Rankings* (Usher & Medow, 2010) is the second iteration of a comparison of higher-education affordability and accessibility for residents in 17 countries. The study presents data on six different indicators of affordability and four different indictors of accessibility. The overall winner in both affordability and accessibility in 2010 was Finland. Indeed, currently more than 60% of upper-secondary school graduates enroll in higher education. All higher education in Finland is free of charge for all students, as of this writing in 2011.

STUDENT LEARNING

The ultimate criterion of the quality of a national education system is how well students learn what they are expected to learn. International comparisons of education systems put a strong emphasis on scores in standardized achievement tests. Although it is difficult to compare students' learning outcomes today with those in 1980, some evidence of progress of student learning in Finland can be offered using IEA (International Educational Assessment) and PISA surveys recorded since the 1970s (Kupari & Välijärvi, 2005; Martin et al., 2000; Robitaille & Garden, 1989). Since it is impossible to conclude whether there has been progress of student learning in general, let us look at some school subjects individually.

Mathematics is often used as a proxy for general academic educational performance. The studies available include the Second International Mathematics Study (SIMS) in 1981 (8th grade, 20 nations), Trends in Mathematics and Science Repeat Study (TIMSS-R) in 1999 (8th grade, 38 nations) and the PISA survey in 2000 (15-year-olds, all 30 OECD-member countries). These are the international student assessment surveys in which Finland has participated since 1980. Since the nations participating in each international survey are not the same and the methodologies of IEA and OECD surveys are different, the international average as a benchmarking value does not always provide a fully comparable or coherent picture.

Table 2.2 shows Finland's performance in major international student assessment studies since the early 1960s when the First International Mathematics Study was launched (Sahlberg, 2009). These studies normally compare student achievement in reading comprehension, mathematics, and science at three points of education: at the end of elementary school (age 10), lower-secondary school (age 14), and upper-secondary school (age 17). Finnish students' performance in the Second International Mathematics Study (published in 1981) was, in all areas of mathematics, at the international average. The national average performance of Finland was clearly behind Hungary, the Netherlands and Japan in lower- and

Table 2.2. Performance of Finnish Students in International Student Assessment Studies Since the early 1960s

Assessment Study	Population Tested	Participating Countries	Rank of Finland
IEA First International Mathematics Study (FIMS) 1962–1967	13-year-olds and high school completion	12	Average performer
IEA First International Science Study (FISS) 1967–1973	10- and 14-year-olds and high school completion	18	Average performer
IEA Study of Reading Comprehension 1967–1973	10- and 14-year-olds and high school completion	14	Average performer (in one area, 3rd)
IEA Second International Mathematics Study (SIMS) 1977–1981	13-year-olds and high school completion	19 (13-year-olds) 15 (high school)	Average performer
IEA Second International Science Study (SISS) 1980–1987	At primary, middle and high school completion	23	10-year-olds: High 14-year-olds: Average performer
IEA Written Composition Study 1980–1988	At primary, middle and high school completion	14	Average performer
IEA Reading Literacy Study 1988–1994	9 and 14-year-olds	32	Top performer
IEA Third (later "Trends in") International Mathematics and Science Study (TIMSS)	4th and 8th grade	1995: 45 1999: 38 2003: 50 2007: 59	Above average performer in 1999 (only participation)
IEA Progress in International Reading Literacy Study (PIRLS)	4th grade	2001: 35 2006: 45	Did not participate
IEA International Civic and Citizenship Education Study (CIVED and ICCS)	8th grade	1999: 31 2009:38	Top performer
OECD Programme for International Student Assessment (PISA)	15-year-olds	2000: 43 2003: 41 2006: 57 2009:65	Top performer

upper-secondary education. In 1999, the Third International Mathematics and Science Study ranked Finland 10th in mathematics and 14th in science among 38 participating countries. Since the first cycle of PISA in 2000, Finland has been one of the top-performing nations in mathematics among all OECD member states. Progress has been similar also in science since the Second International Science Study in the early 1980s. It is noteworthy that Finnish students have always performed well internationally in reading: Finnish 4th-grade students were the best readers in the Reading Literacy Study in the late 1980s and 15-year-olds achieved top rankings in all four PISA cycles.

What might explain this evident improvement in mathematics learning in Finnish schools? There is some research on this question, but it has produced more speculation and qualitative analysis than reliable answers (Hautamäki et al., 2008; Linnakylä, 2004; Ofsted, 2010; Välijärvi et al., 2007). In this analysis three possible explanations appear. First, mathematics teaching is strongly embedded in curriculum design and teacher education in Finnish primary schools. For example, in the University of Helsinki each year about 15% of students in primary school teacher-education programs specialize in teaching mathematics. This allows them to teach mathematics in lower-secondary schools as well. As a consequence, most primary schools in Finland have professionals who understand the nature of teaching and learning—as well as assessing—mathematics. Second, both teacher education and mathematics curriculum in Finland have a strong focus on problem solving, thereby linking mathematics to the real world of students. Mathematics tasks on PISA tests are based on problem solving and using mathematics in new situations rather than showing mastery of curriculum and syllabi. Third, the education of mathematics teachers in Finland is based on subject didactics and close collaboration between the faculty of mathematics and the faculty of education. This guarantees that newly trained teachers with master's degrees have a systemic knowledge and understanding of how mathematics is learned and taught. Both faculties have a shared responsibility for teacher education that reinforces the professional competences of mathematics teachers.

PISA is increasingly being adopted as a global measure to benchmark the nations' student achievement at the end of compulsory education. In 2009, the fourth cycle of this global survey was conducted in all 34 OECD member nations and in 31 other countries or jurisdictions. It focused on young people's ability to use their knowledge and skills to meet real-life challenges. "This orientation," as the OECD says, "reflects a change in the goals and objectives of curricula themselves, which are increasingly concerned with what students can do with what they learn at school and not merely with whether they have mastered specific curricular content" (OECD, 2007, p. 16).

Finland was the top overall performer among the OECD countries in 2000 and 2003 PISA studies and the only one that was able to improve performance. In the 2006 PISA survey, Finland maintained its high performance in all assessed areas of student achievement. In science, the main focus of the PISA 2006 survey, Finnish students outperformed their peers in all 56 countries, some of which are shown in Figure 2.4 (OECD, 2007, p. 16). In the 2009 PISA study Finland was again the best performing OECD country with high overall educational performance and equitable learning outcomes with relatively low cost. Significant in this national learning profile is a relatively large number of best performers (level 6) and a small proportion of low achievers (level 1 and below). More than half of Finnish students reached level 4 or higher in comparison to the United States, where approximately one quarter of all students was able to do the same. The Canadian provinces Alberta, British Columbia, Ontario, and Quebec also have more than 40% of students showing at least level 4 performance.

Figure 2.5 shows another divergence in Finnish students' learning performance trend as measured in the PISA science scale in comparison to some other OECD countries over time (OECD, 2001, 2004, 2007, 2010b). It is noteworthy that student achievement in Finland also consistently demonstrates progress according to the PISA data, contrary to many education super powers. It is important to note that any effects that teaching may have had on the results in a given education system primarily reflects the influence of education policies and reforms implemented in the 1990s—not the most recent education reforms.

Again a question emerges: Why do Finnish students perform exceptionally well in science? Some factors suggested by Finnish science educators include the following: First, primary school teacher education has for the past 2 decades focused on redesigning science teaching and learning in schools so that students would have opportunities for experiential and hands-on science. At the same time, more and more new primary school teachers have studied science education during their teacher education—more than 10% of graduates of the University of Helsinki have studied some science education in their masters' degree programs. These university studies, as part of the normal teacher education program, have focused on building pedagogical content knowledge and an understanding of scientific process in knowledge creation. Thus, the science curriculum in comprehensive school has been transformed from traditional academic knowledge-based to experiment- and problem-oriented curriculum. This change has been followed by massive national professional development support for all primary school science teachers. Third, teacher education in all Finnish universities, including the faculties of science, has been adjusted to the needs of the new school curriculum. Today, science teacher education is coherent and consistent with the current pedagogical principles of contemporary science teaching and learning that have been inspired by ideas and innovation from the United States and England.

There are few international student assessments that focus on subjects other than reading, mathematics, and science. The IEA International Civic and Citizenship Education Study (ICCS) is one such assessment, and it is the third IEA

Figure 2.4. Percentage of Students at Each Proficiency Level on the PISA 2006 Science Scale in Selected OECD Countries and Some Canadian Provinces (*)

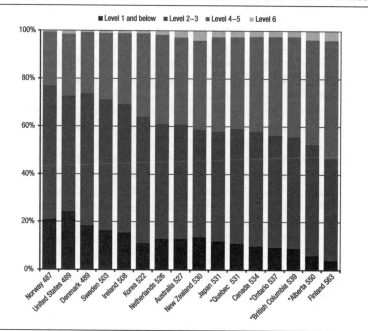

Source: OECD (2007).

Figure 2.5. Performance of Students in Science on PISA Surveys between 2000 and 2009 in Selected OECD Countries

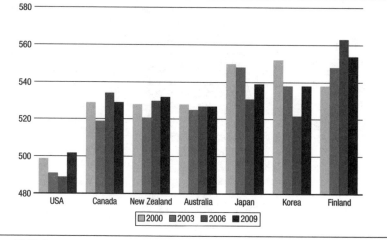

Source: OECD (2001, 2004, 2007, 2010b).

study designed to measure contexts and outcomes of civic and citizenship education (Schulz, Ainley, Fraillon, Kerr, & Losito, 2010). The ICCS of 2009 that built
on IEA's Civic Education Study 1999 studied the ways in which young people in
lower-secondary schools (typically grade 8) are prepared to undertake their roles
as citizens in 38 countries in Europe, Latin America, and the Asian-Pacific region.
A central aspect of the study was the assessment of student knowledge about a wide
range of civic- and citizenship-related issues. In this study *civic knowledge* refers
to the application of the civic and citizenship cognitive processes to the civic and
citizenship content. Civic knowledge is a broad term that is inclusive of knowing,
understanding, and reasoning. It is a key outcome of civic and citizenship education programs and is essential to effective civic participation.

In the 2009 ICCS, Finnish 8th-grade students scored the highest average score in
civic knowledge, alongside their Danish peers (see Figure 2.6). Similarly to PISA and
TIMSS, Finland has the smallest between-school variation of student performance in
the ISSC 2009 study. The ICCS 2009 shows that there is a strong relationship between
the Human Development Index (HDI) and civic knowledge at the country level. The
variation in HDI explains 54% of the between-country variation in civic knowledge.
This shows that national averages of civic knowledge are related to factors reflecting

**Figure 2.6. Civic Knowledge Scores of 8th-Grade Students in the OECD Countries
That Participated in the 2009 International Civic and Citizenship Education
Study (ICCS)**

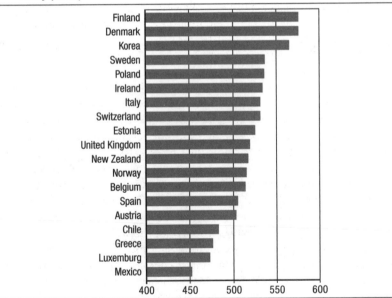

Source: Schulz et al. (2010).

the general development and well-being of a country. This finding is similar to those from other international studies of educational outcomes, but it does not necessarily indicate a causal relationship between civic knowledge and the overall development of a nation. Paradoxically, this study also found that Finnish youth feel the least engaged in politics and civic issues in their everyday lives.

All four PISA survey cycles since 2000 indicate that Finnish educational performance is consistent over all assessed educational domains, and that Finnish students on average score high in every survey across all measured subjects (reading, mathematics, and science). The quality of Finnish public education as measured by international student assessment studies has been steadily improving since the early 1970s. PISA 2009 was the second cycle that focused on reading literacy after 2000. It therefore provides a unique opportunity to look at the trend in how well students understand and can use what they read. Although the national average of student performance in 2009 slightly declined from 2000, as Figure 2.7 shows, Finnish students' reading literacy remains at an internationally high level. What is alarming in the PISA 2009, however, is related to finding that Finnish young people read less for pleasure than they did 10 years ago. Half of 15-year-old Finnish boys reported that they don't read for pleasure. This is clearly visible also in national studies of reading comprehension and habits in Finland.

According to the OECD, "Finland is one of the world's leaders in the academic performance of its secondary school students, a position it has held for the past decade. This top performance is also remarkably consistent across schools. Finnish schools seem to serve all students well, regardless of family background, socio-economic status or ability" (OECD, 2010c, p. 117). The strength of the educational performance of Finland is its consistently high level of student learning, equitably distributed across schools throughout the country.

Since its inauguration in 2000, PISA has had a huge impact on global education reforms as well as national education policies in the participating countries. It has become a significant pretext for educational development in Asia, Europe, and North America, and is gaining interest in the rest of the world. Large-scale education reforms have been initiated (in the United States, England, New Zealand, Germany, Korea, Japan, and Poland), new national institutions and agencies have been created, and thousands of delegations have visited well-performing education jurisdictions, including Finland, Alberta, Ontario, Singapore, and Korea, to discover the "secrets" of good education. In most of the more than 65 participating education systems, PISA is a significant source of education policy development and the reason for many large-scale education reforms.

Perhaps it is surprising to many that Finnish educators are not as excited by PISA results as many foreigners would expect. Many teachers and school principals think that PISA measures only a narrow band of the spectrum of school learning. There are also Finns who see that PISA is promoting the transmission of educational policies

Figure 2.7. Performance of Finnish Students in Reading, Math, and Science on PISA Surveys, 2000–2009

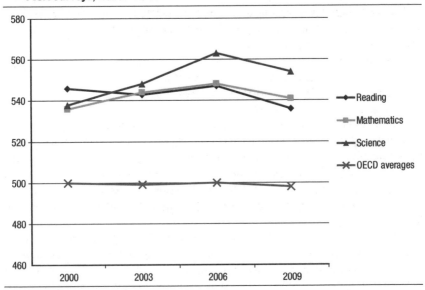

Source: OECD (2010b).

and practices that are not transferrable. This will, they maintain, lead to a simplistic view of educational improvement. Just like in sports, too strong an emphasis on international comparisons (or competitions) may lead to unethical means of temporarily boosting performance just to get a better position in the results tables. A good education system and high educational performance is much more than measured academic scores. Some teachers in Finland are afraid that the current movement, which judges quality of education systems by using academic units of measurement only, will eventually lead to narrowing curriculum and teaching at the expense of social studies, arts, sports, music, and whole-person development.

There is, indeed, an increasing debate about what these international tests really measure and whether PISA alone can be used to judge the quality of education systems. Critics' and proponents' arguments are available in educational literature (Adams, 2003; Bautier & Rayon, 2007; Bracey, 2005; Dohn, 2007; Goldstein, 2004; Prais, 2003; Prais, 2004; Riley & Torrance, 2003; Schleicher, 2007; Mortimore, 2009). The reader should note that PISA is not the only available international student assessment, and that others actually measure different aspects of student learning than PISA. Nevertheless, the PISA study is the only international benchmark instrument that covers all OECD countries and also focuses on competences beyond the curriculum taught in schools. It is also worth noting that there is growing criticism among Finnish educators about the ways that students' performance and success in education systems are determined using solely the test scores from academic student assessments. Many—myself included—would like to see a broader scope of student learning reflected in these assessments, including learning-to-learn skills, social competencies, self-awareness, and creativity.

COST OF EDUCATION

It seems that Finland has been able to reform its education system by increasing participation at all levels, making good education achievable to a large proportion of its population, and attaining comparatively high learning outcomes in most schools throughout the nation. All of this has been accomplished by financing education, including higher and adult education, almost exclusively from public sources. One more question regarding good educational performance remains to be addressed: How much do Finnish taxpayers pay for education?

In OECD nations for which data on comparable trends are available for all educational levels combined, public and private investment in Finnish education increased 34% from 1995 to 2004 in real terms, while the OECD average for the same period was 42%. Total public expenditure on educational institutions as a percentage of GDP in Finland was 5.6% in 2007 (Sahlberg, 2009; OECD, 2010a). This is less than the 5.7% OECD countries spent on average and significantly less than spending in the United States (7.6% of GDP) and Canada (6.1% of GDP). As mentioned earlier, only 2.5% of total Finnish expenditure on education institutions comes from private sources.

The Relationship between Cost and Student Performance

Figure 2.8 summarizes students' mean performance on the PISA science scale in relation to cumulative educational spending per student (between 6 and 15 years of age) in 2006 in U.S. dollars and adjusted to purchasing power parities (OECD, 2007; 2010a). These data indicate that good educational performance in Finland has been attained at reasonable cost. Figure 2.8 also suggests that there is no correlation between the quality of an education system as measured by the PISA study and the level of financial investment in education. For example, the United States and Norway have the highest level of spending in education but their student outcome results are low. This, of course, does not suggest any causal logic between education expenditures and learning outcomes, although regression indicates a very small negative interdependency ($R^2=0.03$) between education cost and student achievement. Efficiency is therefore more important to good educational performance than level of expenditure. Money rarely is *the solution* to the problems in education systems.

Figure 2.8. Relationship between PISA Performance in Science and Cumulative Expenditure per Student between Ages 6 and 15 in Selected OECD Countries in 2006

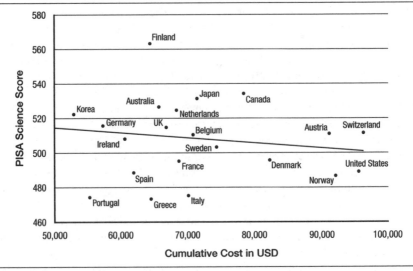

Source: OECD (2007, 2010a).

The Cost of Grade Repetition

One of the cost factors in education is grade repetition. It means that a student is asked to repeat a grade because he or she failed to successfully master the subjects covered the first time. This is a commonly used remedy and form of treating individual deficits and problems. Not only is grade repetition an ineffective way to help students in need of help, but it is also expensive for education systems. Let us look at how Finland has been coping with this common global phenomenon.

Grade repetition in the old Finnish parallel school system was not rare in elementary schools, and it was an integral educational principle of grammar school. In some cases, a student repeated the 3rd grade of elementary school in order to improve knowledge and skills required in the grammar school admission test at the end of the 4th grade. At the time of the introduction of the new 9-year school, approximately 12% of students in each grammar school grade did not progress from their grade. Grade repetition at that time was not evenly distributed between schools or grades. For example, in general upper-secondary school, one in six students repeats a grade. We have estimated that up to half of those graduating from upper-secondary grammar school repeated one or more grades at some point of their schooling (Välijärvi & Sahlberg, 2008). Furthermore, significant numbers of students dropped out of school before completion—often after not being able to progress from one grade to the next. In adequate progress in mathematics and Swedish (as a second language) were the most commonly cited reasons for grade repetition, although some students had to repeat due to behavioral or attitude problems.

Peruskoulu was built on the social value of equity and was driven by the idea that all students are able to achieve common academic and social goals through choice-based educational streams in the upper grades of comprehensive school. In the old school system, grade repetition was a method of differentiation for teachers. Problems related to retention were well known at the inception of the new school system in the early 1970s. The impact of being sent back to the same grade with younger students was often demoralizing and rarely made way for the expected academic improvements among students (Brophy, 2006; Jimerson, 2001). After all, repeating an entire grade was an inefficient way of promoting learning because it did not focus on those parts of the curriculum in which a student needed targeted help. Studying for a second time those subjects that a student had already successfully completed was rarely stimulating for students or their teachers. Students were sent to the same class without a plan to specify the areas of improvement, let alone the methods of achieving most effectively the required levels of knowledge and skills.

In the early days of comprehensive school reform grade repetition was seen as an inadequate and wrong strategy for fixing individual learning or social deficiencies. In the elementary school, grade repeaters who had difficulties in one or two subjects were often labeled as "failing" students who also had behavioral and personality problems. This educational stigma normally had a dramatic negative impact on students' self esteem and thereby their motivation and efforts to learn. It also lowered teachers' expectations regarding these students' abilities to learn. Grade repetition created a vicious circle that for many young people cast a negative shadow right into adulthood. Educational failure is linked to an individual's role in society and is characterized by unfavorable attitudes to learning and further education. Leaving this role behind was possible only for young people with strong identities and high social capital in the form of friends, teachers, and parents. Finnish experience shows that grade repetition, in most cases, led to increased social inequality rather than helping students to overcome academic and social problems.

Peruskoulu quickly changed grade repetition policies and practices. While the new system did not completely remove the problem of repeating grades, the number of students who repeated grades in the comprehensive school decreased significantly. Personalized learning and differentiation became basic principles in organizing schooling for students across society. The assumption that all students can achieve common educational goals if learning is organized according to each student's characteristics and needs became another foundation. Retention and ability grouping were clearly against these ideals. Different students have to learn to work and study together in the same class. Diversity of students' personalities, abilities and orientations has to be taken into account in crafting learning environments and choosing pedagogical methods in schools. This turned out to be one of the most demanding professional challenges for teachers. Even today, schools are searching for an optimal educational and economic solution for the increasing diversity.

Minimizing grade repetition has been possible primarily because special education has become an integral part of each and every school in Finland. Every child has the right to get personalized support provided early on by trained professionals as part of normal schooling. This special support is arranged in many different ways today. As described earlier, special education in Finland is increasingly organized within general mainstream schooling. Special education has a key role to play in improving equity and combating educational failure in Finnish schools.

Upper-secondary schools—both general and vocational—operate using modular curriculum units rather than year-based grades. Thus, grade repetition in its conventional form has vanished from Finnish upper-secondary schools. Today students build their own personalized learning schedules from a menu of courses offered in their school or by other education institutions. Studying in upper-secondary school is therefore flexible, and selected courses can be completed at a different pace depending on the students' abilities and life situations. Rather than repeating an entire grade, a student only repeats those courses that were not passed satisfactorily. Most students complete upper-secondary school in the prescribed time of 3 years, although some progress faster and some need more time than others. This nonclass structure has also abolished classes in which the same group of students move from one lesson to another and from one grade to the next.

Finland has chosen the policy of automatic promotion combined with the principle of early intervention. Such attention to dynamic inequalities in all schools, as professor Norton Grubb points out, is what distinguishes Finland from many other countries (Grubb, 2007). This requires systematic counseling and career guidance as young people start to think about their educational pathways. Indeed, fewer than 2% of students who leave the compulsory 9-year comprehensive school today at the age of 16 have repeated a grade at some point of schooling. Grade repetition is at a similar level in other Nordic countries but much higher elsewhere in Europe: 40% in France; more than 30% in Belgium, the Netherlands, and Spain; and 25% in Germany and Switzerland repeat a grade in school (Välijärvi & Sahlberg, 2008).

FINNISH PARADOXES OF EDUCATION

Finnish educational success has encouraged people to search for reasons for such favorable international performance. Most visitors to Finland discover elegant school buildings filled with calm children and highly educated teachers. They also recognize the large amount of autonomy that schools enjoy: little interference by the central education administration in schools' everyday lives, systematic methods for addressing problems in the lives of students, and targeted professional help for those in need. Much of this may be helpful in benchmarking their country's practice in relation to a leading education nation such as Finland. However, much of the secret of Finland's educational success remains undiscovered:

- What has the educational change process been like?
- What is the role of other public sector policies in making the education system work so well?
- What role does the culture play?
- How much did Finnish educators take note of global education reform movements in creating their own approaches?

In many ways, Finland is a nation of strange paradoxes. Home of the leading telecommunication industry and one of the highest mobile phone densities, Finland is also known for its less-talkative (or silent) people. Known as reserved individuals who prefer isolation rather than social interaction, Finns love to dance the tango. They even select a national tango queen and king during the annual tango festival. Furthermore, with its tough, northern climate, Finns rank among the world's happiest people and live in one of the world's most prosperous nations. Finnish *sisu*, a cultural trademark that refers to strength of will, determination, and purposeful action in the face of adversity, coexists with calmness and tenderness (Lewis, 2005; Steinbock, 2010). Indeed, paradoxes are more helpful than pure logic in understanding some of the key features of Finnish education.

Avoidance of "small talk" is a well-known cultural characteristic of the Finns, as the following traditional story illustrates. Two men met unexpectedly after a long time. Because they had been good friends since boyhood they decided to go and celebrate their pleasant encounter with a drink or two. They soon found a bar, looked for a quiet table, and ordered first drinks. No words were exchanged and the drinks were soon finished. Second drinks were ordered and enjoyed, yet no talk. Third drinks went down in silence, but when the fourth drinks were about to be sipped the other man raised his glass for a toast and cheerfully said: "Kippis" (which is equivalent to "cheers" in English). The companion gave him a puzzled look and replied, "Did we come here to drink or to talk?"

Minimalism is also favored in other walks of life in Finland. Arts, music, design, and architecture all draw their inspiration from small, clear, and simple ideas. Finnish people think that "small is beautiful." In business, politics, and diplomacy, Finns rely on straight talk and simple procedures. They want to solve problems, not to talk about them. Inventions and innovations in Finland are often such that simple ideas make a big difference. It is perhaps not surprising then that these same principles and values are embedded in Finnish education. One of the Finnish educational values is to put teaching and learning before anything else when education policies and reforms are under consideration. Most of all, Finns don't seem to believe that doing more of the same in education would necessarily make any significant difference for improvement.

Paradox 1: Teach Less, Learn More

The Finnish experience challenges the typical logic of educational development that tries to fix lower-than-expected student performance by increasing the length of education and duration of teaching. For example, when students are not learning enough mathematics, a common cure is a revised curriculum with more hours of classroom instruction and homework. This also requires in most education systems more teaching time for teachers. Two international indicators provide a vivid picture of national variances in how much students are exposed to instruction and how long teachers spend time in teaching.

First, as Figure 2.9 shows, there are big differences in the total number of intended instruction hours in public institutions between the ages of 7 and 14 in OECD countries (OECD, 2010a). There appears to be very little correlation between intended instruction hours in public education and resulting student performance, as assessed by PISA study. Interestingly, high-performing nations in all academic domains included in PISA rely less on formal teaching time as a driver of student learning (Finland, Korea, Japan), whereas nations with much lower levels of academic achievement (Italy, Portugal, and Greece) require significantly more formal instruction for their students. When these differences are converted into school years, Italian 15-year-olds, for example, have attended at least 2 more years of schooling than have their Finnish peers. Moreover, in Finland, children start school at the age of 7, whereas many Italian children start school at the age of 5, which adds even more formal learning time for them. There is no comparable data available regarding compulsory instruction time in the United States or in Canada in the OECD database. However, estimates from some states of the United States and Canadian provinces suggest that total instruction time between 7- and 14-year-old students is about 7,500 hours; that is close to what students have in France, England, and Mexico. Furthermore, according to the OECD statistics, Finnish 15-year-old students spend less time on homework than do any of their peers in other nations. This is yet another striking difference between Finland and many other countries where "minimum homework minutes" and other means have been introduced to make sure that students are kept busy studying after school.

With school days running shorter in Finland than in many other countries, what do children do when their classes are over? In principle, pupils are free to go home in the afternoon unless there is something offered to them in the school. Primary schools are encouraged to arrange after-school activities for youngest pupils and educational or recreational clubs for the older ones. Finnish youth and sport

Figure 2.9. Total Intended Instruction Hours in Public Institutions for Students Ages 7–14 in 2008 in Selected OECD Countries

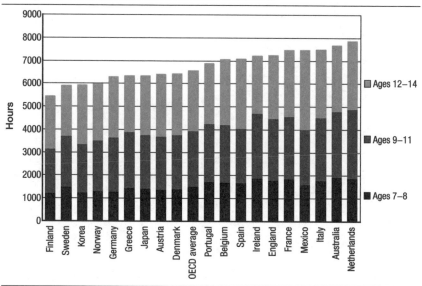

Source: OECD (2010a).

associations play an important role in offering youth opportunities to participate in activities that support their overall learning and growth. Two thirds of 10- to 14-year-olds and more that half of 15- to 19-year-olds belong to at least one youth association. Third Sector, as the network of these nongovernmental groups are called in Finland, contribute significantly to social and personal development of young Finns and thereby also educational performance of Finnish schools.

Another way to illustrate the *quantity* versus *quality* paradox is to examine how teachers spend their working time across the nations. Again, variance among countries is significant, as shown in Figure 2.10 (OECD, 2010a). In lower-secondary schools, on average, Finnish teachers teach about 600 hours annually (i.e., 800 lessons of 45 minutes each). This corresponds to four teaching lessons daily. According to the OECD, in the United States the average annual total teaching time in lower-secondary grades is 1,080 hours, which, in turn, equals six or more daily lessons or other forms of instruction of 50 minutes each. Although there are no comparable data from Canada, it is estimated that Canadian teachers teach approximately 900 hours annually. Lower teaching hours provide teachers more opportunities to engage in school improvement, curriculum planning, and personal professional development during their working hours.

How is a typical school day different in Finnish and American lower-secondary schools? First of all, the American teacher spends almost twice as long every week teaching than her Finnish peer. Teaching 6 hours daily is a tough job and leaves

Figure 2.10. Total Average Teaching Hours per Year in Lower Secondary Education in 2008 in Selected OECD Countries

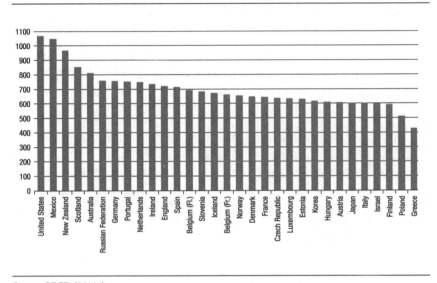

Source: OECD (2010a).

many teachers too tired to engage in anything professional when teaching is done. Teachers' work is therefore primarily defined as teaching in and out of classroom. In a typical Finnish lower-secondary school teachers teach, on average, four lessons a day. Despite the fact that teachers are paid by the number of lessons they teach, there is also time every day to plan, learn, and reflect on teaching with other teachers. Teachers in Finnish schools have many other responsibilities besides teaching: They assess their students' achievement and overall progress, prepare and continuously develop their own school curriculum, participate in several school health and well-being initiatives concerning their students, and provide remedial support to those who may need additional help. Many Finnish schools are, by virtue of a unique definition of teachers' work and by their nature, professional learning communities. Of course there are exceptions to this general image of teachers' work. Most primary schools, nevertheless, are truly professional learning communities where teaching is a holistic profession combining work with students in the classroom and collaboration with their colleagues in the staff room.

Interestingly, evidence from the most recent studies indicates that Finnish students experience less anxiety and stress in school than many of their peers in other countries (OECD, 2004, 2007). The national PISA report concludes that only 7% of Finnish students said they feel anxiety when working on mathematics tasks at home, compared to 52% and 53% in Japan and France, respectively (Kupari & Välijärvi, 2005). Similar observations from Finnish classrooms have been reported by scores of foreign journalists in newspapers around the world. A relaxed culture of learning and a lack of stress and anxiety certainly play a role in the achievement of good overall results in Finnish schools.

Finnish educators don't believe that doing more homework necessarily leads to better learning, especially if pupils are working on routine and intellectually unchallenging drills, as school homework assignments unfortunately often are. According to some national surveys and international studies, Finnish students in primary and lower-secondary school have the lightest load of homework of all. The *Wall Street Journal* reported that Finnish students rarely get more than a half-hour of homework per day (Gameran, 2008). It is true that many primary and lower-secondary school pupils are able to complete most of their homework before leaving school for the day. According to the OECD, Finnish 15-year-old students don't take private tutoring or additional lessons other than what is offered by their school (OECD, 2010b). In this light, high achievement of Finnish students in international tests is amazing. In Korea, Japan, Singapore, and Shanghai, China, jurisdictions that are on par with Finland in reading, mathematics and science, most children spend hours and hours after their regular school days and on their weekends and holidays in private classes and test preparation schools.

Paradox 2: Test Less, Learn More

The global educational reform thinking includes an assumption that competition, choice, and more-frequent external testing are prerequisites to improving the quality of education. Since the Education Reform Act 1988 in England, test-based accountability policies have increased the frequency of standardized testing in many school systems around the world (Hargreaves & Shirley, 2009). Judging the annual progress of students' and schools' performance improvements is almost without exception based on these external standardized tests of reading, mathematics, and science achievements. *Are those education systems where competition, choice, and test-based accountability have been the main drivers of educational change showing progress in international comparisons?*

Using the PISA database to construct such a comparison, a suggestive answer emerges. Most notably, the United States, England, New Zealand, Japan, and some parts of Canada and Australia can be used as benchmarks. Figure 2.11 demonstrates how the 15-year-old students' average performance in mathematics in three 2000–2006 PISA surveys has changed in these countries as compared to Finland's performance (OECD, 2001, 2004, 2007; Sahlberg, 2010a).

The trend of students' performance in mathematics in all test-based accountability-policy nations is similar—it is in decline, in cycle after cycle, between 2000 and 2006. The situation does not change significantly if we look at students' performance in science or reading literacy. Stronger school accountability with intensified standardized testing became common policy options in these nations in the 1990s,

Figure 2.11. Mathematics Performance Scores of 15-Year-Old Students on Three PISA Surveys in Selected OECD Countries, 2000–2006

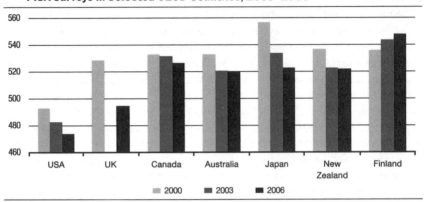

Source: OECD (2001, 2004, 2007).

whereas education policies in Finland at that time emphasized teacher professionalism, school-based curriculum, trust-based educational leadership, and school collaboration through networking. Finland has, unlike any other nation, illustrated in Figure 2.11, improved its average performance from its already high level in 2000. Although this does not constitute evidence of the failure of test-driven educational reform policies per se, it suggests that frequent standardized student testing is *not* a necessary condition for improving the quality of education as has been insisted upon by many advocates of competition-based public sector policies. Lessons from Finland suggest that there is another route to sustained improvement.

Although students are not tested in Finland as they are in many other countries, this does not mean that there is no assessment of students in Finland—quite the opposite. In principle, student assessment in Finland can be divided into three categories. First is classroom assessment by teachers; this includes diagnostic, formative, and summative assessment of students as part of teaching and learning. In all schools, this is solely the responsibility of teachers. All teachers are prepared to design and use various assessment methods in their work. Classroom assessment occupies a significant amount of out-of-classroom working time for teachers.

The second category of student assessment is comprehensive evaluation of students' progress after each semester. Students receive a report card that indicates their performance in academic and nonacademic subjects as well as in behavior and engagement. A student's report card is always a collective professional judgment by her or his teachers. It is up to the school to decide the criteria for this evaluation based on the national student assessment guidelines. This means that report cards issued by different schools are not necessarily fully comparable because they are not based on standardized and objective measures. Many teachers, however, believe that this is less of a problem than having standardized criteria and tests that would impersonalize schools and lead to "teaching to the test."

Third, students' achievement in Finland is also assessed externally. Regular national assessments are carried out using sample-based methodology that includes about 10% of the age cohort (6th- and 9th-grade students, for example). These assessments measure students' learning in reading, mathematics, science, and other subjects in 3- or 4-year cycles. Subjects are included in these assessments according to the needs or requests of national authorities. Schools not included in these samples may purchase one or more of these tests from the National Board of Education to benchmark their performance to that of other schools. About one fifth of all students of the grade cohort take part in this voluntary assessment. As an example, a school of 500 students pays about 5,000 U.S. dollars for each such test, including an analysis of results. The annual student assessment in the state budget in Finland is less than 5 million U.S. dollars for the entire school system. In an equal-size state or province in North America, for example, in Massachusetts or Alberta, a student testing budget can be 10 times higher than this.

Testing itself is not a bad thing and I am not an antiassessment person. Problems arise when they become higher in stakes and include sanctions to teachers or schools as a consequence of poor performance. There are alarming reports from many parts of the world where high-stakes tests have been employed as part of accountability policies in education (Au, 2009; Nichols & Berliner, 2007; Amrein & Berliner, 2002; Popham, 2007). This evidence suggests that teachers tend to redesign their teaching according to these tests, give higher priority to those subjects that are tested, and adjust teaching methods to drilling and memorizing information rather than understanding knowledge. Since there are no standardized high-stakes tests in Finland prior to the matriculation examination at the end of upper-secondary education, the teacher can focus on teaching and learning without the disturbance of frequent tests to be passed.

Other signs of weakening reliance on competition and testing in education come from recent policy changes in England and Wales, and the Canadian province of Alberta, where some of the national standardized tests have been banned and replaced by smarter ways of assessing students and schools. Alberta, for instance, had established a system of provincial achievement tests (PATs) that was used to measure pupils' performance in reading, mathematics, and science to inform decision makers of overall educational quality in the jurisdiction. Although the province authorities avoided using the testing data to rank schools or point out failing districts, there were some others who did so. Teachers and parents became very frustrated with the situation, in which much of good teaching was sacrificed in pursuit of raising test scores. In the spring of 2009 the Albertan Provincial Assembly voted in favor of removing grade 3 tests. As a consequence, the following year the minister of education dissolved the entire Accountability Department in Alberta Education (Ministry of Education). This indicated shifts away from testing toward more intelligent education policies. In other jurisdictions around the world, however, winds are blowing in the opposite direction.

Paradox 3: More Equity Through Growing Diversity

The main policy principle of Finland's comprehensive school reform of the 1970s was to provide equal educational opportunities for all, as was described in Chapter 1. This also included the idea that student achievement should be evenly distributed across the social groups and geographic regions. It is true that Finland long remained ethnically homogeneous. However, since it joined the European Union in 1995, cultural and ethnic diversification has progressed faster than in other European Union countries, especially in larger cities' districts and schools, where the proportion of first- and second-generation immigrant population accounts for one-quarter of the total population. Table 2.3 shows how the number of foreign-born citizens and residents issued Finnish citizenship has grown in Finland since 1980. In 2010 approximately 4.7% of inhabitants in Finland were foreign-born citizens and thus non-Finnish native speakers. The low number of citizenships issued in Finland is mostly due to the requirement that all citizens must be proficient in one of the domestic languages. All these—Finnish, Swedish, and Sami—are not spoken anywhere outside of Scandinavia and therefore are rarely spoken by those immigrating to Finland.

Finnish schools have had to adapt to this changing situation within a very short time. As a consequence, some municipalities are introducing limits to the proportion of immigrant students attending each school to avoid segregation. For example, in the city of Espoo there are schools with more than 40% immigrant student populations, while some schools have practically none. City authorities believe that a more even distribution of immigrant students in their schools would benefit both students and schools. However, school principals are doubtful of such forceful policies and their impact on communities. In comprehensive schools in Helsinki, the proportion of immigrant children is approaching 10% and languages spoken in these schools number 40 (http://www.hel.fi/hki/opev/en/). This trend is evident in all major cities in Finland.

Table 2.3. Foreign-Born Citizens and Residents Issued Citizenship in Finland Between 1980 and 2010

Year	Foreign-born citizens	Residents issued a citizenship
1980	12,853	621
1990	26,255	899
2000	91,074	2977
2010	248,135	4334

Source: Statistics Finland (2011).

The Finnish education system follows the principle of inclusiveness regarding the treatment of students with differing characteristics and needs. Students are placed in regular schools unless there is a specific reason to do otherwise. Therefore, in a typical Finnish classroom, one finds teachers teaching different abilities, interests, and ethnicities, often with the help of assistant teachers. The increased diversity in Finnish schools also suggests that variance in student performance within schools may increase. Cultural heterogeneity in Finnish society would suggest that variance in student learning among schools may become wider. However, as Figure 2.11 shows, a very high overall student performance in science, mathematics, and reading is evenly distributed throughout schools across Finland.

The Finnish sociocultural situation, which is experiencing a rapid diversification of schools and communities, offers an interesting case for research. Professor Jarkko Hautamäki has explored the influence of increased immigration on student learning in schools. Two interesting findings emerge. First, based on the PISA data, immigrant students in Finnish schools seem to perform significantly better than immigrant students in many other countries in PISA before 2009 (Hautamäki et al., 2008). Immigrant students in Finland scored on average 50 points higher than their peers in other countries. Second, according to this same study, in the proportion of immigrant students per class there seems to be a threshold after which learning achievement of all students in that class begins to decline. That proportion of immigrant pupils in Helsinki when notable affects of diversity on student achievement are observable is about 20%.

Poverty is a difficult factor that affects teaching and learning in schools. Child poverty can be defined as the percentage of children living in homes with an income that is below 50% of the national average. According to the UNICEF Innocenti Research Centre, 3.4% of children in Finland live in poverty based on that definition. This is the smallest child poverty rate after Denmark (2.4%). In the United States 21.7% and in Canada 13.6% of children live in poverty (UNICEF, 2007). The equitable Finnish education system is a result of systematic attention to social justice and early intervention to help those with special needs, and close interplay between education and other sectors—particularly health and social sectors—in Finnish society. It is important to understand how the level of student performance has continuously increased and student performance variance has decreased, while Finnish society has become more culturally diverse and socially complex. In other words, Finland has attained success in building increased equity through increased ethnic and cultural diversity in its society.

CHAPTER 3

The Finnish Advantage: The Teachers

But where there's a will, there's a way.

—Aleksis Kivi, *Seven Brothers* (1870/2005)

Many factors have contributed to Finland's educational system's current fame, such as its 9-year comprehensive school (*peruskoulu*) for all children, modern learning-focused curricula, systematic care for students with diverse special needs, and local autonomy and shared responsibility. However, research and experience suggest that one factor trumps all others: the daily contributions of excellent teachers.

This chapter examines the central role that Finnish teachers play and describes how teacher education is making major contributions to transforming Finland's educational system into a global focus of interest and object of study. This chapter suggests, however, that it is not enough to improve teacher education and elevate student admission requirements. Finnish experience shows that it is more important to ensure that teachers' work in schools is based on professional dignity and social respect so that they can fulfill their intention of selecting teaching as lifetime careers. Teachers' work should strike a balance between classroom teaching and collaboration with other professionals in school, as this chapter argues. This is the best way to attract young talented professionals into teaching. Before describing current principles and policies related to Finnish teachers and teacher education, it is useful to review some relevant cultural aspects of teaching and teachers' work in Finland.

THE CULTURE OF TEACHING

Education has always been an integral part of Finnish culture and society. While access to 6-year basic education became a legal obligation and right for all as far back as 1922, Finns have understood that without becoming literate and possessing broad general knowledge it would be difficult to fulfill their lifetime aspirations. Before formal public schooling began to spread during the 1860s, cultivating public literacy was the responsibility of priests and other religious brethren in Finland as early as the 17th century. Catechist schools offered religious-oriented initial literacy education in Sunday schools and itinerant schools within villages and in remote parts of Finland. By tradition, the ability to read and write was required for legal marriage by the church for both women and men. Becoming literate, therefore, marked an individual's entry into adulthood, with its associated duties and rights. Teachers also gradually assumed these responsibilities as the Finnish public school system began expanding in the early 20th century. Primarily due to their high social standing, teachers enjoyed great respect and also uncontested trust in Finland. Indeed, Finns continue to regard teaching as a noble, prestigious profession—akin to physicians, lawyers, or economists—driven mainly by moral purpose, rather than by material interest, careers, or rewards.

Until the 1960s, the level of Finnish educational attainment remained rather low, as Figure 2.1 showed. For example, in 1952, as Finland hosted its first—and last—Summer Olympics, nine out of ten adult Finns had completed only 7 to 9 years of basic education. A university degree was regarded as exceptional attainment at that time in Finland (Sahlberg, 2010a). Compared with other countries, the Finnish educational level was close to that of Malaysia or Peru, and lagged significantly behind its Scandinavian neighbors, Denmark, Norway, and Sweden. In the 1960s, elementary school teachers were still prepared in 2- or 3-year teacher-education seminars, not by academic institutions, but rather by units offering shorter practical training in teaching. One graduate of a teacher-preparation seminar in the late 1950s, Martti Ahtisaari, went from being a primary school teacher, to being an international diplomat, to being President of Finland (1994–2000), and now a Nobel Peace Prize laureate and praised global peacemaker. Today, when celebrating its educational achievements, Finland publicly recognizes the value of its teachers and implicitly trusts their professional insights and judgments regarding schooling. Stated quite plainly, without excellent teachers and a modern teacher education system, Finland's current international educational achievement would have been impossible.

The Finnish education system is distinctly different from public education in the United States, Canada, or the United Kingdom. Some differences are closely related to the work of teachers. For example, the Finnish education system lacks rigorous school inspection, and it does not employ external standardized student testing to inform the public about school performance or teacher effectiveness. Teachers also have professional autonomy to create their own school-based work plan and curriculum. All education in Finland is publicly financed and there are no fee-charging schools or universities.

Finnish teacher education today is fully congruent with these characteristics of educational policy in Finland. Five categories of teachers exist:

1. *Kindergarten teachers* work in kindergartens and are also licensed to teach preschool children.

2. *Primary school teachers* teach in grades 1 to 6 in 9-year comprehensive schools. They normally are assigned to one grade and teach several subjects.

3. *Subject teachers* teach particular subjects in the upper grades of basic school (typically grades 7 to 9) and in general upper-secondary school, including vocational schools. Subject teachers may teach one to three subjects, e.g., mathematics, physics, and chemistry.

4. *Special education teachers* work with individuals and student groups with special needs in primary schools and upper grades of comprehensive schools.

5. *Vocational education teachers* teach in upper-secondary vocational schools. They must possess at least 3 years of classroom experience in their own teaching field before they can be admitted to a vocational-teacher preparation program.

In addition to these five teacher categories, teachers in adult education institutions are required to have similar pedagogical knowledge and skills. Each academic year, approximately 5,700 new openings become available in all teacher education programs in Finland. This chapter focuses on the education of primary and subject teachers in the K–12 part of the Finnish educational system, which constitutes about two-thirds of all teacher-education students.

Teaching as a profession is closely tied to sustaining Finnish national culture and building an open and multicultural society. Indeed, one purpose of formal schooling is transferring the cultural heritage, values, and aspirations from one generation to another. Teachers are, according to their own opinions, essential players in building the Finnish welfare society. As in countries around the world, teachers in Finland have served as critical transmitters of culture. Through the centuries Finland has struggled for its national identity, mother tongue, and its own values, first, during 6 centuries under the Kingdom of Sweden; next for more than a century under the Russian Empire and its five tsars; and then another century as a newly independent nation positioned between its former patrons and the powers of globalization. There is no doubt that this history left a deep mark on Finns and their desire for personal development through education, reading, and self-improvement. Literacy is the backbone of Finnish culture and has become an integral part of the cultural DNA of all Finns.

It is no wonder, then, that teachers and teaching are highly regarded in Finland. The Finnish media regularly report results of opinion polls that document favorite professions among general upper-secondary school graduates. Surprisingly, *teaching* is consistently rated as one of the most admired professions, ahead of medical doctors, architects, and lawyers, typically thought to be dream professions (Liiten, 2004). Teaching is congruent with core social values of Finns, which include social justice, caring for others, and happiness, as reported by the National Youth Survey (2010). Teaching is also regarded as an independent high profession that enjoys public respect and praise. It is particularly popular among young women—more than 80% of those accepted for study in primary teacher education programs are female (Ministry of Education, 2007).

In a national opinion survey, about 1,300 adult Finns (ages 15 to 74) were asked if their spouse's (or partner's) profession had influenced their decision to commit to a relationship with them (Kangasniemi, 2008). Interviewees were asked to select 5 professions from a list of 30 that would be preferred for a selected partner or spouse. The responses were rather surprising. Finnish males viewed a *teacher* as the most desirable spouse, rated just ahead of a nurse, medical doctor, or architect. Women, in turn, identified only a medical doctor and a veterinarian ahead of a teacher as a desirable profession for their ideal husband. In the entire sample, 35% rated teacher as among the top five preferred professions for their ideal spouse. Apparently, only medical doctors are more sought in Finnish mating markets than are teachers. This clearly documents both the high professional and social status teachers have attained in Finland—both in and out of schools.

BECOMING A TEACHER

Due to the popularity of teaching and becoming a teacher, only Finland's best and most committed are able to realize those professional dreams. Every spring, thousands of Finnish general upper-secondary school graduates, including many of the most talented, creative, and motivated youngsters, submit their applications to departments of teacher education in eight Finnish universities. Thus, becoming a primary school teacher in Finland is highly competitive. It is normally insufficient simply to complete general upper-secondary school successfully and pass a rigorous matriculation examination (see Chapter 1). Successful teacher-education candidates must also possess high scores, positive personalities, excellent interpersonal skills, and commitment to work as a teacher in school. Annually, only about 1 of every 10 applicants will be accepted to prepare to become a teacher in Finnish primary schools. The total annual Finnish applicants in all five categories of teacher education programs number about 20,000.

Primary school teacher-education candidates are selected in two phases: First, a group of applicants is selected based on their matriculation examination scores, the upper-secondary school diploma issued by the school, relevant records of each student's out-of-school accomplishments, and a national entrance exam in which questions focus on a wide range of educational issues. In the second selection phase, top candidates from the first phase are interviewed and asked, among other things, to explain why they have decided to become teachers.

BOX 3.1: Why Do I Want to Be a Teacher?

Becoming a teacher was easy for me. Actually, it was not a choice at all, but rather a process that grew from a childhood dream into a realistic goal as an adult. I have many educators in my family and teaching is in my blood. My parents have encouraged me to take this direction. They helped me to find summer jobs and hobbies where I had a chance to work with children. I always found those jobs rewarding, fun, and morally fulfilling. It was that fun aspect of working with children that influenced me when I graduated high school and moved on in my career.

During my part-time teaching in school and also currently in teacher education in the university, the rosy picture of teaching has from time to time been tarnished, but every time shines again. Now, when I am about to graduate and get my masters' degree to teach in primary school, I have started to think about what it is to be a teacher. Why do I do this? First is the internal drive to help people to discover their strengths and talents, but also to realize their weaknesses and inadequacies. I want to be a teacher because I want to make a difference to children's lives and to this country. My work with children has always been based on love and care, being gentle and creating personal relations with those with whom I work. This is the only way that I can think will give me fulfillment in my life.

But I also understand that in my work, I will face huge responsibility, for a modest salary and heavy workload. I also know that shrinking financial resources for schools will continue and will influence my work in school. In Helsinki the social problems that children increasingly face in their lives will also be part of my work in the classroom. I need to be able to observe diverse individuals and offer help in situations for which I am probably not yet prepared. I accept that my work is not only teaching the things I like but it is working out conflict situations, working with colleagues who do not necessarily think the same way as I do, and collaborating with different parents in educating their children. Without a doubt, I will continue to ask myself whether this work is really worth all that.

The well-known Finnish educator Matti Koskenniemi used the term "pedagogical love" that is also a corner stone of my own theory-of-action as a teacher. Teaching is perhaps, more than any other job, a profession that you can successfully do only if you put your heart and personality into play. Each teacher has her own style and philosophy of teaching. There may be many motives for becoming a teacher. My own is that I want to do good for other people, care and love them. I do love them and thus I will be a teacher.

Veera Salonen
Teacher-education student
University of Helsinki

As these two selection phases suggest, access to Finnish teacher education is highly competitive. Normally, at least some prior experience in teaching or working with children is required from successful candidates. In 2010, total applications to primary school teacher education programs reached an all-time record. More than 6,600 applicants competed for 660 available student positions in Finnish universities. For the academic year 2011–2012, there were nearly 2,400 new applicants to the 120 available spaces in the primary school teacher-education study program in the Department of Teacher Education at the University of Helsinki. Figure 3.1 summarizes the trend in total annual applicants between 2001 and 2010, disaggregated by gender (Sahlberg, 2011b).

Two phenomena are apparent. The Finnish teaching profession in primary schools has become increasingly attractive, except for a slight decline in the middle of this decade. Also, the proportion of male primary school teachers remains relatively small. The state of the Finnish economy is reflected in the number of teacher-education applicants; when prospects of employment are dimmer, young people head toward teaching, as can be seen during the latest economic downturn in Finland starting in 2008. Although the number of Finnish students who do not complete their studies and thus fail to earn a degree is small, a relatively larger number of male students end up studying in other disciplines or working before they graduate.

Figure 3.1. Total Annual Applicants to Finnish Primary School Teacher Education Programs in 2001–2010

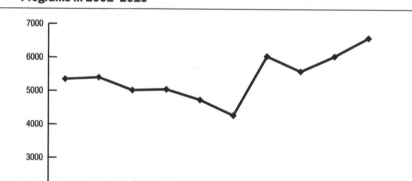

Source: Sahlberg (2011b).

Finland is perhaps the only nation that is able to select its primary school teacher-students from the top quintile of all high school graduates year after year. This ability has created a strong moral and professional foundation for teaching in Finnish primary schools, where Finnish children spend their first 6 school years with able, effective educators. Thus, I call this phenomenon the "Finnish advantage," while other nations continue to wonder how to get the "best and brightest" into teaching.

What makes teaching a top job?

If we use Finnish education as a reference, three conditions for attracting the best young people into teaching and keeping them in schools emerge. First, and most importantly, it is paramount that teachers' workplaces allow them to fulfill their moral missions. In Finland, as in many other countries, a teaching career is a result of an inner desire to work with people and help them and their societies through teaching. Teachers in Finland possess a strong sense of being esteemed professionals similar to medical doctors, engineers, or economists. Teachers at all levels of schooling expect that they are given the full range of professional autonomy to practice what they have been educated to do: to plan, teach, diagnose, execute, and evaluate. They also expect to be provided time to accomplish all of these goals inside and outside of normal classroom duties. Indeed, in Finland, teachers spend relatively less time teaching than their peers in many other countries. For example, in North American schools, teachers are engaged in teaching during the vast majority of their daily working time in school, which leaves little space for any other professional activities. The concept of the professional learning community (PLC) is often applied to how teachers work in schools, frequently on their own time. However, in Finland, Korea, and Japan, for example, schools are regarded as professional learning communities due to the inherent nature and balance of teachers' daily professional work.

I have talked with Finnish primary school teachers in early phases of their careers in order to understand what would prompt them to leave their chosen profession (Sahlberg, 2011b). Interestingly, practically nobody cites salary as a reason for leaving teaching. Instead, many point out that if they were to lose their professional autonomy in schools and their classrooms, their career choice would be called into question. For example, if an outside inspector were to judge the quality of their work or a merit-based compensation policy influenced by external measures were imposed, many would change their jobs. Finnish teachers are particularly skeptical of using frequent standardized tests to determine students' progress in school. Many Finnish teachers have told me that if they encountered similar external pressure regarding standardized testing and high-stakes accountability as do their peers in England or the United States, they would seek other jobs. In short, teachers in Finland expect that they will experience professional autonomy, prestige, respect, and trust in their work. First and foremost, the working conditions and moral professional environment are what count as young Finns decide whether they will pursue a teaching career or seek work in another field.

Second, teacher education should be sufficiently competitive and demanding to attract talented young high school graduates. Teacher education attracts many of Finland's top high school graduates because it constitutes a master's degree program and is therefore challenging enough for them. In addition, due to the high quality of Finnish students entering teacher education programs, the curricula and requirements have become very demanding, comparable to other degree programs offered by Finnish academic universities. Graduates who hold a master's degree can, without further work, apply to doctoral studies. That same degree also qualifies an individual to work in government or local administration, teach in the university, or compete with other master's degree holders in private sector employment. It has been questioned in Finland now and then whether primary school teachers necessarily need master's-level academic and research-based qualifications. However, Finnish experience suggests that if the primary school teaching degree requirement were lowered, many would seek studies in professional fields that would give them higher academic status and thus open more employment opportunities later in their careers.

Third, the salary level is not the main motive to become a teacher in Finland. Teachers earn slightly more than the national average salary. The annual statutory teacher's salary in the upper grades of *peruskoulu* (lower-secondary school) after 15 years of experience (in equivalent U.S. dollars, converted by using purchasing-power parity) is about 41,000 U.S. dollars (OECD, 2010a). That is close to what teachers earn, on average, in OECD countries. Comparable annual salary in the United States is 44,000 U.S. dollars, and in Korea, 55,000 U.S. dollars. Although making money is not the main reason for becoming a teacher, there should be a systematic way for salaries to increase. Finnish teachers climb the salary ladder as their teaching experience grows; their pay is not merit based.

There is a striking difference between Finnish and American teachers with respect to salaries. (OECD, 2010a). In Finland, first of all, teachers earn comparatively more, depending on the level of school at which they teach. There are approximately 7% to 10% higher average salaries for mid-career teachers in lower-secondary school than in primary schools. A similar gap exists between average salaries in lower-secondary schools and upper-secondary schools. In the United States, teacher salaries are roughly the same at all levels of schooling. Although the international statistics don't provide a full picture, it seems that American teachers can expect a 21% to 26% increase in earnings from the beginning of their careers to the midpoint (15 years of service in K–12 schools). Finnish teachers are in a more favorable situation. Their starting salaries will increase by approximately one third by the time they reach mid-career. The top-scale salaries in Finland are 58% (lower-secondary school teachers) to 77% (upper-seconadry school teachers) higher than starting salaries, respectively.

ACADEMIC TEACHER EDUCATION

Until the end of the1970s, primary school teachers were prepared in teacher colleges or special teacher-education seminars. Lower- and upper-secondary school subject teachers studied in specific subject-focused departments within Finnish universities. By the end of the 1970s, all teacher-education programs became a part of academic higher education and, therefore, were only offered by universities. A master's degree became the basic qualification to teach in Finnish schools. Simultaneously, scientific content and educational research advances began to enrich teacher-education curricula. Finnish teacher education is now *academic*, meaning that it must be based on and supported by scientific knowledge and be focused on thinking processes and cognitive skills needed to design and conduct educational research (Niemi, 2008; Jakku-Sihvonen & Niemi, 2006). A particular principle of research-based teacher education in Finland is systemic integration of scientific educational knowledge, didactics (or pedagogical content knowledge), and practice to enable teachers to enhance their pedagogical thinking, evidence-based decision making, and engagement in the professional community of educators. Consequently, the basic requirement today for permanent employment as a teacher in all Finnish comprehensive and upper-secondary schools is possession of a research-based master's degree, as shown in Table 3.1.

Teacher education is an important and recognized part of higher education in Finland. In many other nations, the situation is different: Teacher preparation is frequently viewed as semiprofessional training arranged outside of academic universities. In the Acts on Teacher Education in 1978–79, the minimum requirement for permanent employment as a teacher was raised to a master's degree that includes an approved master's thesis with scholarly requirements similar to those in any other academic field. This legislative policy served as the impetus to transfer all teacher-education programs from colleges to Finnish universities. The seeds were sewn for believing that the teaching profession is based on scholarly research. An important side effect of this transition was unification of the Finnish teaching cohort, which had become divided by the Comprehensive School Reform of the 1970s into primary school teachers and subject teachers working in lower- and upper-secondary schools.

The role of the Trade Union of Education in Finland (OAJ),established in 1973, has been both a negotiator of the terms of teachers' employment contracts and speaker for education (www.oaj.fi). The union represents teachers at various school levels and institutes, ranging from kindergarten teachers to instructors in vocational schools, school principals and lecturers in universities. More than 95% of teachers in Finland are OAJ members.

As mentioned above, all Finnish teachers must hold a master's degree. The major subject in primary school teacher-education programs is *education*. In subject-focused teacher-education programs, students concentrate within a particular

Table 3.1. Required Teacher Qualifications by Type of Finnish School

Type of school	Age of pupils	Grades	Required teacher qualifications
Kindergarten	0–6		Kindergarten teacher (BA)
Pre-school	6		Kindergarten teacher (BA) Primary school teacher (MA)
Comprehensive School (Peruskoulu)	7–16	1–9	Comprehensive school teacher (MA)
Primary School	7–12	1–6	Primary school teacher (MA)
Lower-Secondary School	13–15	7–9	Subject teacher (MA)
General Upper-Secondary	16–18	10–12	Subject teacher (MA)
Vocational Upper- Secondary			Vocational teacher (BA) Subject teacher (MA)
University	19–		Higher academic degree (MA/ PhD)
Polytechnic			Higher education degree (MA/ PhD)

Source: Sahlberg (2011b).

subject, for example, mathematics or foreign languages. Subject-focused teacher candidates also study didactics, consisting of pedagogical content knowledge (subject didactics) within their own subject specialty. Today, successful completion of a master's degree—that includes a bachelor's degree—in teaching takes from 5 to 7 years, according to the Finnish Ministry of Education (Ministry of Education, 2007). There are no alternative ways to earn a teacher's diploma in Finland; only the university degree constitutes a license to teach. In the United States, for example, the Teach for America program admits college graduates, immerses them in pedagogy courses over a summer for several weeks, and then sends them to schools in need of teachers—where they often find that classroom challenges are exceedingly difficult. There are similar teacher-certification initiatives in some other nations, such as Teach First in the United Kingdom and Norway.

Academic teacher education focuses on balanced development of a prospective teacher's personal and professional competences. Particular attention is devoted to building pedagogical thinking skills, enabling teachers to manage instructional processes in accord with contemporary educational knowledge and practice (Westbury, Hansen, Kansanen, & Björkvist, 2005; Toom et al., 2010). In Finnish primary teacher education, this is characterized by the study of education as a main subject, composed of three thematic areas:

1. Theory of education
2. Pedagogical content knowledge
3. Subject didactics and practice

Finnish research-based teacher-education programs culminate in a required master's thesis. Prospective primary school teachers normally complete their theses in the field of education. Typically, the topic of a master's thesis is focused on or close to a teacher's own school or classroom practice, such as mathematics teaching, or learning. Subject-focused teacher students, in turn, select a thesis topic within their major subject. The level of scholarly expectations for teacher-education studies is similar across all teacher-preparation programs, from elementary to upper-secondary school.

Teacher education in Finland is aligned to the framework of the European Higher Education Area that is being developed under the ongoing Bologna Process.1 Currently, Finnish universities offer a two-tier degree program. First, an obligatory 3-year bachelor's degree program qualifies students for a 2-year master's degree program that is the minimum qualification for the license to teach in Finland. These two degrees are offered in multidisciplinary programs consisting of studies in at least two subjects. Studies are quantified in terms of credit units within the European Credit Transfer and Accumulation System (ECTS) within 46 European nations. ECTS, which will become the guiding policy for the European Higher Education Area, is a student-centered system based on student workload required to achieve program objectives.

The objectives are normally specified in terms of learning outcomes and competencies to be acquired. ECTS is based on the assumption that 60 credits represent the workload of a full-time student over 1 academic year. The annual student workload for a full-time study program in Europe equals, in most cases, about 1,500 to 1,800 hours. Therefore, one ECTS credit represents about 25 to 30 working hours. Teacher education requires 180 ECTS credits for a bachelor's degree (which doesn't meet qualifications for a teaching diploma or enable permanent employment as a teacher), followed by 120 ECTS credits for a master's degree.

A broad-based teacher-education curriculum ensures that newly prepared Finnish teachers possess well-balanced knowledge and skills in both theory and practice. It also implies that prospective teachers develop deep professional insight into education from several perspectives, including educational psychology and sociology, curriculum theory, student assessment, special-needs education, and didactics (pedagogical content knowledge) in their selected subject areas. It is noteworthy that contemporary Finnish teacher education has been strongly influenced by research and development in this field in American, Canadian, and British universities.[2] To illustrate what teachers study during their preparation program, Table 3.2 summarizes primary school teacher-education topics with required credit units, as offered by the Department of Teacher Education, University of Jyväskylä. All eight Finnish universities offering teacher education have their own nationally coordinated teacher-education strategies and curricula, ensuring coherence but encouraging local initiative to make best use of each university's resources and nearby opportunities.

Table 3.2. Summary of Primary Teacher-Education Master's Degree Program at the University of Jyväskylä in 2010

Curriculum Component	European Credit Transfer and Accumulation System Credit
Basic Studies in Education*	25
Language and Communication Studies	25
Intermediate Studies in Education*	35
Multidisciplinary School Subject Studies	60
Minor Subject Studies	60
Advanced Studies in Education**	80
Elective Studies	15
Total European Credit Transfer and Accumulation Credits	300

* Including 12 ECTS credits from teaching practice.
** Including 16 ECTS credits from teaching practice.

As a general rule, primary school teacher education preparing teachers for the lower grades (typically, grades 1 to 6 of comprehensive schools) includes 60 ECTS credits of pedagogical studies and at least 60 additional ECTS credits for other courses in educational sciences. An integral part of these additional educational studies is a master's thesis requiring independent research, participation in research seminars, and defending of the completed educational study. The commonly assigned credit for this research work within all universities is 40 ECTS credits.

The revised teacher-education curriculum in Finland requires primary school teacher candidates to complete a major in educational sciences and earn 60 ECTS credits in minor studies within subjects included in the National Framework Curriculum for Comprehensive School, which is regularly updated by the National Board of Education and the Ministry of Education. Mathematics is one of the popular minor subjects among students. This is an important factor in securing high-quality mathematics teaching in many primary schools in Finland.

Most students in primary teacher-education programs enter their studies with solid knowledge and skills in the range of subjects studied in upper-secondary school. In Finland, unlike in the United States or England, all upper-secondary school students are obliged to complete successfully a study program including up to 18 required subjects—such as physics, chemistry, philosophy, music, and at least two foreign languages in addition to two domestic languages. Normally, students accepted in primary school teacher-education programs have earned higher than average grades in these subjects. For example, in the University of Helsinki, some 15% of students select mathematics as their minor subject, which earns them a license to teach mathematics as subject teachers in grades 7 to 9 (Lavonen et al., 2007). Science education is also quite popular among primary school teacher students; each year approximately 10% take basic or advanced studies in science teaching. It is clear that primary school teachers in Finland, in general, possess strong mastery of subjects that they teach due to their broadly based upper-secondary school studies and primary teacher-education programs that build upon that solid base.

Finnish subject teacher education follows the same principles as primary school teacher education but is arranged differently. There are two main pathways to becoming a subject teacher. Most students first complete a master's degree in their academic programs with one major subject, such as the Finnish language, for example, and one or two minor subjects, such as literature and drama. Students then apply to the Department of Teacher Education for their subject-teacher-education program. In pedagogical studies, the main focus is on subject-oriented teaching strategies equivalent to 60 ECTS credits, and requires one academic year to complete. The other pathway to becoming a subject teacher is for a student to apply directly to teacher education to pursue a major subject in their academic program. Normally, after 2 years of subject studies, students start their pedagogical studies in their university's faculty of education. The curriculum for this second pathway is identical to that of the first route, only scheduled differently within bachelor and master tracks, typically over four academic terms, as illustrated by the program at the University of Helsinki shown in Table 3.3.

Prospective subject teachers decide to major in fields that they will be teaching, such as mathematics or music. For major subjects, advanced studies involving

Table 3.3. Structure of the Pedagogical Component of the Subject Teacher Education Program at the University of Helsinki in 2010

Bachelor's level (25 European Credit Transfer and Accumulation credits)	Master's level (35 credits)
FIRST TERM (18 CREDITS)	THIRD TERM (17 CREDITS)
Developmental psychology and learning (4)	Social, historical, and philosophical foundations of education (5)
Special education (4)	Evaluation and development of teaching (7)
Introduction to subject didactics (10)	Advanced teaching practice in Teacher Training School or Field School (5)
SECOND TERM (7 CREDITS)	FOURTH TERM (12 CREDITS)
Basic teaching practice in Teacher Training School (7)	Research seminar (Teacher as a researcher) (4)
	Final teaching practice in Teacher Training School or Field School (8)
AS PART OF MASTER'S PROGRAM: Research methodology (6)	

90 ECTS credits are normally required. In addition, 60 ECTS credits are required in a second subject that will be taught in schools. Generally, the Department of Teacher Education organizes courses in pedagogical studies in collaboration with subject-matter programs offered by subject departments responsible for teacher education of their own students. Exceptions include teacher education for some subjects included in the National Curriculum Framework for the comprehensive school, such as textile work and crafts, special education, student counseling, and music, which are organized within departments of education. Teacher education for music, arts, and physical education usually occurs in separate departments or institutes within a university. It is also internationally unique that Finnish academic subject faculties—not the department of teacher education—issue Master's degrees for subject teachers and thus play important roles in Finnish teacher education.

TEACHERS AS RESEARCHERS

Instruction in Finnish teacher-education departments is arranged to support peda-gogical principles that newly prepared teachers are expected to implement in their own classrooms. Although all university teachers have full pedagogical autonomy, every department of teacher education in Finland has a detailed and often bind-ing strategy for improving the quality of their teacher-education programs. Subject-focused pedagogy and research in science education within Finnish universities, for example, are regarded as advanced by international standards (Lavonen et al., 2007). Moreover, cooperative learning, problem-based learning, reflective practice, and computer-supported education are now implemented—at least to some extent—in all Finnish universities. A Finnish higher-education evaluation system that offers public recognition of and financial prizes for effective, innovative university teaching practice has served as an important driver of these positive developments.

Research-based teacher education means that integration of educational the-ories, research methodologies, and practice all play important roles in Finnish teacher-education programs. Teacher-education curricula are designed so that they constitute a systematic continuum from the foundations of educational thinking, to educational research methodologies, and then on to more advanced fields of edu-cational sciences. Each student thereby builds an understanding of the systemic, interdisciplinary nature of educational practice. Finnish students also acquire skills of designing, conducting, and presenting original research on practical or theoreti-cal aspects of education. An integral element of Finnish research-based teacher education is practical training in schools, a key component of the curriculum, as documented in Tables 3.2 and 3.3.

There are, in principle, two kinds of practicum experiences within Finnish teacher-education programs. A minor portion of clinical training occurs in seminars and small-group classes within a department of teacher education (part of a faculty

BOX 3.2: Research-based Teacher Education

In my long career as a teacher-educator the most significant policy change was the requirement that all teachers must hold a academic masters' degree in education or in the subject they teach in school. It launched a development chain that elevated all teachers as professionals who, among other things, are able to understand teaching holistically and improve their own work continuously. In Finland it took more than 20 years to build common understanding among teacher educators, university professors, and practitioners about the complexity of the teaching profession. Research-based teacher education has the following three key principles:

- Teachers need a deep knowledge of the most recent advances of research in the subjects they teach. In addition, they need to be familiar with the research on how something can be taught and learned.
- Teachers must adopt a research-orientated attitude toward their work. This means learning to take an analytical and open-minded approach to their work, drawing conclusions for the development of education based on different sources of evidence coming from the recent research as well as their own critical and professional observations and experiences.
- Teacher education in itself should also be an object of study and research.

Many people ask why Finnish students perform so well in school and many young Finns choose teaching as their life career. There is no regular standardized testing, school inspection, teacher evaluation, or ranking of schools in Finland. Public education has a central role in enhancing equality and well-being in Finnish society. High-quality academic teacher education ensures readiness to work in many other areas of the Finnish labor market. Most importantly, in Finland teachers and schools enjoy strong public confidence. Parents trust teachers the way that they trust their dentists. Parents do not need to worry about finding a good school for their children. Many think that the nearest school in their community is good enough. I believe that because teachers—as a result of academic education—have clear moral purpose and independent professional ethos, they are trusted. Research-based teacher education is essential in making that possible.

Hannele Niemi
Professor of Education
University of Helsinki

of education), where students practice basic teaching skills with their peers. Major teaching practice experiences occur mostly within special teacher training schools governed by universities, which have curricula and practices similar to ordinary public schools. Students also use a network of selected field schools for practice teaching. In primary school teacher education, students devote approximately 15% of their intended study time (for example, in the University of Jyväskylä, 40 ECTS credits) practice-teaching in schools. In subject teacher education, the proportion of teaching practice in schools constitutes about one-third of the curriculum.

The Finnish teacher-education curriculum, as summarized in Tables 3.2 and 3.3, is designed to integrate teaching practice in theoretical and methodological studies systematically. Teaching practice is normally divided into three phases over the 5-year program: basic practice, advanced practice, and final practice. During each phase, students observe lessons by experienced teachers, complete practice teaching observed by supervisory teachers, and deliver independent lessons to different pupil groups, all evaluated by supervising teachers and department of teacher education professors and lecturers. Evaluations of Finnish teacher education have repeatedly identified the systematic nature of teacher education curricula as a key strength and a characteristic that distinguishes Finnish teacher education from that of many other nations (Darling-Hammond, 2006; Jussila & Saari, 2000; Saari & Frimodig, 2009).

The Finnish teacher education program represents a spiral sequence of theoretical knowledge, practical training, and research-oriented enquiry of teaching. Teacher-education responsibilities are integrated within the activities of academic university units. For example, at the University of Oulu, three faculties, namely science, humanities, and education, deliver teacher education courses for their students. They include staff (normally university lecturers and professors) specialized in subject-oriented teaching methodologies. Their curricula are coordinated with the Department of Teacher Education, responsible for the overall organization of teacher education.

Although teacher training schools constitute the main portion of the network within which Finnish students complete their practice teaching, some ordinary municipal public schools (municipal field schools) also serve the same purpose. One-third of all teaching practice at the University of Oulu occurs in these municipal field schools (MFS). Teacher training schools where practice teaching occurs have higher professional staff requirements; supervising teachers must prove their competency to work with student teachers. Teacher training schools (but not MFSs) are also expected to pursue research and development roles in teacher education in collaboration with the university's department of teacher education, or sometimes also with the academic units' teacher education staff. For example, at the University of Oulu, the Faculty of Science and the Faculty of Humanities assume teacher-education roles and support appropriate staff. All teacher training schools can, therefore, introduce sample lessons and alternative curricular designs to student teachers. These schools also have teachers experienced in supervision, teacher professional development, and assessment strategies. There are no specific qualifications to be designated as such a teacher—it is each individual's responsibility to build the needed knowledge and skills required for employment in a teacher training school.

PROFESSIONAL DEVELOPMENT

Since teaching is a much-desired profession in Finland, most new graduates from Finnish departments of teacher education and subject-focused programs seek immediate school employment. During their studies, students develop their impressions of what school life from a teacher's viewpoint may be like. However, graduates do not necessarily acquire experience of participating in a community of educators, assuming full responsibility for a classroom of students, or interacting with parents. All these considerations are part of the curriculum, but many licensed graduates discover that there is a chasm between lecture-hall idealism and school reality.

Induction of a new teacher into a first classroom assignment is relatively less developed in Finland, although research and development work on teacher induction is rather active (Jokinen & Välijärvi, 2006; OECD, 2005b). It is up to each school and municipality governing these schools to address new teachers' needs for induction or mentoring into their teaching responsibilities. Thus, practices regarding Finnish teacher induction are, admittedly, diverse. Some schools, as part of their mission, have adopted advanced procedures and support systems for new staff, whereas other schools merely bid new teachers welcome and show them to their classrooms. In some schools, induction is a well-defined responsibility of school principals or deputy principals, while in other schools, induction responsibilities may be assigned to some experienced classroom teachers. Teacher induction is an area that requires further development in Finland, as recent European recommendations have correctly pointed out (European Commission, 2004).

It is recognized that professional development and in-service programs for teachers are not aligned with initial teacher education and often lack focus on essential areas of teaching and school-development. Perhaps the main criticism deals with weak coordination between initial academic teacher education and continuing professional development of teachers (Ministry of Education, 2009). Municipalities, as the overseers of primary and lower- and upper-secondary schools, are responsible for providing teachers opportunities for professional development or in-service training, based on their needs. According to the employment contract, there are 3 mandatory professional development days annually that all teachers must take part in that are offered by the local education authorities. It is up to individual teachers or school principals to decide how much time beyond those 3 days, and what type of professional development, is needed, and whether such interventions, in fact, can be funded.

In Finland, a significant disparity exists among municipalities' and schools' ability to finance professional development for teachers. The main reason for this situation is the way that education is financed. The central government has only limited influence on budgetary decisions made by municipalities or schools. Therefore, some schools receive significantly more allocations for professional development and school improvement than do others, particularly during times of economic downturn when professional development budgets are often the first to vanish.

Governance of Finnish education is inconsistent throughout the nation. Some schools experience relatively higher autonomy over their operations and budgeting. Others do not. Therefore, Finnish teacher professional development appears in many forms. Ideally, the school is the prime decision maker regarding the design and delivery of professional development. Schools may also be motivated to lower operating expenses, such as for textbooks, heating and maintenance, and divert those funds to teacher-development priorities. However, some Finnish municipalities still organize in-service programs uniformly for all teachers and allow little latitude for individual schools to decide what would be more beneficial for them. According to a large national survey conducted by the University of Jyväskylä in 2007, on average, teachers devoted about 7 working days (or 50 hours) annually to professional development; approximately half of that was drawn from teachers' personal time (Piesanen, Kiviniemi, & Valkonen, 2007).

Moreover, approximately two thirds of primary and secondary school teachers in 2007 participated in professional development (Kumpulainen, 2008). This suggests that within a total Finnish teacher population of 65,000, more than 20,000 failed to participate in any professional development during that year. Participation in professional development, according to a recent report by the Finnish Ministry of Education, is decreasing (Ministry of Education, 2009). The government, therefore, is considering ways to strengthen the legal groundsa for teacher professional development by requiring that all teachers must have access to adequate professional in-service support, funded by municipalities.

The Finnish state budget allocates normally about 30 million U.S. dollars each year to professional development of teachers and school principals through various forms of university courses and in-service training (compared with 5 million U.S. dollars for student assessment and testing!). The main purpose of this investment in human development is to ensure equal access to further training, particularly for teachers working in more disadvantaged schools. This professional development support is contracted to service providers on a competitive basis. The government initially determines the focus of the desired training, based on current national educational-development needs. Local education authorities that own the schools and also employ all the teachers make an investment of similar scale in professional development of their education personnel each year. The Ministry of Education, in collaboration with municipalities, plans to double public funding for teacher professional development by 2016.

Finnish teachers possessing a master's degree have rightful access to doctoral studies to supplement their normal professional development opportunities. Primary school teachers can easily begin their further studies in the faculty of education; their PhD dissertations will then focus on a selected topic in educational sciences. Many primary school teachers take advantage of this opportunity, often while simultaneously teaching in schools. Doctoral studies in education for subject teachers who have their previous degrees in some other academic field require more work. These teachers must first complete advanced studies in the educational sciences because the main subject requires a shift from a student's initial academic major, for example, chemistry, into education, so that students are qualified to complete their research in education.

TIME FOR PEDAGOGICAL REFLECTION

Teaching is commonly viewed in Finland as a demanding profession requiring superior academic qualifications, even for teachers of very young students. Since teacher education became part of academic university studies in the 1970s, Finnish teachers' identity and sense of belonging to a highly regarded profession have gradually increased. During the course of Finland's education reforms, as explained in Chapter 1, teachers have demanded more autonomy and responsibility for curriculum planning and student assessment. The professional context of teaching in Finland differs significantly from other countries regarding how teachers experience their work. The professionally respectful environment that teachers experience in Finland is an important factor not only for teacher education policies but also for explaining why so many young Finns regard teaching as a most admired career.

Curriculum planning is the responsibility of teachers, schools, and municipalities, not the State. Most Finnish schools today have their own customized curriculum coordinated with and approved by their local education authorities. This correctly implies that teachers and school principals have key roles in curriculum development and school planning. The National Framework Curricula for comprehensive school and for upper-secondary school provide guidance and necessary regulations that each school must keep in mind in its curriculum-development activities. However, there are no strict national standards for or descriptions of student learning outcomes that Finnish schools must include in their curriculum, as is true in the United States, Great Britain, or Canada, for example. That is why curriculum planning varies from school to school and why the actual school curricula can look very different depending on the school. The teachers' key role in pedagogical decision making clearly requires teacher education to install in all prospective teachers well-developed knowledge and skills related to curriculum development and student assessment theory and practice. Moreover, it has shifted Finnish teacher professional development focus from fragmented in-service training toward more systemic school improvement that builds better ethical and theoretical grounding for effective teaching.

Another important teacher responsibility is student assessment. As mentioned earlier, Finnish schools do not employ standardized census-based tests to determine their progress or success. There are four primary reasons for this:

1. Education policy in Finland gives high priority to personalized learning and creative teaching as important components of schooling. Therefore, students' progress in school is primarily judged against their respective characteristics and abilities, rather than by reliance on uniform standards and statistical indicators.

2. Education developers insist that curriculum, teaching, and learning are priority components in education that should necessarily drive teachers' thinking and school practice, rather than focusing on assessment and testing, as is the case in some other education systems. Student assessment in Finnish schools is embedded in teaching and learning processes and is thereby used to improve both teachers' and students' work in school.

3. Determining students' personal and cognitive progress is regarded as a responsibility of the school, not of external assessments or assessors. Most Finnish schools acknowledge some shortcomings, such as comparability or consistency, when teachers do all student assessments and grading. At the same time, there is wide acknowledgment that problems often associated with external standardized testing can be even more troublesome. These problems, according to teachers, include a narrowing curriculum, teaching for testing, and unhealthy competition among schools and teachers. Classroom assessment and school-based evaluation are therefore important and valued components of Finnish teacher education curricula and professional development.

4. The Finnish national strategy for student assessment is based on the principle of diversified evidence in which test-based performance data are just one part of the whole. Data regarding student achievement in various subjects are collected using sample-based standardized tests and thematic reviews. Municipalities are autonomously designing their quality assurance practices according to their needs and aspirations.

The only external "standardized" assessment of student learning is the National Matriculation Examination at the end of upper-secondary school when students are at the age of 18 or 19, as described in Chapter 1. It occurs at the close of upper secondary education and serves as a general requirement for academic higher education. It assesses students' knowledge, skills, and competences through essay-type exams in various subjects, and is fully financed by students and administrated by an external examination board. It has exerted, many Finnish education specialists argue, a discernable effect on curriculum and teaching in general upper-secondary school.[3]

Although Finnish teachers' work consists primarily of classroom teaching, many of their duties are outside of class. Formally, teacher's working time in Finland consists of classroom teaching, preparation (in the case of lab-based subjects such as biology), and 2 hours weekly of planning and development work with colleagues. Unlike in many other nations, Finnish teachers do not need to be present at school if they do not have classes or if the school principal has not requested them to perform some other duties. From an international perspective, Finnish teachers devote less time to teaching than do teachers in many other nations.

Average net teaching hours as reported by the governments to the OECD are presented in Figure 3.2. Schools in Finland are autonomous in terms of scheduling their work but it is still common to have a 15-minute recess after a 45-minute lesson. Every school serves a warm three-course lunch for all during a lunch break that can range from 20 to 75 minutes depending on the school schedule. Recently schools have sought alternative arrangements to release more time for teachers' collaboration, for example, combining lessons or classes into longer periods or larger groups and thereby providing more discretionary time during the school day for teachers.

Figure 3.2 reveals notable differences in average teaching hours of all teachers between the United States and Finland. Even if teaching time is adjusted to annual school days, it appears that teachers in Finland spend much less time each day in teaching. A question arises: What are Finnish teachers doing when teachers in some other countries are still teaching their students? An important—and still voluntary—part of Finnish teachers' work is devoted to school improvement and work with the community. It is worth recalling that Finnish schools are responsible for the design and continuous development of their school curriculum. Also, teachers serve as the main assessors of students' educational progress and their school's performance. Students receive their grades from teachers whose duties include designing and conducting appropriate assessments and tests to monitor their students' progress in school. Finnish teachers have accepted curriculum development, experimentation with teaching methods, responsibility to engage in student welfare support, and collaboration with parents as important aspects of their work outside of classrooms.

Foreign visitors in Finnish schools often ask how teachers are assessed based on their effectiveness. Or how do administrators know who are effective teachers and who need to upgrade their teaching competences? The overall finding is clear: There are no formal teacher evaluation measures in Finland. Since there are no standardized census-based data about student achievement available, it is not possible to compare school performance or teacher effectiveness. The only exception is the use of matriculation examination results by certain media every spring to rank Finnish high schools according to their students' grades in the exams. That news rarely gets any significant attention among parents or schools.

Figure 3.2. Average Net Teaching Hours per School Year in Finland, the United States, and in OECD Countries

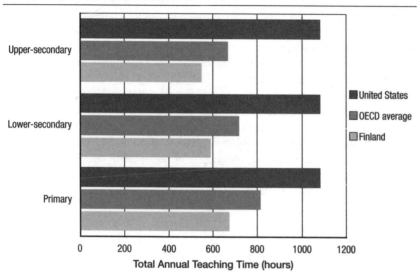

Source: Sahlberg (2011b).

The question of teacher effectiveness or consequences of being an ineffective teacher is not relevant in Finland. As described earlier, teachers have time to work together during a school day and understand how their colleagues teach. This is an important condition for reflecting on teacher's own teaching and also building shared accountability between teachers. The school inspection system that previously provided external feedback and evaluation of how teachers taught and schools operated was abolished in the early 1990s. Today school principals, aided by their own experience as teachers, are able to help their teachers to recognize strengths and areas of work that need improvement. The basic assumption in Finnish schools is that teachers, by default, are well-educated professionals and are doing their best in schools. In real professional learning communities teachers trust each other, communicate frequently about teaching and learning, and rely on their principal's guidance and leadership.

Internationally, identifying teacher effectiveness has become a new trend in finding ways to improve education. Novel statistical techniques, called value-added modeling (VAM), are intended to resolve the problem of socioeconomic and other differences by adjusting for students' prior achievement and demographic characteristics. Although VAM approaches are fairer comparisons of teachers than judgments of their students' test scores, closer analysis of VAM results has led researchers to doubt whether this methodology can identify good or bad teachers as its designers claim (Baker et al., 2010). It is safe to believe that rarely are such quantitative measures the sole or even the primary factor of a good or poor teacher. Even some management experts from the business world warn against using such measures for making salary or bonus decisions, as has been done, for example, in paying teachers by their performance merits (using student test scores as the main source of evidence). "In both the United States and Great Britain," reports a review of the problems with using student test scores to evaluate teachers by the Education Policy Institute, "governments have attempted to rank cardiac surgeons by their patients' survival rates, only to find that they had created incentives for surgeons to turn away the sickest patients" (Baker et al., 2010, p. 7). Paying teachers based on their performance is an alien idea in Finland. Authorities and most parents understand that teaching, caring, and educating children is too complex a process to be measured by quantitative metrics alone. In Finnish schools, the operational principle is that the quality of teaching and of the school is defined through the mutual interaction between the school and the students, together with their parents.

LEADERS ARE TEACHERS

Regardless of how well teachers are trained in any education system, consistent high educational performance requires good professional leadership at the school level. Some countries allow their schools to be led by noneducators hoping that business-style management would raise the efficiency and improve performance. Similarly, local education authorities and administrators are sometimes persons without experience in teaching or leading schools. In Finland educational leadership in municipal education offices is without exception in the hands of professional educators who have experience in working in the field of education. This is an important factor in enhancing communication and building trust between schools and educational administration.

In Finland school principals have to be qualified to teach in the school that they lead. They also have to have successfully completed academic studies on educational administration and leadership offered by universities in Finland. This means that a corporate-CEO without these merits would not be able to lead a school. In most Finnish schools the principal is an experienced teacher with proven leadership competences and suitable personality. In many schools principals also have a small number of classes to teach each week. Pedagogical leadership is one of the key areas of professional school leadership in Finland. Teachers rely on their leader's vision and the principal understands teachers' work. Therefore leadership and management in Finnish schools are informal but effective as foreign observers witnessed (Hargreaves et al., 2008).

Before the 1990s, becoming a school principal was often a reward of successful service as a teacher. In some cases, however, a rather young teacher was appointed as a school leader. Leadership experience or qualities were rarely examined when filling an open principal's post in schools. Nor did school principals need to be experts in administration, financial management, or political lobbying as they do today. In the early 1990s this situation rapidly changed. One driver of this change was the sudden decentralization of public sector management and educational administration in Finland at that time. A new financing scheme that increased autonomy of the municipalities immediately affected schools in most parts of the country. School principals offered to control their school budgets; in some cases that included teachers' salaries and all recurrent costs.

Second, and a related driver of change, was an unexpected financial crisis that hit Finland harder than many other Western countries in the early 1990s. School principals became the operational arms of the municipalities in deciding how forthcoming budget cuts, that were typically double-digit in magnitude, would be managed. Finnish school principals found themselves in a situation similar to corporate CEOs who had to adjust their firms into shrinking markets. The image of the nostalgic head of the school had changed. Major educational changes—such as curriculum reforms of 1994—have been implemented successfully primarily due to professional attitude and pedagogical leadership by the school principals. Ever since, this leadership community in Finland has served as a critical voice in shaping education policies and steering school improvement based on the needs of teachers, students, and the society. Based on these experiences it is difficult to imagine that market-based education reforms that often undermine the central role of pedagogical leadership could have been implemented in Finland. School principals have been first to stand between these intentions and the well-being of schools.

GOOD TEACHERS, GREAT SCHOOLS

In summary, what are the relative strengths of teacher education in Finland, based on international perspectives? First, although the Bologna Process directs overall European higher-education structures and policies, it doesn't stipulate how signatory nations should design curricula or arrange their teacher education. There are, and will continue to be, significant differences in national teacher education policies and practices among European education systems. Within this mosaic of European teacher-education systems, Finland has these three peculiarities.

1. The most able and talented individuals go into teaching. Since it shifted primary school teacher education to the universities and upgraded teacher diplomas to a required master's degree in late 1970s, Finland has attracted some of its most able and talented youth to become teachers. As described earlier, there is a strong cultural influence in career planning of young Finns, but that alone does not explain the sustained popularity of teaching. Two other salient factors may be identified. First, the required master's degree in educational sciences provides a competitive professional foundation, not only for becoming employed as a primary school teacher, but also for many other careers, including education administration and work in the private sector. All graduating teachers are fully eligible to enroll in doctoral studies, which are still tuition-free in Finland. Second, many young Finns select teaching as their primary life career because work in schools is perceived as an autonomous, independent, highly regarded profession, comparable to working as a medical doctor, lawyer, or architect, for example. Increased external control over teachers' work in schools through test-based accountability or centrally mandated regulation would likely deflect more bright young people to professional careers where they have freedom to make use of their own creativity and initiative.

2. There is close collaboration between subject faculties and schools of education. Subject teacher education is organized collaboratively and is coordinated to ensure both solid mastery of subjects to be taught and state-of-the-art pedagogical competences for all graduates. Faculties in Finnish universities perceive teacher education as an important component of their academic programs. Lecturers and some professors in the subject faculties have specialized in the teaching of their own disciplines that has enhanced cooperation among teacher educators. Faculties of education and various subjects within the university are also positively interdependent: They can achieve sustainable success only when all of them do their best.

3. Teacher education is research oriented. Teacher education in Finland is also recognized because of its systematic and research-based structure. All graduating teachers, by the nature of their degree, have completed research-based master's theses accompanied by rigorous academic requirements of theory, methodology and critical reflection equal to any other field of study in Finnish universities at that level. Research-orientation to teacher education prepares teachers, at all levels, to work in complex, changing societal and educational environments. Research-based academic training has also enabled implementation of more radical national education policies. For example, enhanced professional competences have led to increased trust in teachers and schools regarding curriculum planning, student assessment, reporting of student performance, and school improvement. Finland has successfully integrated research, knowledge of content and didactics, and practice into its teacher-education programs.

Indeed, this research focus carries a twofold significance for teacher education. Research findings establish the professional basis for teachers to teach and work effectively within a complex knowledge society. Teacher education—within any society—has the potential to progress as an effective field of professional activity only through and from robust contemporary empirical, scientific inquiry. *Professionalism* as the main characteristic of teaching requires that teachers are able to access and follow ongoing development of their own profession and that they can freely implement new knowledge within their own instructional work. Thus, further development of

Finnish teacher education must necessarily be built upon on-going, high-quality, internationally relevant research and development achievements.

Finnish teacher education's greatest potential lies in hundreds of talented and motivated young people who, year after year, seek enrollment in teacher education programs. This is a crucial factor for the continued and future success of teacher education in Finland. Young Finns gravitate toward teaching because they regard it as an independent, respected, and rewarding profession within which they will have freedom to fulfill their aspirations. However, general upper-secondary school graduates also weigh the quality of teacher education programs when making decisions about their future career. It is therefore paramount that Finnish teacher education continues to develop to ensure that, in the future, it remains an attractive and competitive option for highly able young people.

Teachers' professional status in Finnish society is a cultural phenomenon, but how teachers become prepared to teach in classrooms and work collaboratively in professional communities is attributable to systematically designed and implemented academic teacher education. For other nations, imitating the Finnish curriculum system or organizational aspects of schools may not be a wise strategy. However, a positive lesson that Finns themselves have learned by raising the level of teacher education on par with other academic pursuits certainly merits closer examination. A critical condition for attracting the most able young people year after year to teacher education, however, is that a teacher's work should represent an independent and respectful profession rather than merely focus on technical implementation of externally mandated standards, endless tests, and administrative burdens.

CHAPTER 4

The Finnish Way:
Competitive Welfare State

Real winners do not compete.

—Samuli Paronen
(Finnish author, 1917–1974)

What makes Finnish education unique is its steady progress from a system that was barely at international averages to one of the rare strong public educational performers today. Equally important, Finland has been able to create a network of schools where nearly everybody succeeds and failure is rare. Simultaneously, participation in and graduation from post-compulsory education in Finland—both upper-secondary and higher education—have increased significantly during that time. The success of Finnish education has been frequently noted by global media and various education development agencies. This exceptional development was not accomplished by following the same education reform principles that are dominant in the United States, England, Canada and much of the rest of the world.

Finland has a competitive national economy, low levels of corruption, good quality of life, a strong sustainable-development lifestyle, and gender equality. These qualities make Finland one of the most prosperous nations in the world. The success of Finland as a small, remote European nation has been built upon flexibility and solution-orientation in all aspects of society. In its education system, these principles have enabled schools to experiment with creativity and assume risks while seeking to reach set goals, whether these goals represent effective teaching or productive learning. This is in harmony with policies and strategies in other areas of the public sector. Especially interesting has been the close interplay between education policies and economic strategies since the early 1990s.

This chapter discusses in more detail how education policies in Finland have responded to international educational reform ideas and how they are linked to the overall development of the knowledge economy and welfare state. It describes the increased interdependency among public sector policies in Finland since 1970, and presents a tentative typology to compare education reform principles and economic development policies in Finland. The main point of this chapter is that education policies in dynamic-knowledge societies need to be based on a systems view of policy making and sustainable leadership that does not undermine complex relationships between different public sector policies in these societies.

THE POWER OF GLOBALIZATION

Internationalization has shaped Finland and the lives of its people during the past 2 decades. Membership in the European Union and an active role in the OECD have increased individual mobility and the exchange of policies between Finland and the rest of the developed world. Finnish people, however, remain divided regarding globalization. Many think that globalization is leading to a diminishing role for nation-states and loss of their sovereignty, as a result of the emergence of global hegemony of transnational money, media, and entertainment corporations. Others argue that standardization in economies, policies, and cultures has become a new norm for competitive corporations and nations, thus diminishing Finnish customs and traditions. Changes in global culture also deeply affect educational policies, practices, and institutions. It is obvious that there is no straightforward view of the consequences of the globalization process on educational policies.

Indeed, globalization is a cultural paradox: It simultaneously unifies and diversifies people and cultures. It unifies national education policies by integrating them with broader global trends. Because problems and challenges are similar from one education system to the next, solutions and education reform agendas are also becoming similar. Due to international benchmarking of education systems, by using common indicators and the international comparisons of student achievement, the distinguishing features of different education systems are becoming more visible. For example, the OECD PISA has mobilized scores of politicians and education experts to visit other countries, especially Finland, Canada, and Korea, in order to learn how to redefine their own education policies and improve schools. As a consequence, globalization has also accelerated international collaboration, the exchange of ideas, and the transfer of education policies among education systems.

Analyzing global policy developments and education reforms has become a common practice in many ministries of education, development agencies, and consultant firms. Therefore, the world's education systems are beginning to share some core values, functions, structures, and evidently they look alike. The question arises whether increased global interaction among policy makers and educators, especially benchmarking of education systems through agreed indicators and borrowing and lending educational policies, has promoted common approaches to education reform throughout the world.

Change knowledge in education has been created and disseminated predominantly by English-speaking countries. The United States, Canada, and the United Kingdom in the West and Australia and New Zealand in the East have become the centers of gravity for research and debate on school improvement, school effectiveness, and educational change. Two academic journals, *School Effectiveness and School Improvement* (established in 1990) and the *Journal of Educational Change* (established in 2000), are the key forums within which contemporary change knowledge is communicated.[1] Beyond the Anglo-Saxon world, the Netherlands, Sweden, Spain, and Norway have engaged most actively in international dialogue and research on educational change. Surprisingly, Finland, Korea, and Japan—all countries with high-performing and equitable education systems—have had only a modest role in the generation of global change knowledge. Each of these countries has heavily relied on the research and innovation from the United States, England, Australia, and Canada.

In the business of global education development it is important to be a critical consumer of available change knowledge. Indeed, rather than shifting emphasis toward standardized knowledge of content and mastery of routine skills, some advanced education systems are focusing on flexibility, risk taking, creativity, and problem solving through modern methods of teaching, such as cooperative learning, and through the use of community networks and communication technologies in teaching. The number of examples is increasing, including China (or at least its larger cities like Shanghai, Beijing, and Hong Kong, an economic power that is loosening its standardized control on education by making a school-based curriculum a national policy priority. Japan and Singapore are adopting the idea of "less is more" in teaching in order to make room for creativity and innovation (see Chapter 11 in OECD, 2010c). The highest performing Canadian province, Alberta, is loosening its grip on schools by removing standardized provincial assessments and creating more intelligent accountability policies, which focus on authentic learning. Wales has done so already. Even in England, the most test-intensive education system in the world, the government is putting an end to all standardized testing in primary schools.

As a reaction to the overemphasis on knowledge-based teaching and test-based accountability, authorities around the world are considering more dynamic forms of curriculum, introducing smarter forms of accountability and enhancing leadership in education in order to find alternative instructional approaches that promote the productive learning required in knowledge economies. Instead of focusing on single institutions, education reforms are beginning to encourage networking of schools and communities. At the core of this idea is *complementarity*, that is, cooperation between schools and districts and striving for better learning in the network. Clustering and networking also appear to be core factors in nations' economic competitiveness and efforts to cope with globalization.

Although improvement of education systems is a global phenomenon, there is no reliable, recent comparative analysis about how education reforms in different countries have been designed and implemented. However, the professional literature indicates that the focus on educational development has shifted from structural reforms to improving the quality of and access to education (Hargreaves & Fink, 2006; Hargreaves & Goodson, 2006). As a result, curriculum development, student assessment, teacher evaluation, integration of information and communication technologies into teaching and learning, proficiency in basic competencies (i.e., reading and writing), and mathematical and scientific literacy have become common priorities in education reforms around the world. These changes in schools and classrooms are then ensured by employing management models from the business world, such as test-based accountability, merit-based pay and data-driven administration. I call this the Global Educational Reform Movement (see Sahlberg, 2006a, 2007, 2010a).

THE GLOBAL EDUCATIONAL REFORM MOVEMENT

The idea of the Global Educational Reform Movement, or simply GERM, evolves from the increased international exchange of policies and practices. It is not a formal global policy program, but rather an unofficial educational agenda that relies on a certain set of assumptions to improve education systems (Sahlberg, 2011a; Hargreaves, Earl, Moore, & Manning, 2001; Hargreaves & Shirley, 2009). GERM has emerged since the 1980s and is one concrete offspring of globalization in education. It has become accepted as "a new educational orthodoxy" within many recent education reforms throughout the world, including reforms in the United States, many parts of Australia, Canada and the United Kingdom, some Scandinavian countries, and increasing number of countries in the developing world.[2]

Tellingly, GERM is promoted through the strategies and interests of international development agencies, bilateral donors, and private consultants through their interventions in national education reforms and policy-making processes. Professor Diane Ravitch has described how venture philanthropy injects billions of dollars into public education systems in the United States—and, to lesser extent, in some other countries—and often insists on employing management concepts and principles borrowed from the business world in the school systems (Ravitch, 2010c). By doing so it promotes the viral spread of GERM globally. There are only a small number of private foundations providing funds to public education in Finland, and they have to operate under close supervision of the authorities. Their influence on education policies or the direction of education reforms is diminishing.

The inspiration for the emergence of GERM comes from three primary sources. The first is the new paradigm of learning that became dominant in the 1980s. The breakthrough of cognitive and constructivist approaches to learning gradually shifted the focus of education reforms from teaching to learning. According to this paradigm, intended outcomes of schooling emphasize greater conceptual understanding, problem solving, emotional and multiple intelligences, and interpersonal skills, rather than the memorization of facts or the mastery of irrelevant skills. At the same time, however, the need for proficiency in literacy and numeracy has also become a prime target of education reforms.

The second inspiration is the public demand for guaranteed, effective learning for all pupils. The global campaign called Education for All has been influential in shifting the policy focus in education from teaching of some to learning for all. Inclusive education arrangements and the introduction of common learning standards for all have been offered as means to promote the ideal of education for all. This has led, generally speaking, to raising the expectations for all students through national curriculums and common programs.

The third inspiration is the competition and accountability movement in education that has accompanied the global wave of decentralization of public services. Making schools and teachers compete for students and resources and then holding them accountable for the results (i.e., student test scores), this movement has led to the introduction of education standards, indicators and benchmarks for teaching and learning, aligned assessments and testing, and prescribed curricula. As James Popham has noted, various forms of test-based accountability have emerged where school performance and raising the quality of education are closely tied to the processes of accreditation, promotion, sanctions, and financing (Popham, 2007). In other words, education has become a commodity where the efficiency of service delivery ultimately determines performance.

Since the 1980s, at least five globally common features of education policies and reform principles have been employed in attempts to improve the quality of education, especially in terms of raising student achievement. The first is *standardization* in education. Outcomes-based education reform became popular in the 1980s, followed by standards-based education policies in the 1990s, initially within Anglo-Saxon countries. These reforms, quite correctly, shifted the focus of attention to educational outcomes, i.e., student learning and school performance. Consequently, a widely accepted—and generally unquestioned—belief among policy makers and education reformers is that setting clear and sufficiently high performance standards for schools, teachers, and students will necessarily improve the quality of desired outcomes. Enforcement of external testing and evaluation systems to assess how well these standards have been attained emerged originally from standards-oriented education policies. Since the late 1980s centrally prescribed curricula with detailed and often ambitious performance targets, frequent testing of students and teachers, and high-stakes accountability with merit-based pay for teachers have characterized globalized education policies, promising quick fixes and standardized solutions at increasingly lower cost for those desiring to improve school quality and effectiveness.

A second common feature of the global education reform movement is *increased focus on core subjects* in curriculum, such as literacy and numeracy (Hargreaves, 2003). Basic student knowledge and skills in reading, writing, mathematics, and natural sciences are elevated as prime targets and indices of education reforms. Due to the acceptance of international student assessments such as PISA, TIMSS, and PIRLS as criteria of educational performance, reading, mathematical, and scientific literacy have now become the main determinants of perceived success or failure of pupils, teachers, schools, and entire education systems. Literacy and numeracy strategies that increased instruction time for so called core subjects in England and Ontario are concrete programmatic examples of the global educational reform movement. In the United States, the No Child Left Behind legislation led most school districts to steal teaching time from other subjects, especially from social studies, arts, and music, to be better prepared for state tests that measured student performance in literacy and mathematics (Jennings & Stark Rentner, 2006).

The third characteristic that is easily identifiable in global education reforms is teaching with *prescribed curriculum*; in other words, searching for safe and low-risk ways to reach predetermined learning goals. This minimizes experimentation, reduces use of alternative pedagogical approaches, and limits risk taking in classrooms and schools. Research on education systems that have adopted policies emphasizing achievement of predetermined standards and prioritized core subjects suggests that teaching and learning are narrower, and teachers focus on guaranteed content to best prepare their students for the test (Au, 2009). The higher the test-result stakes, the lower the degree of freedom for experimentation in classroom learning.

The fourth globally observable trend in educational reform is the *transfer of models from the corporate world* as a main logic of change management. This process, where educational policies and their implementation principles are borrowed from outside the education system, is often supported by private corporations, consultant firms, and private venture philanthropy. Moral goals of human development are often combined with national hegemony and economic profit. Faith in educational change that depends on innovations brought from outside the education system undermines two important elements of successful educational improvement. First, it often limits the role of national policy development and the enhancement of an education system's own capability to maintain renewal (Levin, 1998). Perhaps more important, it paralyzes teachers' and schools' attempts to learn from the past and to learn from each other. Or, it prevents lateral professional development in the system that is the main source of energy needed for sustained educational improvement.

The fifth, and a corollary of the previous global trend, is adoption of *high-stakes accountability policies* for schools. Within that trend, school performance—especially raising student achievement—is closely tied to processes of accrediting, promoting, inspecting, and, ultimately, rewarding or punishing schools and teachers. Merit-based pay is one popular approach to holding teachers accountable for their students' learning. Success or failure of schools and teachers is often determined by standardized tests and external evaluations that devote attention to limited aspects of schooling, such as student achievement in mathematical and reading literacy, exit examination results, or intended teacher classroom behavior.

Race to the Top (RTTT), launched in 2009, is a $4.35 billion U.S. Department of Education program designed to spur reforms in state and local district education, and includes many of the elements of GERM. It encourages competition among states and also between schools as they seek more effective practices and practitioners. Teacher and leader effectiveness as measured by standardized student tests have a central role in this initiative. Table 4.1 also illustrates how education policies in Finland since the 1980s have been almost orthogonal to those of the RTTT.

There are also others who have analyzed the global educational change efforts. Andy Hargreaves and Dennis Shirley have done so in their book *The Fourth Way* (2009), to which I will return later in this chapter. Michael Fullan, a Canadian educational change scholar, has come to a similar conclusion in his analysis of whole-system reform policies and strategies (2011). He speaks about "drivers of change," such as education policy or strategy levers, which have the best chances of driving intended change in education systems. "In the rush to move forward," writes Fullan, "leaders, especially from countries that have not been progressing, tend to choose the wrong drivers" (p. 5). "Wrong drivers" include accountability (vs. professionalism), individual teacher quality (vs. collegiality), technology (vs. pedagogy), and fragmented strategies (vs. systems thinking). These ineffective elements of education reform that resonate closely with the aspects of GERM discussed above have fundamentally missed the targets and continue to do so, according to Fullan. In his analysis of whole-system reforms in the United States and Australia, he goes even further:

> There is no way that these ambitious and admirable nationwide goals will be met with strategies being used. No successful system has ever led with these drivers. They cannot generate on a large scale the kind of intrinsic motivational energy that will be required to transform these massive systems. The US and Australian aspirations sound great as goals but crumble from a strategy or driver perspective. (Fullan, 2011, p. 7)

None of the elements of GERM shown in Table 4.1 has been adopted in Finland in the ways that they have within education policies of many other nations. This, of course, does not imply that there is no educational standardization, learning of basic skills, or accountability in Finnish schools. Nor does it suggest that there is a black-and-white distinction between each of these elements in Finland vis-à-vis other countries. But, perhaps, it does imply that a good education system can be created using alternative policies orthogonal to those commonly found and promoted in global education policy markets.

GERM has had significant consequences for teachers' work and students' learning in schools wherever it has been a dominant driver of change (Sahlberg, 2011a). The most significant consequence is standardization of educational and pedagogical processes. Performance standards set by the educational authorities and consultants have been brought into the lives of teachers and students without

Table 4.1. The Key Elements of Global Educational Reform Movement in Comparison with Finnish Education Policies Since the Early 1990s

Global Education Reform Movement (GERM)	The Finnish Way
Standardizing teaching and learning	*Customizing teaching and learning*
Setting clear, high, and centrally prescribed performance expectations for all schools, teachers, and students to improve the quality and equity of outcomes. Standardizing teaching and curriculum in order to have coherence and common criteria for measurement and data.	Setting a clear but flexible national framework for school-based curriculum planning. Encouraging local and individual solutions to national goals in order to find best ways to create optimal learning and teaching opportunities for all. Offering personal learning plans for those who have special educational needs.
Focus on literacy and numeracy	*Focus on creative learning*
Basic knowledge and skills in reading, writing, mathematics, and the natural sciences serve as prime targets of education reform. Normally instruction time of these subjects is increased.	Teaching and learning focus on deep, broad learning, giving equal value to all aspects of the growth of an individual's personality, moral character, creativity, knowledge, and skills.
Teaching prescribed curriculum	*Encouraging risk-taking*
Reaching higher standards as a criterion for success and good performance. Outcomes of teaching are predictable and prescribed in uniform way. Results are often judged by standardized and externally administrated tests.	School-based and teacher-owned curricula facilitate finding novel approaches to teaching and learning, and encourage risk-taking and uncertainty in leadership, teaching, and learning.
Borrowing market-oriented reform ideas	*Learning from the past and owning innovations*
Sources of educational change are management and administration models brought to schools from corporate world through legislation or national programs. Such borrowing leads to aligning schools and local education systems to operational logic of private corporations.	Teaching honors traditional pedagogical values, such as teacher's professional role and relationship with students. Main sources of school improvement are proven good educational practices from the past.
Test-based accountability and control	*Shared responsibility and trust*
School performance and raising student achievement are closely tied to processes of promotion, inspection, and ultimately rewarding schools and teachers. Winners normally gain fiscal rewards, whereas struggling schools and individuals are punished. Punishment often includes loose employment terms and merit-based pay for teachers.	Gradually building a culture of responsibility and trust within the education system that values teacher and principal professionalism in judging what is best for students. Targeting resources and support to schools and students who are at risk to fail or to be left behind. Sample-based student assessments.

full understanding that most of what pupils need to learn in school cannot be formulated as a clear standard. New forms of student assessments and testing that have been aligned to these standards are often disappointments and bring new problems to schools. However, because the standardization agenda promises significant gains in efficiency and quality of education, it has been widely accepted as a basic ideology of change, both politically and professionally.

The voices of practitioners are rarely heard in the education policy and reform business. Educational change literature is primarily technical discourse created by academics or change consultants. Therefore, I give space here to a school improvement practitioner from Scotland. This example is particularly relevant because Scotland is currently recovering from a rather serious GERM infection a few years back. The symptoms included top-heavy planning, rigid curriculum, fixed measures through audits, external snapshot-inspection and externally judged accountability. Many of them are gradually now fading away and giving room to more intelligent curriculum and evaluation policies. Niall MacKinnon, who teaches at Plockton Primary School, makes a compelling appeal for "locally owned questions and purposes in realising practice within the broader national policy and practice frameworks" (MacKinnon, 2011, p. 98). He gets right to the point of how GERM affects teachers and schools:

> There is the real practical danger that without an understanding of rationale and theoretical bases for school development, practitioners may be judged by auditors on differing underlying assumptions to their own developmental pathways, and the universalistic grading schemas come to be applied as a mask or front giving pseudoscientific veneer to imposed critical judgments which are nothing more than expressions of different views and models of education. Through the mechanism of inspection, a difference of conceptual viewpoint, which could prompt debate and dialogue in consideration of practice, is eliminated in judgmental and differential power relations. One view supplants another. Command and control replaces mutuality, dialogue and conceptual exploration matched to practice development. Those who suffer are those innovating and bringing in new ideas. (MacKinnon, 2011, p. 100)

GERM has gained global popularity among policy makers and change consultants because it emphasizes some fundamental new orientations to learning and educational administration. It suggests strong guidelines to improve quality, equity, and the effectiveness of education, such as putting priority on learning, seeking high achievement for all students, and making assessment an integral part of the teaching and learning process. However, it also strengthens market-like logic and procedures in education. First and most importantly, GERM assumes that external performance standards, describing what teachers should teach and what students should do and learn, lead to better learning for all. By concentrating on the basics and defining explicit learning targets for students and teachers, such standards place strong emphases on mastering the core skills of reading and writing and mathematical and scientific literacy. Systematic training of teachers and external inspection are essential elements of this approach.

Second, GERM relies on an assumption that competition between schools, teachers, and students is the most productive way to raise the quality of education. This requires that parents choose schools for their children, that schools have enough autonomy, and that schools and teachers are held accountable for their students' learning.

By contrast, a typical feature of teaching and learning in Finland is high confidence in teachers and principals regarding curriculum, assessment, organization of teaching and inspection of the work of the school. Another feature is the encouragement of teachers and students to try new ideas and approaches, in other words, to make school a creative and inspiring place to teach and learn. Moreover, teaching in schools aims to cultivate renewal while respecting schools' pedagogic legacies. This does not mean that traditional instruction and school organization are nonexistent in Finland; it is quite the opposite. What is important is that today's Finnish education policies are a result of 3 decades of systematic, mostly intentional, development that has created a culture of diversity, trust, and respect within Finnish society, in general, and within its education system, in particular.

I have named this alternative approach to the global educational reform movement the *Finnish Way*. A similar attempt in development of the information society and economic system is called the *Finnish Model* (Castells & Himanen, 2002; Routti & Ylä-Anttila, 2006; Saari, 2006). What distinguishes Finland from most other nations is that the proven level of performance of the education system has occurred simultaneously in learning outcomes and equity in education. These are both the next generation applications of the Third Way, or radical centrism, that became well-known in the 1990s through the leadership of Tony Blair, Bill Clinton and Gerhard Schröder. In education, the Finnish Way seems to have strongly inspired the Fourth Way (2009):

> The Fourth Way is a way of inspiration and innovation, of responsibility and sustainability. The Fourth Way does not drive reform relentlessly through teachers, use them as final delivery points for government policies, or vacuum up their motivations into a vortex of change that is defined by short-term political agendas and the special interests with which they are often aligned. Rather, it brings together government policy, professional involvement, and public engagement around an inspiring social and educational vision of equity, prosperity and creativity in a world of greater inclusiveness, security and humanity. (Hargreaves & Shirley, 2009, p. 71)

In the quote above, the word *Fourth* could be replaced by the word *Finnish*. The Finnish Way is a professional and democratic path to improvement that grows from the bottom, steers from the top, and provides support and pressure from the sides.

"Through high quality teachers committed to and capable of creating deep and broad teaching and learning," as Hargreaves and Shirley describe the Fourth Way, "it builds powerful, responsible and lively professional communities in an increasingly self-regulating but not self-absorbed or self-seeking profession" (Hargreaves & Shirley, 2009, p. 107). In the Finnish Way teachers design and pursue high standards and shared targets, and improve their schools continuously through professional collaboration and networks, from evidence, and from literature in their trade.

A KNOWLEDGE-BASED ECONOMY

The major economic transformation and need for sophisticated knowledge and skills in new high-tech industries provided the Finnish education system with unique opportunities for radical renewal in the 1990s. This happened at the same time as three significant economic and political processes unfolded: the collapse of the Soviet Union; a deep and severe economic recession triggered by a Finnish banking crisis (1990–1993); and integration with the European Union (1992–1995). Each of these changes influenced the Finnish education sector either directly or indirectly. By the middle of the 1990s, a clear Finnish consensus emerged that mobile communication technologies would eventually foster the transformation to a knowledge economy and that this was perhaps the best way out of the economic crisis and into the heart of European power (Routti & Ylä-Anttila, 2006). It was also realized that the knowledge economy is not only about preparing human capital for higher know-how, it is also about having highly educated and critical consumers able to benefit from innovative technological products in markets requiring better technological literacy.

In the beginning of 1993, Finland was in the most severe economic recession since the 1930s. Unemployment was reaching 20%, gross domestic product volume had declined 13%, the banking sector was collapsing, and public debt had gone through the roof. The government responded to this national crisis in an unexpected way. First, investments were heavily targeted to innovation instead of promoting a range of traditional activities. The survival strategy addressed diversification away from timber and conventional industries toward high-technology and mobile communication. It introduced new national competitiveness policy and accelerated the privatization of government-owned companies and public agencies, and accelerated the liberalization of fiscal markets and foreign ownership in Finland. The key assumption was that the facilitation of private sector innovation and reciprocal collaboration between public and private actors would be superior to traditional direct intervention and investment in broader research and development policy. The overcoming of crisis was mainly due to the strong concentration on the telecommunication industry, and the support of Nokia Corporation in particular.

Nokia gave birth to a completely new electronics industry in Finland, an essential part of the successful Finnish economic comeback in the 1990s.

Second, knowledge accumulation and development became the key turn-around feature in pulling Finland up from depression. Without many natural resources to rely on, Finland's main determinants for growth strategies became knowledge and the active internationalization of its economy and education. In 1998, the World Economic Forum (WEF) ranked Finland as 15th in its global competitiveness index. By 2001 Finland had climbed to the pole position in this influential ranking that covers more than 130 economies of the world (Sahlberg, 2006a; Alquézar Sabadie, & Johansen, 2010). Gross expenditure on research and development, commonly used as a proxy for competitiveness in knowledge-based economies, increased from 2.0% in 1991, to 3.5% in 2003, and to 3.7% in 2008, at the same time the OECD average fluctuated between 2.0% and 2.3% (Statistics Finland, n.d.b). The number of knowledge workers in the Finnish labor force also increased significantly. The total research and development labor force in 1991 was exactly an OECD average at that time, slightly more than five people per thousand workers. By 2003 this number climbed to 22 people, almost three times higher than the concurrent OECD average.

The transformation of the Finnish economy into a knowledge-economy is described as "remarkable, not only in light of its earlier economic difficulties . . . [but because] it is interesting to see that a knowledge economy can be built suc-cessfully in a small and comparably peripheral country" (Routti & Ylä-Anttila, 2006, p. 4). Trust and increased investment in innovation resulted in education policies in the 1990s that focused on better knowledge and skills in coherence with creativity and problem solving. The strong focus on mathematics, science, and technology contributed markedly to the growth of Nokia as a world leader in mobile communication and Stora Enso in paper manufacturing. Several Finnish universities were closely connected to research and development in these firms. Indeed, governmental innovation agencies actively facilitated innovation as a third element in the Finnish knowledge and innovation triangle. Finnish economists who endorsed the importance of innovation and education in national develop-ment policy also played an important role. Education was seen as necessary and a potential investment—not just expenditure—in helping to develop innovation and adopting more innovation throughout the economy. Highly educated people are certainly "irreplaceable for the implementation of new technologies from home and abroad" (Asplund & Maliranta, 2006, p. 282).

The information society and knowledge economy have been important con-textual factors for educational change in Finland since the 1970s. The economic sector in Finland has expected the education system to provide the needed quanti-ties of skilled and creative young people with appropriate competences to deal with rapidly changing economic and technological environments. In their call for raising standards of knowledge and skills, Finnish employers, for example, were reluctant to advocate for narrow specialization and early selection to schools, contrary to many other countries at that time. While Finnish industry actively promoted better learning of mathematics, sciences, and technology, it simultaneously supported rather innovative forms of school–industry partnerships as part of the formal curriculum. The rapid emergence of innovation-driven businesses in the mid-1990s introduced creative problem solving and innovative cross-curricular projects and teaching methods to schools.[3] Some leading Finnish companies reminded education policy makers of the importance of keeping teaching and learning creative and open to new ideas, rather than fixing them to predetermined standards and accountability through national testing.

Membership in the European Union in 1995 marked a mental challenge and change for, and within, Finland. The Soviet Union had disappeared only a few years earlier, an event that boosted consolidation of Finland's identity as a full member of Western Europe. The accession process of becoming a European Union member-state was equally important as attaining actual membership in 1995. As a new Finnish identity emerged during the years of the European Union accession, Finnish people were motivated to ensure that they and their institutions, including schools, were up to the level of other European nations. In fact, the poor reputation of mathematics and sciences in Finnish schools, compared to European peers in the 1970s and 1980s, became a reason to try harder to improve Finnish educational performance to a good European level. Although education is not included in formal European Union membership requirements or common policies, the accession process had a tangible positive impact on strengthening public institutions, including the education system in Finland, especially in the midst of the worst economic recession described earlier in this book. Moreover, Finnish educators became increasingly aware of various European education systems. This certainly drove the ongoing education reform and adoption of new ideas as more information became readily available about practices within other systems.

History and the personal mindset of Finns suggest that they are at their best when faced with these kinds of global challenges. For example, experiences such as the 1952 Olympics, the war against the Soviet Union, and the deep economic recession of the early 1990s provide good evidence of the competitive and resilient Finnish spirit, or *sisu* as the Finns say. These educational and cultural attitudes were complemented by key economic, employment, and social policies that evolved since the 1970s, while the establishment of a welfare state and its institutions and policies was completed by the end of the 1980s. Survival has always been the best source of inspiration and energy for the Finns to go beyond expectations.

Analysis of educational change often includes speculation about the basic nature of change, that is, whether it is evolutionary or revolutionary. These terms refer to change as either continuous with smooth development from one stage to another, or radical transition, where new institutions and rules are created. Educational change in Finland has displayed periodic evolution, meaning that the nature of educational change has changed during these periods of change. What is important to realize, as shown in Table 4.2, is that 1990 marks an important watershed in Finnish history that distinguishes two periods in educational time. The time prior to 1990 was characterized by the creation of institutions and frameworks for a welfare-based education system. Post-1990 has been more concerned with interests, ideas, and innovations that have formed the education system as an integral part of the complex social, economic, and political system. Part of the success of the Finnish Way emerges from an ability to create punctuated equilibrium between these two periods of educational change.

Two simultaneous processes have played an important role in developing the education system in Finland since 1970. On the one hand, increased interaction among various public-sector policies has strengthened the coherence of economic and social reforms and, therefore, created conditions for what Hargreaves and Fink term "sustainable leadership" in education (Hargreaves & Fink, 2006). This increased coherence enables systematic commitment to longer-term vision and intersector cooperation among different policies and strategies. On the other hand, internationalization and Finland's integration into the European Union have harmonized and intensified consolidation and development of public institutions and their basic functions. In this light, three conclusions can be drawn regarding how Finnish educational success can be understood from an economic and political perspective:

1. The success of Finnish education reform is mainly based on institutions and institutional structures established in the 1970s and 1980s, rather than on changes and improvements implemented from the 1990s. This state-generated social capital that is created through government regulations and motivated by the responsibility to provide basic conditions of well-being for all has provided a favorable social context for educational achievement.
2. Changes in Finnish primary and secondary education after 1990 have been more about interests, ideas, and innovations than about new institutional structures. Institutional changes in the 1990s have been smaller, except in higher education where a new polytechnic system was introduced. Nonetheless, directions remain clear and are based on the earlier policies.
3. The emphasis on national competitiveness that has been a key driving force in most public-sector policies in the European Union, has not been converted to clear targets or operations in Finnish public-policy sectors during the 1990s and 2000s. At the same time, equity principles promulgated in the early 1970s have gradually lost influence in these policies.

Table 4.2. Increased Interdependency Among Public Sector Policies in Finland Since 1970

		Strategy	Economic Policies
Interdependency between public sector policies strengthens	Establishment of institutions	1970s: Institutionalization Consolidation of the pillars of welfare state and strengthened state-driven social capital. Fostering conventional industrial production structures.	Small, open economy that depended on exports and was state-regulated. Investments mainly in physical capital.
		1980s: Restructuring Welfare state completed. Restructuring economic regulations, information technology infrastructure, and public administration.	Rapid public sector growth. Industrial production concentrates on metal and wood sectors.
	Interests, ideas, and innovations	1990s: Ideas and Innovation Public sector liberalization. Diversification of exports through innovation-driven markets and dissemination of ideas through a network society.	Public sector growth halts and starts to decline. Private service sector starts to grow and new ICT industries emerge. Investments in R&D increased. Restructuring of banking sector.
		2000s: Renewal Strengthening well-performing parts of economy and renewing social policies (further privatization) to match financial realities.	Focus on services increases. Central administration loses its role and productivity of public sector is emphasized.

Employment Policies	Social Policies	Education Reform Principles
Establishing active employment policies and unemployment benefit system. Strengthening direct training for labor markets.	New risk-management systems for adults. Systems for unemployment, work-life balance, access to further education and housing.	Emphasis on equity and equal access to good primary and secondary education for all. Securing public provision of education.
Restructuring unemployment benefit system. Using early retirement as part of new employment policies.	Student welfare services and medical-care system. Student loan and social benefit systems. Restructuring unemployment legislation.	Restructuring upper secondary education to increase access for all students. Transferring upper-secondary schools to municipal authority.
Recession cuts employment benefits. New labor market benefit system to encourage employment. Employment policy system reform.	Fixing social consequences of Big Recession, especially for in-debt and long-term unemployed. Re-training and further education of unemployed.	Empowering teachers and schools through school-based curricula, coordinated innovations, and networking schools and municipalities for sharing ideas and change. Expansion of higher education sector.
Aging population casts a shadow on employment. Accent on rights and obligations of unemployed. Cross-sector approach emphasized.	Renewing immigration legislation. Adapting social system for further diversification.	Renewing education legislation, strengthening evaluation policies, and tightening state control over schools and productivity in education sector. Sizes of schools increases.

To sum up, since 1970 there have been two differing yet interconnected educational change periods, which differ in terms of the theories of change and sources of ideas and innovation driving them. On one hand, education reform principles have increasingly been created interdependently with other public-policy sectors, following a *complementarity* principle. On the other hand, ideas for educational change—particularly improving teaching and learning in schools—have been built upon past good practices and traditions in Finland. This has sometimes been labeled *pedagogical conservatism* and has created a pedagogical equilibrium between progressivism and conservatism through learning from the past and teaching for the future (Simola, 2005). A common conclusion about the role of social and economic policies in building the education system in Finland since the 1970s is that it is a demonstration of how context makes a difference in educational achievement. In other words, it demonstrates that individual well-being, equitable distribution of income, and social capital can explain student learning in international comparisons. Let's take a closer look at how social policies and the welfare state are linked to education system performance in Finland.

WELFARE, EQUALITY, AND COMPETITIVENESS

Social policy decisions in the 1950s and 1960s underscored the economic importance of farms run by families. However, the general perceived image of Finland remained agrarian despite rapid industrialization and agriculture's declining contribution to the GDP over the second half of the 20th century. Regardless of drastic changes in the way of life and emerging cosmopolitanism among Finnish people, traditional social values endured. According to Richard Lewis, who has studied the Finnish culture closely, these values included such cultural hallmarks as a law-abiding citizenry, trust in authority including schools, commitment to one's social group, awareness of one's social status and position, and a patriotic spirit (Lewis, 2005). Policies that guided education reforms since the 1970s relied on these cultural values and principles of consensus-building that have been distinguishing characteristics of Finnish society.

Finland followed the main post-war social policies of other Nordic countries. This led to the creation of a type of welfare state where basic social services, including education, became public services for all citizens, particularly for those most in need of support and help. It increased the level of social capital, as did national government policies that affected children's broader social environment and improved their opportunities and willingness to learn. Professor Martin Carnoy calls this "state-generated social capital" (Carnoy, 2007). State-generated social capital is the social context for educational achievement created by government social policies. The influence of social restructuring and educational reform in Finland was profound and immediate. Eager to improve their children's economic and social opportunities, Finnish parents turned to the education system that has served as an equalizing institution in Finnish society.

Income inequality is often claimed to affect people's lives in more ways than just how much they can afford to spend on their living. Are education systems in more equal societies performing better than elsewhere? Richard Wilkinson and Kate Pickett argue in their book, *The Spirit Level,* that indeed these systems are doing better in more ways than just one (Wilkinson & Pickett, 2009). Actually, they show how income inequality is related to many other issues in our societies as well. Income inequality can be measured in different ways. One common method calculates the gap between the wealthiest and poorest quintile in each country. In Figure 4.1, I use the data from the United Nations 2006 Human Development Report (UNDP, 2007) and PISA 2006 (OECD, 2007) to construct a relationship between income inequality and science learning for 15-year-olds. It appears that there is a not strong but still recognizable relationship between wealth distribution and student learning: In more equal societies, pupils seem to learn better in science. Wilkinson and Pickett show how more equitable countries (statistically) have more literate citizens, rarer school drop-out, less obesity, better mental health, and fewer teenage pregnancies than those where the income gap between poor and wealthy is wider.

Figure 4.1. Income Inequality and Student Learning in Science (PISA) in Selected Developed Countries in 2006

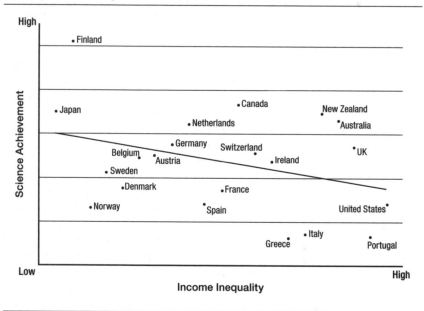

Source: OECD (2007) and UNDP (2007).

It seems understandable that income inequality, child poverty and lack of appropriate pupil welfare in schools play an important part in improving teaching and learning in national education systems. This has been well understood in Finland during the last half a century. Complimentary school lunches, comprehensive welfare services, and early support to those in need have been made available for all children in all Finnish schools—free of charge. Every child has, by law, a right to these welfare services in their school.

This chapter urges that educational progress in Finland should be viewed in the broader context of economic and social development and renewal, both nationally and globally. Interestingly, the growth of the Finnish education sector coincided with an impressive economic transformation from an agrarian, production-driven economy to a modern information society and knowledge-driven economy. Indeed, Finland has transformed itself into a modern welfare state with a dynamic knowledge economy in a relatively short time. The Finnish experience of the 1990s represents one of the few documented examples of how education and therefore knowledge can become driving forces of economic growth and transformation. During that decade, Finland became the most specialized economy in the world in telecommunication technology and thus completed its transition from resource-driven to a knowledge- and innovation-driven economic and educational system.

In the 2000s, Finland consistently scored high in international comparisons of national economic competitiveness, transparency and good governance, communication network readiness, implementation of sustainable development policies, and, surprisingly, in happiness of people. Finland has been ranked as the most competitive economy several times in the first decade of the 21st century by the World Economic Forum's *Global Competitiveness Index*.[4] This is significant given that Finland experienced a severe economic crisis in the early 1990s. Becoming a competitive economy and the first country to make a broadband Internet connection a human right for all citizens, required a major restructuring of the economy. Moreover, Finland also has a reputation of rule of law and, as a consequence, a low level of corruption that plays an important role in economic development and performance of public institutions. In 2009, the British think tank Legatum ranked Finland the most prosperous nation, before Switzerland, Sweden, Denmark, and Norway (the United States was ranked ninth) (http://www.prosperity.com). The late summer 2010 issue of *Newsweek* labeled Finland as the best country in the world, trailed by Switzerland, Sweden, Australia, and Luxemburg (United States was 11th) (*Newsweek*, 2010). Education was the driving force in both of these indexes.

After the historic economic crisis of the 1990s, good governance, strong social cohesiveness, and an extensive social safety net provided by the welfare state made an exceptionally rapid economic recovery possible. A similar turnaround of Finnish economic progress was recorded after the global financial crisis in 2008. One of the strategic principles in pulling the Finnish economy out of downturn has been continuous high levels of investment in research and development, as described earlier in this chapter. Despite severe cuts in public spending, both in the early 1990s and after the most recent fiscal crisis, belief in knowledge generation and innovation has remained strong. In 2010, Finland spent nearly 4% of GDP in research and development—the highest of the OECD countries after Sweden.

As noted, this chapter asserts that education system performance has to be seen in the context of other systems in the society, for example, health, environment, rule of law, governance, economy, and technology. It is not only that the education system functions well in Finland, but that it is part of a well-functioning democratic welfare state. Attempts to explain the success of the education system in Finland should be put in the wider context and seen as a part of the overall function of democratic civil society. Economists have been interested in finding out why Finland has been able to become the most competitive economy in the world. Educators are trying to figure out the secret of Finland's high educational performance. The quality of a nation or its parts is rarely a result of any single factor. The entire society needs to perform harmoniously.

Four common features are often mentioned as contributory factors for positive educational and economic progress. First, policy development has been based on integration rather than exclusive subsector policies. Education sector development is driven by medium-term policy decisions that rely on sustainable basic values, such as equal opportunities to good education for all, inclusion of all students in mainstream publicly financed education, and strong trust in public education as a civil right rather than an obligation. These medium-term policies integrate education and training, and involve the private sector and industry in the creation and monitoring of their results. Similarly, economic and industrial policies have integrated science and technology policies and innovation systems with industrial clusters. Integrated policies have enhanced systemic development and the interconnectedness of these sectors and have thus promoted more sustainable and coherent political leadership for their successful implementation.

Second, strategic framework development and change have been built upon longer-term vision. National development strategies, such as the Information Society Program in 1995, National Lifelong Learning Strategy in 1997, and Ministry of Education Strategy 2020 in 2009, have served as overarching frameworks for the sector strategies (these strategies can be found on the website of the Ministry of Education, www.minedu.fi). These and other strategies have emphasized increasing flexibility, coherence between various sectors, and development of local and regional responsiveness and creativity in institutions.

Third, the roles of governance and public institutions have been central in policy developments and the implementation of both education and economic reforms. Good governance, high-quality public institutions, and rule of law play important roles in policy development and implementation of planned changes. Evaluation approaches in both sectors are development-oriented and various players in the system are held accountable for process and outcomes. Specific institutions, such as the Parliamentary Committee of the Future are shared by private and public representatives as well as the key stakeholders of the society for consensus-making purposes.

Fourth, a highly educated labor force and broad participation in education at all levels guarantee the stock of *human capital* that is necessary for both good education service delivery and economic growth. For instance, all teachers are required to hold a master's degree, and most workers are encouraged to participate in continuous professional development as part of their work. Teachers are professionals in their schools and therefore actively involved in planning and implementing changes in their work.

Flexibility is one of the key denominators of education and economic development in Finland. The education system went through a major transformation in the early 1990s when most state regulations were abolished and pathways to education opportunities were dramatically increased. Similarly, private sector regulations were loosened and more flexible standards were introduced, especially to foster networking between firms, universities, public research, and development institutions.

Strong integrated policy frameworks and longer-term strategic visions have enhanced sustainable leadership in education and private sector developments. Due to this sustainability factor the education system has been reluctant to adopt market-oriented principles of the Global Education Reform Movement. For example, learning and teaching standards, high-stakes tests, or consequential accountability, have never been favored in Finnish education policies. Frequent and open dialogue between private business leaders and the public education sector has increased the mutual understanding of what is important in achieving the common good and promoting the development of a knowledge economy. Indeed, active cooperation between education and industry has encouraged schools to experiment with creative teaching and learning practices, especially in nurturing entrepreneurship and building positive attitudes toward work. Most importantly, the main principle in the development of Finnish society has been encouraging intellectual growth and learning of each individual. Developing cultures of growth and learning in education institutions as well as in work places has proved to be one of the key success factors.

TWO FINNISH ICONS: NOKIA AND *PERUSKOULU*

When people are asked what they associate with Finland, most say: "Nokia." According to Finnish diplomats around the world, next comes "Education." In the middle of 2011 Nokia still is the leading mobile communication company, with about a 40% share of all mobile phones sold in 2010 in the world. Its head office is located in Espoo, just west of Helsinki. Nokia employs some 133,000 people around the world with net sales of 60 billion U.S. dollars (in 2010). The global reputation of Finnish education, in turn, draws primarily from *peruskoulu*, a 9-year comprehensive school model launched in 1972 that has become the bedrock of all other forms of education in Finland. There are 2,900 such schools in Finland with 550,000 students and 40,000 teachers in 2010. Although Nokia as an enterprise and *peruskoulu* as a public institution are very different and serving different purposes, they share some interesting similarities. These similarities reflect the principles of being Finnish and doing big things in the Finnish way.

Both Nokia and the Finnish public school system have roots dating back to the 1860s. The story of Nokia begins in 1865. Fredrik Idestam, mining engineer and founder of Nokia Company, brought a new paper manufacturing process from Germany to Finland and built a wood pulp mill on the banks of the Tammerkoski River near the city of Tampere. Idestam's invention was recognized with an award at the Paris World Exposition in 1867, and he is often referred to as the father of Finland's paper industry. A little later he opened a second mill by the Nokianvirta River. This is where Nokia got its name.

The Finnish school system evolved at the same time. Pastor Uno Cygnaeus, a student of my grandfather's grandfather's father, Professor Carl Reinhold Sahlberg, and a travel companion of his son Reinhold Ferdinand to Sitka, Alaska, in the 1840s, was sent to Germany and Switzerland by the Finnish Senate in the 1850s to find out how public education should be organized in Finland. Cygnaeus recommended that the first teacher preparation seminar, based on what he saw in Switzerland, should be established in Jyväskylä, Finland. The first teacher education seminar began there in 1863. He also advised that the Finnish *Folk School,* as it was called, should be based on practical learning and the development of manual skills for all students, boys and girls. The Senate passed the Act of Basic Education in 1866. The first Finnish public school for all children was established in Jyväskylä in that same year, and it followed the model of German education. The pedagogy of Cygnaeus significantly shaped the future of public education, and he has come to be known as the father of Finnish public school, although there are those who question whether this title can be given to only one person.

Nokia grew quickly and expanded its business from forestry to rubber works, cables, and electronics. During the first half of the 20th century, Nokia became an important player in the Finnish economy. By 1967, Nokia had become the Nokia Corporation, a conglomerate with rubber, cable, forestry, electronics, and power generation divisions and global reach. With its range of expertise, Nokia was ideally positioned for a pioneering role in the early evolution of mobile communications. When European telecommunications markets were deregulated in the 1970s and 1980s and mobile networks became global, Nokia quickly took the leading role with some iconic innovations: The first international mobile phone network was built in 1981 and the first new technology GSM (global system for mobile communications) phone call was made by Nokia in 1991. Under the leadership of its new CEO, Jorma Ollila, Nokia decided to focus on mobile telecommunication. As a result, Nokia became the world leader of the mobile telephone industry by the end of that decade. This transformation of Nokia happened in a relatively short period of time and is often cited as an example of dramatic organizational transformation.

Education in Finland has gone through a similar transformation, as has been described in previous chapters of this book. In the beginning of the 1960s, barely 10% of adults in Finland had earned a secondary degree or higher. Most young people sought employment right after completing 7 or 8 years of basic education. Until the beginning of the 1970s, further education opportunities were based on private grammar schools that many families could not afford. The transformation of the education system in Finland that kicked off from the introduction of the new *peruskoulu* was fundamental and rapid. It led to the immediate expansion of upper- secondary education and created pathways to higher education for two thirds of the age cohorts by the end of the 1990s. Building on the ideas of upgrading teacher education to the master's degree level in universities, abolishing streaming and ability grouping, and investing early on in special education and student counseling positively affected the quality of education in *peruskoulu* and beyond. As a consequence, by the end of the 1990s, Finnish *peruskoulu* became the world leader in reading, science, and math. This shift from an elitist and socially divided system of education into the most equitable public education system in the world happened in such a short time that it has been frequently cited as an example of dramatic organizational transformation.

By the 1990s, Nokia and Finnish schooling entered an era of fruitful engagement. My work with the Finnish Ministry of Education in the 1990s included, among other duties, chairing the national task force to create the National Framework for Science Curriculum. The task force included not only educators from schools and universities but also business leaders and entrepreneurs who had an interest in what young people should learn in school. Nokia was the key player in the Finnish industry at that time and also an outspoken advocate of high-quality education, especially in *peruskoulu*, where the foundation for knowledge and skills is built. It was understandable, therefore, that we gave a particularly attentive ear to the opinions and perspectives of leaders at Nokia. In our dialogue with Nokia, to our surprise, we heard quite unexpected ideas of developing Finnish *peruskoulu*.

The logic of the Nokians and some others with similar points of view was simple. In order to be on the cutting edge of innovation in the mobile communication business, they contended that people must be the key. Their objective in this regard was to hire the most innovative as well as the most collaborative people they could find and to give them the freedom to work together and take risks. They explained to us that if people work or learn in an environment where avoidance of mistakes and fear of failure are dominant, they typically don't think for themselves. Fear of

---

BOX 4.1: The Finnish School Principal

School sizes in Finland are increasing. One hundred fifty years ago, when the Finnish public school was born, most schools had only one teacher. Today these schools do not exist. In today's schools, teachers have to be able to work together in shared spaces and also educate students together. Each teacher has to adjust his or her pedagogical thinking and principles to those of other teachers. It is therefore essential that the school has a common culture that enables consistent teaching and learning for shared purposes. That is why a principal is needed in each school.

The Finnish school principal is always also a teacher. Almost all Finnish principals teach some classes each week. Finnish school principals have an increasing amount of administrative duties. Many complain that the workload is becoming too heavy. The principal needs a good theory of leadership in order to cope successfully with all tasks and responsibilities in school. I would say that principals should also have a vision of what a good school is and know how leadership can help to achieve that vision.

In my work as a principal I make basic values the foundation on which I lay my leadership. In good schools daily routines work well and teaching is effective. My task is to help my teachers to do their best, and I make necessary decisions so that my school operates well. I work hard to create a good atmosphere in school and inspire teachers and students. As a leader of my own school and part of the network of other public schools in my district I must know national and local level policies. It is important to guarantee that public money is wisely spent in all schools, including mine. That's what makes a good school principal.

I strive to be a good principal in my school. It means that I have to do my best as a manager, leader, director, and pedagogic guide for teachers and students: In other words, I want to be a good and trusted person. The biggest challenge for me is to combine all these aspects of my work. Being a school principal is not like being an administrator or coach of a sports team. A school principal is in charge of the part of a complex social system that is continuously changing. Without experience as a teacher this work would be very difficult to fulfill successfully.

Martti Hellström
School Principal of Aurora School
City of Espoo

failure does not engender creativity. It was as simple as that. One of the members of the Nokia top management put it to us this way:

> If we hire a youngster who doesn't know all the mathematics or physics that is needed to work here, we have colleagues here who can easily teach those things. But if we get somebody who doesn't know how to work with other people, how to think differently or how to create original ideas and somebody who is afraid of making a mistake, there is nothing we can do here. Do what you have to do to keep our education system up-to-date but don't take away creativity and open-mindedness that we now have in our schools.[5]

Another significant message articulated by the Nokians concerned shared leadership and strong trust in people. Dan Steinbock writes in his recent book, *Winning Across Global Markets*, "Nokians believe that in a rapidly changing and highly complex technology and marketing business, a broad and diverse executive team can provide stability, flexibility, and simplicity in decision making" (Steinbock, 2010, p. 47). Indeed, informality, quick decision making, and freedom to act have been typical principles within the leadership of education in Finland since the early 1990s. Just like in Nokia, the objective of educational management in Finland has been to have decisions made by the people who have the best knowledge and skills. The education management system is not only less hierarchical than many other education systems, but decidedly antihierarchical. The objective of meritocratic management in both Nokia and the education system is to encourage creativity, entrepreneurship, and personal responsibility.

Smart phone sales became the weak component of Nokia in 2010. Nokia continued to make mobile phones that were smarter but they were also more complicated for users. These new products were not able to compete in North America with the iPhone and other hand-held media devices that could do more than traditional phones. The Finnish CEO of Nokia was replaced in mid-2010 by a Canadian from Microsoft. Analysis of what went wrong at Nokia reveals some telling aspects of leadership that may resonate with education sector management later on. Some observers argued that 10 years ago Nokia had reached a state of complacency with its domination of the world's mobile phone market. There were those who claimed that top management procedures were too slow when they relied on building consensus on every possible technical issue.[6] And then there were those who believed that Nokia had lost much of its creative capacity to come up with new ideas when set goals had been realized. All these are also potential risks for the Finnish education system as it moves on as a celebrated model of public education in the world. The fourth OECD PISA study in 2009 conveyed the first signs of possible turn of the course of the Finnish comprehensive school, although the overall performance is still excellent (OECD, 2010b). As will be discussed in Chapter 5, certain complacency and inability to build joint and inspiring vision of the future in Finnish education will serve as factors that inevitably lead the system into trouble.

Yet, Nokia and Finnish education are fundamentally different. Nokia is an international corporation in the fiercely competitive market of communication technology and innovation. Finnish education, especially its *peruskoulu,* is a strictly domestic system of human development. Nokia is a commercial enterprise driven by the purpose of private good, while education in Finland is a public service for social good. Finally, Nokia relies heavily on its own proprietary research and development to keep its competitive edge. The Finnish school system does not have this type of built-in source of innovation on which to rely.

Foreign visitors have often asked me about where all the pedagogical ideas and innovations come from in Finnish education. The response surprises them: the United States, England, Canada, Sweden, and Germany, among other countries. Although the educational change is characterized as the Finnish Way, described earlier in this chapter, the source of many pedagogical innovations and research evidence for change are imported from elsewhere. Education in Finland also depends on a truly open-source platform because domestic educational change-knowledge generation is modest in international comparison. In 2009 Nokia spent 8.5 billion U.S. dollars on its own research and development work, with every third staff member employed as a researcher. Finland's budget for higher education in 2009—for 40 institutions of post-secondary learning—was approximately 4 billion U.S. dollars, including research in all fields of science.

THE FINNISH DREAM CHALLENGED

It would be a mistake to think that the education reforms of the 1970s that created Finland's 9-year *peruskoulu* were supported by all business leaders, politicians, and educators. The campaign against *peruskoulu* was particularly harsh from some parts of the business community. Finnish business leaders followed closely how *peruskoulu,* which was built on the ground of former privately governed grammar schools, was implemented. The Finnish Business and Policy Forum (EVA), a policy and pro-market think tank, gave funding to a foundation that was opposed to this ongoing school reform and wanted to see private schools as alternatives to the new schools. The Parliament's conservative right accused advocates of the comprehensive school reform of being socialist or even communist, warning that the model would jeopardize the steady economic progress of Finnish society. The other side of the aisle defended the reforms by saying they would secure a good education for every child in Finland and thereby raise the well-being and prosperity of Finnish society. There was also a debate in the 1970s about the ability of the new *peruskoulu* to keep up with the international race for a knowledgeable and skilled labor force. These critics feared that *peruskoulu* would not allow the most able and talented to progress as far as they should in school.

In the late 1980s, when the opposition to ongoing education reform was particularly strong, some parents as well as politicians and business leaders voiced their criticism and dissatisfaction to *peruskoulu*, where all streaming and tracking had been abolished a few years earlier. According to these critics, the emphasis on social equality had led to a suppression of individuality. This concern was, in fact, voiced by the prime minister at the Finnish School Principals' Annual Meeting in November 1987:

> When believing that anyone can learn everything, the goals of the comprehensive school are set too high. When trying to educate the whole population to the unattainable comprehensive school level, the financial and mental resources of a small nation are being wasted on a hopeless task. These same educational resources would be badly needed to educate those who have proven to be talented in different areas to international high standards. Only that way can we maintain Finland's position in the hard international competition in science and the economy. (Aho et al., 2006, p. 62)

Triggered by this perception of the political leadership, Finnish business leaders launched a survey to find out the actual state of *peruskoulu* as the main medium of education in Finland. In the autumn of 1988, the Finnish media widely reported the findings of that survey. The grim conclusion was that *peruskoulu* kills talent. In other words, it doesn't allow able and gifted pupils to progress to their full potential because it insists on social equality by employing unified curriculum in all classrooms. This coincided with the deregulation of the economy. The education system had to support the transition of Finnish society into a more liberal and competitive market economy. There were those—including the then prime minister of Finland—who argued that the economic transformation from postindustrial to knowledge economy requires that able and talented students should be offered opportunities to progress freely and not to "wait for the mediocre students," especially in mathematics and science.

The campaign to reform the Finnish education system according to the models of the free market continued into the 1990s. The Education Reform Act of 1988 in the United Kingdom with the first national curriculum and common attainment targets to all, the outcome-based education policies of New Zealand, and the standards-based model of the United States were all seen by some Finnish business leaders as suitable alternatives to the new Finnish Way in education. Increasing choice, competition, and specialization were cited as a way to better education. National assessments and regular testing of student achievement were promoted as the necessary means of catching up to other education systems that seemed to increase the gap between them and Finland in education.

Criticism continued and sharpened until the end of the 1990s, although research findings did not support the contention that students were learning less because of *peruskoulu* (Linnakylä & Saari, 1993). Shifting the responsibility of curriculum planning, school improvement, and student assessment to municipalities and schools in the mid-1990s had strengthened the support from teachers and principals to develop the Finnish school system without using the models of marketplace management. The critical voices were suddenly muted in early December 2001 when news of the first PISA study was published in the global media: Finland outperformed all other OECD countries in reading, mathematics, and science when measured at the end of *peruskoulu*. Indeed, the *peruskoulu* was validated. Finnish schooling soon joined Nokia as another Finnish global brand.

CHAPTER 5

Is the Future Finnish?

The future needs a big kiss.

—U2, 360° Tour 2009–2011

Finland has been engaged in comprehensive school reform since the 1970s. Research on specific features of *peruskoulu* led to the development of applied educational sciences, or subject didactics, in Finnish universities. However, more generic understandings of educational change remained relatively untouched. Even today, research on educational change, school improvement, and school effectiveness in Finland is modest. Much more analytical and research work on the Finnish educational system is conducted on the country's educational policies at different phases of its history. It is somewhat paradoxical that with undeveloped domestic educational change knowledge, Finland has been able to transform its education system in 3 decades, as this book describes. Models of change in Finland have often been borrowed from abroad, but educational policies, as discussed earlier, were crafted and then implemented in the Finnish way.

Finland has now come to a fork in the road. Until the end of the 20th century, Finland has been following other countries, learning from them and sometimes adapting their good ideas for its own restructuring and development. Indeed, it is easier to walk the paths that others have paved than to be in the lead. But the future requires new ways of thinking. Finland has shown that in the past it has been able to be innovative when needed and has used its past experience as a basis for new policies and practices. The Country Brand Delegation crystallized Finland's greatest strength as "the unbiased, solution-focused approach to problems, which derives from our history and culture. When faced with an impossible situation, we roll up our sleeves and double our efforts," (Ministry of Foreign Affairs, 2010, p. 3). Therefore, this final chapter first argues that educational excellence has been attained because Finland has chosen an alternative way in its educational reform, often almost in opposition to the global educational reform movement. Finland's approach reflects a particular winning strategy: System-wide excellence in education is possible by doing things differently than others. The chapter next discusses some factors behind educational success in Finland since the 1970s. It then suggests that Finland needs to work out a shared vision of the future that inspires practitioners and communities to continuously renew teaching in schools and education in the communities. Ultimately, the core question considered is this: Will Finland sustain its high educational performance in the future?

EXCELLENCE BY BEING DIFFERENT

In this book I have conveyed my concern that the insistence that nations follow the Global Educational Reform Movement—characterized by increased competition and choice, standardization of teaching and learning, tightening test-based accountability, and merit-based pay for teachers—may jeopardize schools' efforts to teach for the evolving knowledge society and for a sustainable future. This is not the best way to improve learning in our schools, and there is no evidence that it would improve the quality or enhance equity of education systems. Finland, forgoing the tenets of the GERM, is a nation that has demonstrated sustained educational improvement since the early 1970s, shown consistent high performance by students, and maintained an equitable educational system at the same time. Finnish schools operate in congruence with a competitive knowledge economy as was described in previous chapters. It is therefore useful to look at how that society has responded to the global challenge to transform national education systems to increase their overall effectiveness and relevance for 21st-century knowledge and skills needs.

Interestingly, the term *accountability* cannot be found in Finnish educational policy discourse. Finnish educational reform principles since the early 1990s— when much of the public sector administration went through a thorough decentralization—have relied on developing professional responsibility by educators and encouraging learning among teachers and schools, rather than by applying bureaucratic accountability policies. Therefore, sample-based testing, thematic assessments, reflective self-evaluations, and emphasis on creative learning have established a culture of mutual trust and respect within the Finnish education system. Before the end of upper-secondary school, or grade 12, no external high-stakes tests are employed. There is no inspection of teachers, and only loose external standards steer the schools. These practices leave teachers with the opportunity to focus on learning rather than be concerned about frequent testing and public rankings of their schools. Some policy makers predicted in the mid-1990s that Finland would follow the school accountability policy models promoted by GERM. But in a review of policy development in Finland 10 years later, test-based accountability is not even mentioned (Laukkanen, 1998, 2008). Other Nordic countries have moved to adopt policies that are close to GERM, and thus distanced themselves from their eastern neighbor.

Explaining the educational success of nations or schools is by no means easy. Finland is said to have well-prepared teachers, pedagogically designed schools, good school principals, a relatively homogeneous society, an inclusive national educational vision, and emphasis on special education needs—each separately and collectively certainly help the Finnish educational system to perform well (Hargreaves et al., 2008; Kasvio, 2011; Sahlberg, 2010a; Simola, 2005; Välijärvi et al., 2007; Hautamäki et al., 2008; Matti, 2009). Critics claim that since Finland doesn't have the very diverse ethnic population that characterizes many other nations its schools perform better. Others suggest that low levels of child poverty explain part of its students' good educational performance. Fair enough. I argue, however, that because Finland has been able to keep schools as centers of learning and caring, teachers can concentrate on what is most important and what they can do best: teach. They are not disturbed by frequent testing applied to schools, competition against other schools, or performance targets imposed by administrators. Since the beginning of the 1990s, Finnish schools have been systematically encouraged by educational authorities to explore their own conceptions of learning, develop teaching methods to match their own learning theories-in-action, and craft pedagogical environments to meet the needs of all of their students. This is why Finnish students learn well in all schools.

The National Board of Education's (1999) *Framework for Evaluating Educational Outcomes in Finland* and the national Law on Education in 1998 stipulate the requirements and basic principles of student assessment and school evaluation. Teachers are responsible for the overall assessment of their students, using a mix of diagnostic, formative, performance, and summative assessments. The municipality's responsibility is to plan and implement necessary evaluations within and of their schools, based on their own and nationally expressed needs. Thus, current education policies encourage cooperation between schools and try to protect schools from unhealthy competition. Education policies in Finland encourage collaboration and friendly rivalry, not competition and race to the top.

Finland is the land of nongovernmental organizations. There are 130,000 registered groups or societies in Finland with a total of 15 million members. On average, each Finn belongs to three associations or societies. Young Finns are also actively involved in sports and youth associations that normally have clear educational aims and principles. Young people learn social skills, problem solving, and leadership when they participate in these associations. It is commonly accepted in Finland that these associations give a positive added-value to formal education offered by schools.

Finland's response to improving learning of all students since the early 1970s has relied on four strategic principles:

1. Guarantee equal opportunities to good public education for all.
2. Strengthen professionalism of and trust in teachers.
3. Steer educational change through enriched information about the process of schooling and smart assessment policies.
4. Facilitate network-based school improvement collaboration between schools and non-governmental associations and groups.

The key message of this book is that schools in competition-driven education environments are stuck in a tough educational dilemma. The current culture of accountability in the public sector as it is employed in England, North America, and many other parts of the world often threatens school and community social capital; it damages trust rather than support it.[1] As a consequence, teachers and school leaders are no longer trusted; there is a crisis of suspicion, as O'Neill has observed (2002). Although the pursuit of transparency and accountability provides parents and politicians with more information, it also builds suspicion, low morale, and professional cynicism.

SUCCESSFUL EDUCATIONAL REFORM

A typical feature of education in Finland is the encouragement of teachers and students to try new ideas and methods, to learn from innovations, and to cultivate creativity in schools. At the same time, many teachers respect the traditions of good teaching. Education policies today are a result of 3 decades of systematic, mostly intentional, development that has created a culture of diversity, trust, and respect within Finnish society in general and within its education system in particular.

As shown in Table 4.1, the education policies and related strategies to raise student achievement in Finland differ from those found in other countries. Andreas Schleicher suggests that one element of Finland's success has been "the capacity of policy makers to pursue reform in ways that went beyond optimizing existing structures, policies and practices, and moved toward fundamentally transforming the paradigms and beliefs that underlay educational policy and practice until 1960s," (Schleicher, 2006, p. 9). Although education policy discourse in Finland changed dramatically during the 1990s as a consequence of new public sector management and other neoliberal policies, Finland has remained immune to market-based educational reforms. Instead, education sector development has been built upon values grounded in equity and equitable distribution of resources rather than on competition and choice. Importantly, the Trade Union of Education in Finland (OAJ), which represents more than 95% of all teachers in Finland, has consistently resisted adopting business management models in the education sector. Moreover, Finland is a society where achieving consensus on important social and political issues is not rare. Although education is politicized in Finland as it is everywhere, Finns have been able to get together across the political party lines and reach agreements. *Peruskoulu,* the 9-year compulsory school, is a good example of that.

A question asked repeatedly is this: Why are Finnish schools and students doing better in the international comparison studies than most others? This book describes how Finland, by employing alternative approaches in education policies, has been able to improve student achievement.[2] Professor Jouni Välijärvi who has worked on international student assessments for several decades observes that:

Finland's high achievement seems to be attributable to a whole network of interrelated factors in which students' own areas of interest and leisure activities, the learning opportunities provided by school, parental support and involvement as well as social and cultural context of learning and of the entire education system combine with each other. (Välijärvi et al., 2002, p. 46)

One accomplishment of the Finnish education system that is often overlooked is the especially high level of reading literacy that Finnish children have already at early age. There are both educational and sociocultural reasons for it: Teaching to read in schools is based on individual development and pace rather than on standardized instruction. Finnish parents read a lot, books and newspapers are easily available through a dense library network, and children are exposed to subtitled TV and cinema at an early age. Good reading comprehension and ability to understand texts fast is a great advantage in PISA tests that are based on being able to understand descriptive tasks in all measured areas.

Another overlooked direction of Finnish educational development is reform of school architecture along the guidelines set out by the National Curriculum Framework and its pedagogical and philosophical principles. New school buildings are always designed in collaboration with teachers and architects and they are thereby adapted to the teaching and learning needs of the specific communities. Physical environment provides an important context for both students and teachers. "If the building is consciously viewed as an instrument of learning," reasons Kaisa Nuikkinen, "the architecture itself can serve as an inspirational, tangible teaching tool, offering a living example of such things as good ergonomic design and the principles of sustainable development" (Nuikkinen, 2011, p. 13–14). The school building can create a sense of well-being, respect, and happiness—all hallmarks of Finnish school.

The following five interrelated factors are often heard when Finnish experts explain the reasons behind good educational performance. All are related to education or school and should not suggest that social, community, physical environment, or family factors would not have important roles to play.

Peruskoulu offers equal educational opportunities for all. All Finnish children start their formal schooling in August of the year they turn 7. Normally, class-based primary school lasts 6 years and is followed by 3-year lower-secondary school, although today *peruskoulu* is formally a unified 9-year school. Today it is widely recognized that the 6-year primary school provides a solid basis for high-quality education system. Finnish experience and international research show that investment in early childhood development and primary education pays off in later grades through better aptitude and learning skills, as well as through positive overall outcomes (Biddle & Berliner, 2002). Schools are typically small with class sizes ranging from 15 to 30 students. In 2010, one quarter of Finnish comprehensive schools had fewer than 50 pupils; just 6% of all schools had 500 or more pupils. In other words, Finnish schools are rather small. Primary schools (grades 1 to 6) typically have fewer than 300 pupils and often operate separately from upper grades (7 to 9), although the unified *peruskoulu* is gradually closing the gap between these two. As a consequence of the tightening financial conditions in Finnish municipalities, about 1,000 comprehensive schools have been shut down during the first decade of this century. Many of them were small rural schools.

Teaching is an inspiring profession that attracts many young Finns. In Finnish society, the teaching profession has always enjoyed great public respect and appreciation, as explained in Chapter 3. Classroom teaching is considered an independent, high-status profession that attracts some of the best upper-secondary school graduates each year. The main reason for the strong appeal of teaching as a career is the fact that a master's degree is the basic requirement for permanent employment as a teacher in Finnish schools and having it opens other future employment options. Therefore, individuals who choose teaching as their first career do not feel that their lives are limited to working in a school. Indeed, teachers with a master's degree often interest human resource departments within the Finnish private sector and third-sector organizations. They also have access to doctoral studies in Finnish universities. During the past decade, Finnish schools have noted an upsurge in school principals and teachers possessing a PhD in education.

Westbury and colleagues point out that preparing teachers for a research-based profession has been the central idea of teacher education development in Finland since the mid-1970s (Westbury et al., 2005; Toom et al., 2010). Teachers' higher academic qualifications have enabled schools to have an increasingly active role in curriculum planning, evaluating education outcomes, and leading overall school improvement. The OECD review on equity in education in Finland describes how Finland has created a virtuous circle surrounding teaching:

> High status and good working conditions—small classes, adequate support for counselors and special needs teachers, a voice in school decisions, low levels of discipline problems, high levels of professional autonomy—create large pools of applicants, leading to highly selective and intensive teacher preparation programs. This in turn leads to success in the early years of teaching, relative stability of the teacher workforce, and success in teaching (of which PISA results are only one example), and a continuation of the high status of teaching. (OECD, 2005a, p. 21)

Today the Finnish teaching profession is on par with other high professions; teachers can diagnose problems in their classrooms and schools, apply evidence-based and often alternative solutions to them, and evaluate and analyze the impact of implemented procedures. Parents trust teachers as professionals who know what is best for their children.

Finland has a smart policy for accountability. Finland has not followed the global educational accountability movement that assumes that making schools and teachers more accountable for their performance is the key to raising student achievement. Traditionally, the evaluation of student outcomes has been the responsibility of each Finnish teacher and school. There are no external standardized high-stakes tests in Finnish *peruskoulu*. Assessment of student learning is based on teacher-created tests at the school level and on sample-based national assessments. Normally Finnish pupils are not assessed using numerical grades that would enable a direct comparison of pupils with one another before 5th or 6th grade. Only descriptive assessments and feedback are employed, depending on how student assessment is described in the school curriculum or municipal education plan. Primary school is, to a large extent, a "standardized testing-free zone" and pupils are allowed to focused on learning to know, to create, and to sustain natural curiosity. Fear of learning and anxiety are not common in Finnish schools. The national PISA report concludes that only 7% of Finnish students said they feel anxiety when working on mathematics tasks at home compared to 52% and 53% in Japan and France, respectively (Kupari & Välijärvi, 2005).

Educational accountability in the Finnish education context preserves and enhances trust among teachers, students, school leaders, and education authorities, and it involves them in the process, offering them a strong sense of professional responsibility and initiative. Shared responsibility for teaching and learning characterizes how educational accountability is arranged in Finland. Parents, students, and teachers prefer smart accountability that enables schools to keep the focus on learning and permit more degrees of freedom in curriculum planning, compared to the external standardized-testing culture that prevails in some other nations.

People trust schools. Much of what has been previously noted is possible only if parents, students, and authorities trust teachers and school principals. As described earlier in this book, the Finnish education system was highly centralized until the early 1990s. Schools were previously strictly regulated by the central agencies; a dense network of rules and orders regulated the daily work of teachers. The gradual shift toward trusting schools and teachers began in the late 1980s. In the early 1990s, the era of a trust-based school culture, so eloquently described by Director General Vilho Hirvi in the opening pages of this book, formally started in Finland.

The culture of trust meant that education authorities and political leaders believe that teachers, together with principals, parents, and their communities, know how to provide the best possible education for their children and youth. Trust can only flourish in an environment that is built upon honesty, confidence, professionalism, and good governance. Tellingly, Finland also performs well in international transparency rankings that indicate the perceptions of corruption among citizens. Public institutions generally enjoy high public trust in Finland.

Trusting schools and teachers is a consequence of a well-functioning civil society and high social capital. Honesty and trust, as Lewis (2005) observes, are often seen as among the most basic values and the building blocks of Finnish society.

The Finnish education system has sustainable leadership and political stability. The success of Finnish education is not the result of any major national education reform per se. Instead, education development in Finland has been based on the continual adjustment of schooling to the changing needs of individuals and society. Professor Risto Rinne claims that although the emergence of the new public sector management meant revolutionary changes in Finnish educational discourse, this new rhetoric and practices have not been able to take root in education as easily as in other parts of society (Rinne, Kivirauma, & Simola, 2002). As a consequence, the basic values and the main vision of education as public service have remained unchanged since the 1970s. Governments from the political left and right have respected education as the key public service for all citizens and maintained their belief that only a highly and widely educated nation will be successful in world markets.

In education systems that undergo wave after wave of reforms, frequent emphasis often is on implementation and consolidation of externally designed changes. The main result is frustration and resistance to change rather than the desire to improve schools. A rather steady political situation since the 1980s and sustained educational leadership have enabled Finnish schools and teachers to concentrate on developing teaching and learning. Rather than allocating financial resources and time to implement new reforms repeatedly, teachers in Finland have been given professional freedom to develop pedagogical knowledge and skills related to their individual needs. After a decade of centralized in-service teacher education, following the launch of comprehensive school reform in the 1970s, the focus of professional development programs has shifted to meet authentic demands and expectations of schools and individuals.

THE TRANSFER OF CHANGE KNOWLEDGE

Today, Finland is often used as a model of successful educational change. "As societies move beyond the age of low-skill standardization," writes Andy Hargreaves, "Finland contains essential lessons for nations that aspire, educationally and economically, to be successful and sustainable knowledge societies" (Hargreaves et al., 2008, p. 92). However, reform ideas and policy principles that have been employed in Finland since the 1970s will not necessarily work in other cultural or social contexts. For example, in Finland, as in other Nordic countries, people trust each other and therefore also their teachers and principals more than in many other countries (OECD, 2008). Similarly, there are other sociocultural factors that are mentioned by some external observers, such as social capital, ethnic homogeneity, and high professional status of teachers that may have a key role when transferability of education policies is considered.[3]

Indeed, many want to learn how to develop a good education system from the Finns (Barber & Mourshed, 2007; Hargreaves et al., 2008; OECD, 2010c; Ofsted, 2010). Understanding Finnish educational success needs to include an awareness of the sociocultural, political, and economic perspectives discussed in this book. Indeed, there is more to the picture than meets the eye. An external OECD expert review team that visited Finland observed that "it is hard to imagine how Finland's educational success could be achieved or maintained without reference to the nation's broader and commonly accepted system of distinctive social values that more individualistic and inequitable societies may find it difficult to accept" (Hargreaves et al., 2008, p. 92). Another visiting OECD team confirmed that the Finnish approaches to equitable schooling rely on multiple and reinforcing forms of intervention with support that teachers can get from others, including special education teachers and classroom assistants (OECD, 2005a). Furthermore, Finland has shown that educational change should be systematic and coherent, in contrast with the current haphazard intervention efforts of many other countries. The conclusion was that "developing the capacities of schools is much more important than testing the hell out of students, and that some nonschool policies associated with the welfare state are also necessary" (Grubb, 2007, p. 112). Scores of news articles on Finnish education have concluded that trust, teacher professionalism, and taking care of those with special needs are the factors that distinguish Finnish schools from most others.[4]

These observations about the transferability of educational-change knowledge contradict with the thinking of those who claim that context, culture, politics, or governance are not of key importance to a school system and its leaders when seeking real improvement in educational outcomes. The McKinsey report that analyzed education policies and practices in 25 countries concluded that the following three educational reform principles go before anything else: 1. the quality of teachers helps determine the level of student performance; 2. education outcomes will only improve by improving instruction; and 3. systemwide excellence is only possible by "putting in place mechanisms to ensure that schools deliver high-quality instruction to every child" (Barber & Mourshed, 2007, p. 40). This is a rational approach to educational improvement.

An alternative example cited was the United States education reform known as No Child Left Behind. This legislation, according to many teachers and scholars, led to fragmentation in instruction, further interventions uncoordinated with the basic classroom teaching, and more poorly-trained tutors working with students and teachers (Ravitch, 2010c; Darling-Hammond, 2010). As a consequence, schools experienced too many instructional directions for any student, with an increase in unethical behaviors such as students cheating on tests and administrators manipulating student assessment protocols, and a loss of continuity in instruction and systematic school improvement (Nichols & Berliner, 2007). This is a bureaucratic approach to developing education.

Differences between these approaches and the Finnish Way described in this book are notable: The Finns have worked systematically over 30 years to make sure that competent professionals who can craft the best learning conditions for all students are in all schools, rather than thinking that standardized instruction and related testing can be brought in at the last minute to improve student learning and turn around failing schools. The rational and bureaucratic approaches to educational change mentioned above resonate with the key ideas of GERM and can be found in the educational policies of numerous nations and jurisdictions around the world, but not in Finland.

Indeed, importing specific aspects of the education system from Finland, whether it be curricula, teacher training, special education, or school leadership, is probably of little value to those aiming to improve their own education systems. The Finnish welfare system guarantees all children the safety, health, nutrition, and moral support that they need to learn well in school. As the passage from the novel *Seven Brothers* at the beginning of Chapter 1 illustrates, literacy and education in general have historically played a central role in becoming a full member of the Finnish society. One lesson from Finland is, therefore, that successful change and good educational performance often require improvements in social, employment, and economic sectors. As described by Stuart Kauffman (1995), separate elements of a complex system rarely function adequately in isolation from their original system in a new environment. Therefore, rather than borrowing only specific aspects or innovations from other education systems, more transferable aspects may be the features and policy principles of a larger, complex system, in this case, the Finnish Model. In a complex system, interactions among elements of the system determine the behavior of that system as much as its individual elements. Therefore, some concerns that should be considered when contemplating the transfer of ideas from the Finnish education system are:

1. *Technical drivers of good educational performance.* They include common comprehensive school for all, research-based teacher education, professional support to teachers, smart accountability policies, relatively small schools, and good educational leadership, especially within schools.
2. *Sociocultural factors.* They include long reliance on the social value of literacy and education, high work morality, trust in public institutions including schools, and state-driven social capital created by the welfare state.
3. *Links to other public-policy sectors.* Success of one sector depends on the success of all others. Therefore good educational performance may only be explained through larger policy principles, including those of other public policies.

Finnish people also need to be smart to avoid the illusion that the current ways of measuring the performance of education systems is going to last forever. Although there are clear advantages to relying on global education indicators—especially those related to economics of education—and student achievement numbers produced by PISA and other surveys, there will be a growing pressure in the coming years to develop educational units of measurement that better cover a broader range of learning and the changing face of future societies. PISA is looking at one part of that desired outcome of education. At the same time, as Peter Mortimore writes:

> PISA also suffers some limitations: It assesses a very limited amount of what is taught in schools; it can adopt only a cross-sectional design; it ignores the role and contribution of teachers; and the way its results are presented—in some, at least, of its tables—encourages a superficial, "league table" reading of what should be a more interesting but essentially more complex picture. (Mortimore, 2009, p. 2)

Many teachers and principals in Finland have a skeptical view of international measurements and benchmarking tools. They perceive teaching and learning as complex processes and are aware that quantifying their effectiveness is difficult.

Is there anything to learn from the Finns? I am not suggesting that other nations should adopt the Finnish education system or even its elements, such as *peruskoulu* or academic teacher education, as I clearly pointed out above. But there are many things we can learn from one another in education. While sensitivity to the problems of transferring educational ideas from one place to another is essential, I would propose three main lessons from Finland that are relevant to trying to improve quality and equity of education.

First, we should reconsider those education policies that advocate choice, competition, and privatization as the key drivers of sustained educational improvement. None of the best-performing education systems currently rely primarily on them. Indeed, the Finnish experience shows that a consistent focus on equity and shared responsibility—not choice and competition—can lead to an education system in which all children learn better than they did before. Hoping that the problem of inadequate education would be fixed by paying teachers based on their students' test scores or converting public schools into private ones through charters or other means is not included in the repertoire of educational improvement in Finland.

Second, we should reconsider teacher policies by giving teachers government-paid master's degree-level university education, providing better professional support in their work, and making teaching a respected profession. As long as the practice of teachers is not trusted and they are not respected as professionals, young talent is unlikely to seek teaching as their lifelong career anywhere. Or if they do, they will leave teaching early because of lack of a respectful professional working environment. The experience of Finland and other high-performing education systems speaks clearly to this.

Finally, with the international student assessment studies and educational indicators, differences between high-performing education systems and those who are struggling are becoming more visible. There is much to learn from the current leaders. The secret of Finnish rapid and sustained educational improvement is due to a smart combination of national tradition and international ideas. In international education, being a forerunner and the shining star is not necessarily the best position when transforming education systems to meet the needs of the future. Therefore, aiming at being close to the leaders is probably the best plan. Let me explain my position.

THE FUTURE OF FINNISH EDUCATION

In the first decade of this millennium, Finland established a global reputation as a model educational nation. *Newsweek* titled its May 24, 1999 article about Finland: "The Future is Finnish." It praised the smart way Finland has been able to create a national vision for an innovation-based society that combines mobile communications and information technologies unlike any other (*Newsweek*, May 24, 1999). This book has described how Finland's education performance has progressed steadily since the early 1970s. Mobile phone makers, symphony-orchestra conductors, and Formula 1 drivers are symbols of what a Finnish culture and society that values ingenuity, creativity, and risk taking is able to nurture. But will the Finnish education system continue to be a model in the future?

On the one hand, Finland's systemic educational leadership since the 1970s, its stable political structure, and its established complementarity among public-policy sectors would suggest that its educational performance will remain strong. On the other hand, PISA survey results, in particular, have created a feeling of complacency among education policy makers, politicians, and the public-at-large regarding the status of Finnish education. This may lead to a condition favoring the status quo, where education policies and leadership of a high-performing system are motivated by a desire to maintain the current situation, rather than seeing what possible futures might require from a reformed Finnish education system.

Educational change in Finland has been driven by culture and emotion in the context of social, political, and economic survival. Finland has shown to others that there is an alternative way of change to that employed by many other countries. Finns themselves have learned that technical knowledge or political interests are not enough to renew society without emotional engagement. Indeed, global educational reforms show that too rational an approach on change does not work because renewal requires energy, and energy is driven by emotion. In the era of big changes emotional passion often emerges from crisis—or a sense of survival—as it did in Finland. But it can also come from viewing new economical, technological, or cultural opportunities and innovation.

In the beginning of the 21st century Finland has become a model nation for other reasons: It has been able to build a competitive knowledge economy while maintaining much of the social justice of the Nordic welfare state model. A high-level think tank named the New Club of Paris considered possible futures for Finland and stated that survival is no longer the impetus for renewal to keep all the good that Finland has built. In its recommendations to the Finnish Government it suggested that:

> Other drivers with emotional effect need to be identified. The question is how to broaden the scale of emotional recognition and exploitation. Instead of survival the driver for change could be a powerful vision, or the Big Dream of Finland. If people do not love the idea, it is futile to publish new strategies. The new strategy with cultural and emotional dimensions should be simple; a couple of words that people can immediately and emotionally relate to. This is currently missing. (Ståhle, 2007, p. 2)

Some Finns are concerned about how the country is seen by other nations in this competitive, globalized world. Several international comparisons indicate that Finland has become one of the most functional and attractive countries in many ways—well-being, governance, economic performance, sustainable development, education, and happiness. For a rather small and young nation that seems to be good enough. The Ministry of Foreign Affairs invited an influential delegation of specialists from various fields of life to think about how to secure this positive situation—or even strengthen it—in the future. The final report of this group found that functionality, nature, and education are seen as the key themes on which the future of Finland should be built. It also insists that—despite or because of the current positive situation—Finland must continue to ask itself "what shall we do next" in all fields of operations (Ministry of Foreign Affairs, 2010, p. 277).

The spirit of these general recommendations should also be considered in education. The chief instrument that guides Finnish education policies and educational renewal is the Development Plan for Education and Research for 2007–2012. This, like the previous document for 2003–2008, continues earlier policies and development principles. These documents emphasize securing equal opportunities, improving the quality of education, preparing skilled workers, developing higher education, and dignifying teachers as main resources of good education. Furthermore, these documents place strong emphasis on the *complementarity* principle by developing the education system as a whole. All this assumes that the Finnish education system will continue to perform well in the coming years. However, there are some trends within the governance of the education system and in Finnish society in general that provide cause for concern.

BOX 5.1: Leading a Local School District

The Development of the education system is based on systematic and sustainable fiscal policies. Finnish education depends heavily on public funding. As a result of the global financial crisis, the Finnish public sector has been hit hard. Municipalities are experiencing rapidly tightening budgets. During the last decade, the debt burden of Finnish municipalities has tripled and the Finnish government debt is bigger than ever before. Increasing productivity and cutting public spending are now common public policies in Finland. Merging or closing down small schools is one expression of these policies.

From an international perspective, Finland is still a country of small schools. The average size of a comprehensive school in Finland is 200 students. In 2008 there were 2,988 comprehensive schools. Since 2004 the number of these schools has decreased by 14%. A total of 1,900 comprehensive schools have disappeared since 1990. This has radically changed the density and nature of the comprehensive school network in Finland. More students now travel longer distances to school. Many small villages are affected when the school closes down. Much of this structural change has been steered by economic rather than educational considerations.

The worsening situation of the Finnish public sector has also caused many municipalities to use temporary lay-offs of teachers as a cure for their chronic financial crisis. Teachers have been sent home without pay for a few days or in some cases, some weeks. While a teacher has been on this forced unpaid leave other teachers have had to take care of her or his classes and students. Savings have often been minor, but the negative implications for the school severe.

I am concerned about the longer-term affects of these public sector policies. Economic forecasts in Finland do not promise better times ahead. On one hand, we know from experience that simply increasing financial resources does not solve the daily problems of schools. But sustained shrinking of education budgets creates a situation in which some of the essential structures will be jeopardized. Will schools and municipalities be able to achieve more with less in the future? I think that is possible, but it requires a careful analysis of current structures and practices. We need to be clear where the savings can be made and where resources can be transferred to development and renewal. However, without a sufficient slice from the overall public budget to education it will be very difficult. Cutting budgets and worsening the possibility for high-quality education is not a smart way to reward people for their good work, demonstrated by OECD PISA.

Peter Johnson
Director of Education
City of Kokkola

First, national education authorities have tightened the grip of control over schools. This shift signals that confidence in schools' ability to judge what is best for pupils and parents is declining. For example, the new National Curriculum Framework of 2004 reduces schools' role in curriculum planning.

Second, the governmental Education Sector Productivity Program for 2006–2010 and the new government program for 2011–2015 call for municipalities and schools to do more with fewer resources, and often lead to school mergers and increasing school sizes. In some cases, productivity gains are sought by reducing schools' special education and counseling services. This may turn out to be harmful for the development of social capital in Finnish schools. There is, at the moment of this writing, no clear idea within the Finnish education system of what the direction of public education should be in the future. For example, the Development Plan for Education and Research for 2007–2012 is silent about how education should react to needs expressed in the economic sector to intensify innovation and create new products.

Third, Finland is slipping away from its top position as the most transparent nation, the country with the most competitive economy, and a socially equal society. PISA 2009 results sent similar, although weak, signals of Finland's educational performance (OECD, 2010b). Other indicators suggest that inequalities in Finnish society and in its education system are increasing. Countries with higher levels of equality have higher overall levels of attainment in many different fields, including education, as Wilkinson and Pickett have shown (Wilkinson & Pickett, 2009). In terms of income equality, Finland has been among the top countries in the world, together with other Nordic countries. Figure 5.1 shows how income inequality has increased in Finland during the last 2 decades. Increasing inequality is often related to growing social problems, such as a prevalence of violence, diminishing social trust, worsening child well-being, increased poverty, and declining educational attainment. Therefore, the challenge for Finland is not to try to maintain high student performance but to strive to keep the country an equal society and maintain its leading position as having the most equitable education system in the world.

In reforming its education system Finland has actively listened to what other countries have advised as necessary for raising the quality of student learning and meeting the new challenges in education. Finnish education authorities have been particularly attentive to what supra-national organizations—the OECD, the European Commission, and the United Nations agencies—have thought to be the necessary steps in educational policies in Finland. The educational research community in Finland has adopted models and ideas from their foreign colleagues. In Finland's current situation, a new orientation is needed. It is still important for communication and collaboration with international partners to remain active. Today, however, Finland is much more a giving partner than a receiving one. It is

Figure 5.1. Ratio Between Income Shares of the Highest and Lowest Income Quintiles in Finland for 1987–2008

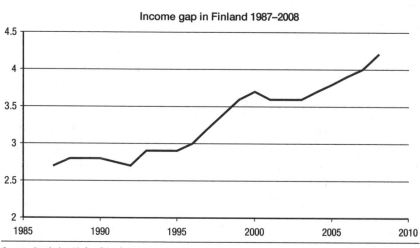

Source: Statistics Finland (n.d.c).

therefore necessary for Finland to be prepared for collaboration and exchange of experiences with other education systems as a trusted source of inspiration, ideas and innovation. I have suggested that a *new global partnership* for the leadership of educational change is needed. This should be based on proven excellence and good practice, capacities and willingness to move fearlessly to implement innovative ideas and solutions for the future of education. Finland has a place in this league of new education leaders. But it can't take that place without an inspiring vision of education.

Any movement needs the foundation that draws from the core set of values, philosophies, and a commonly shared vision. Finnish philosopher Pekka Himanen's vision, *School 2.0*, about future education is truly a transformation of present day schooling. It would be based on a community of learners where learning sparks from individual interests, passion, and creativity and aims to help each learner to find his or her own talent.[5] Whatever the vision of the new school is, or however we call it, completely new forms of school have to be considered. The new global partnership in educational change should kick-off from this question.

The inspiring idea—or *Big Dream*—has often joined Finnish people together and provided a source of emotional energy for change. After World War II, the idea was to provide all Finns with an equal opportunity for good public education regardless of their domicile, socioeconomic status, or other life conditions. This became the main principle in building *peruskoulu* in the early 1970s. The first PISA survey in 2000 proved that the Finnish Big Dream was fulfilled. The fourth PISA survey in 2009 insists that the new Finnish dream is urgently needed.

In the midst of one of the worst post-World War II economic crises in the early 1990s, Finland turned again to education and insisted that nothing less than becoming the leading and most competitive knowledge economy of the world was enough to bring Finland back to the trajectory of other advanced economies. The Big Dream then was to make the education system serve the social cohesion, economic transformation, and innovation that would help Finland to be a full member of the European Union and remain a fully autonomous nation. The education system was, as was discussed in previous chapters, the key driver that raised the nation out of the economic crisis. The past visions of education are accomplished, and it is time to form a new vision that is capable of steering educational change in Finland during the next few decades. As a conclusion to this book I offer some seeds for creating that vision for the future of education in Finland.

The Big Dream for the future of Finnish education should be something like this: *Create a community of learners that provides the conditions that allow all young people to discover their talent.* That talent may be academic, artistic, creative, or kinesthetic, or some other skill set. What is needed is for each school to be a safe learning community for all to engage, explore, and interact with other people. School should teach knowledge and skills as before, but it must prepare young people to be wrong, too. If people are not prepared to be wrong, as Sir Ken Robinson says, they will not come up with new ideas that have value (Robinson, 2009). That is the only way that we in Finland will be able to make the best use of our scarce human resources.

Many changes are required to the existing format of schooling. First and foremost, Finnish school must continue to become more pupil-friendly so that it allows more personalized learning paths. Personalization doesn't mean replacing teachers with technology and individualized study. Indeed, the new Finnish school must be a socially inspiring and safe environment for all pupils to learn the social skills that they need in their lives. Personalized learning and social education lead to more specialization but build on the stronger common ground of knowledge and skills. The following themes of change would emerge:

1. Development of a personal road map for learning. It is important for each young person to acquire certain basic knowledge, such as reading, writing, and using mathematics. In the future, it will be important that students have alternative ways to learn these basic things. Children will learn more and more of what we used to learn in school out of school, through media, the Internet, and from different social networks to which they belong. This will lead to a situation in which an increasing number of students will find teaching in school irrelevant because they have already learned what is meaningful for them elsewhere.

A good solution to address this is to rethink schools so that learning in them relies more on individual customized learning plans and less on teaching drawn from a standardized curriculum for all. The art of future education will be to find a balance between these two. Due to expanding educational possibilities in a digital world, young children enter schools with huge differences in what they already know and are able to do. This also means that young people are interested in a great variety of issues that may be completely foreign to teachers in their schools. Customized study plans or personalized learning must not mean that students will study alone with tools and information from the Internet only. It means that they will have a well-prepared, rich, and educationally justified individual plan for learning that is jointly designed and agreed upon by teachers, parents, and the student.

2. Less classroom-based teaching. Developing customized and activity-based learning eventually leads to a situation in which people can learn most of the what is now taught in schools through digital devices wherever and whenever. Hand-held portable devices will provide online access to knowledge and other learners. Shared knowing and competences that are becoming an integral part of modern expertise and professional work will also become part of schools and traditional classrooms. Finland and some other countries have shown that it is not the length of the school year or school day that matter most. Less teaching can lead to more students learning if the circumstances are right and solutions smart. Such circumstances include trust in schools, adequate support and guidance for all students, and curriculum that can be locally adjusted to meet the interests and requirements of local communities.

Rather than continue thinking of future schooling in terms of subjects and time allocations to them, the time is right now to make a bold move and rethink the organization of time in schools. This would mean having less time allocated to conventional subjects, such as mother tongue, mathematics, and science, and more time for integrated themes, projects, and activities. Naturally, the share of organized lessons should be more available in the lower grades of primary school, and then gradually decrease as pupils' skills of managing their own behavior and learning develops. This would also mean a shift from common curriculum-based teaching to individual learning-plan-based education. This would lead to extended time for all students to spend engaged in personally meaningful workshops, projects, and the arts.

3. Development of interpersonal skills and problem solving. In the future people will spend more time on and give more personal attention to media and communication technologies than they do today. It means two things from the educational point of view. First, people in general will spend less time together in a concrete social setting. Social interaction will be based on using social networking and other future tools that rely on digital technological solutions. Second, people will learn more about the world and other people through media and communication technologies. Especially expanding engagement in social media and networks will create a whole new source of learning from other people who have similar interests. By default, these new social tools will increase opportunities for creative actions as people can be part of open source projects designing games or digital solutions in collaboration with others in these networks.

Schools need to rethink what their core task in educating people will be. It cannot remain as it is today: to provide the minimum basic knowledge and skills that young people need in the future. The future is now and many young people are already using those skills in their lives today. Schools need to make sure that all students learn to be fluent in reading, mathematics, and science concepts, and possess the core of cultural capital that is seen as essential. Equally important, however, is that all students develop attitudes and skills for using available information and opportunities. They will also need to develop better skills for social interaction, both virtual and real, learn to cooperate with people who are very different from themselves, and cope in complex social networks. What most people in the future will need that they are not likely to learn anywhere else is real problem-solving in cooperation with other people. This will become one of the basic functions of future schools: to teach cooperation and problem solving in small groups of diverse people.

4. Engagement and creativity as pointers of success. Current education systems judge individual talent primarily by using standardized knowledge tests. At worst these tests include only multiple choice tasks. At best they expand beyond routine knowledge and require analytical, critical thinking, and problem solving skills. However, they rarely are able to cover the non-academic domains that include creativity, complex handling of information, or communicating new ideas to others. It is important to assess how students learn the basic knowledge and skills in school and to know how they can develop their communication, problem-solving skills, and creativity as a result of school education.

Conventional knowledge tests as we know them now will gradually give space to new forms of assessment in schools. As schools move to emphasize teaching skills that everybody needs in a complex and unpredictable world, the criteria of being a successful school will also change. People will learn more of what they need through digital tools and media, and therefore it will become increasingly difficult to know what role schools have played in students' learning (or not learning if you wish) of intended things. Two themes will be important as we move toward the end of this decade.

First, engaging all students in learning in school will be more important than ever. Lack of engagement is the main reason for the challenges that teachers face in schools and classrooms today. It is well known from research and practice that as children get older their interest in what schools offer declines. By the end of *peruskoulu* a growing number of young people find school learning irrelevant, and they are seeking alternative pathways to fulfill their intentions. Therefore, engagement in productive learning in school should become an important criterion of judging the success or failure of schools.

Second, students' ability to create something valuable and new in school will be more important than ever—not just for some students, but for most of them. If creativity is defined as coming up with original ideas that have value, then creativity should be as important as literacy and treated with the same status. Finnish schools have traditionally encouraged risk taking, creativity, and innovation. These traditions need to be strengthened. When performance of students or success of schools is measured, the creative aspect of both individual learning and collective behavior should be given high value. In other words, a successful school is able to take each individual—both students and teachers—further in their development than they could have gone by themselves.

What is needed to turn these four change themes into reality is not yet another educational reform but renewal, a continuous systemic transformation of teaching and learning, step-by-step toward the Big Dream. Finland has what it takes to do just that. It requires the new global partnership and leadership in educational change that Finland takes part in. An important lesson from Finland is that there are different pathways to educational excellence. These paths differ from the global educational reform movement discussed in the previous chapter. A way of increasing productivity and improved efficiency may lead to financial savings and perhaps temporarily better services. But, as Finnish futurologists Pirjo Ståhle and Markku Wilenius point out, in the economic context shrinking budgets will never create sustainable improvements unless there are simultaneous investments in something new (Ståhle & Wilenius, 2006). There are enough signals through forecasts of the Finnish economy and society in general to suggest that more investments are needed to create new ideas and innovations both in education and in economic development, and to maintain the high level of social capital that has traditionally been the driver of strong educational performance.

At the end of the1990s, Finland was able to benefit from one of the most competitive national economies when experimentation, creativity, and networking were taken to the heart of school improvement, and trust in teachers and schools were endorsed as the key principle of education management. A component of educational change that creates new ideas and innovation should provide enough encouragement and support for risk taking that will enable creativity to flourish in classrooms and schools. This is possible only with continuous renewal of Finnish education, guided by wise educational leadership in close relation to other public sector policies.

What many countries are looking for now is a socially just education system with schools that inspire teachers and students alike to do their best. Seymour Sarason reminded educational reformers that "teachers cannot create and sustain contexts for *productive learning* unless those conditions exist for them" (Sarason 1996, p. 367). Finnish educational policy conforms precisely with this conviction. The Finnish government understands the importance of teachers and accordingly invests heavily in not only teacher education and professional development but also work-conducive environments so that the teaching profession attracts and retains talent.

Well before the surge in attention to Finnish education following the publication of the 2000 PISA results, I had the privilege to host Seymour Sarason in Helsinki for a week in 1995. He was finalizing the revision of his book *The Culture of the School and the Problem of Change*, from which the observation above is drawn. I took Sarason to visit schools, talk to professors, and tell senior education authorities about the laws of school change as he saw them. He also read the Finnish 1994 National Curriculum Frameworks for comprehensive and upper-secondary schools and the education development plans we had prepared for the future of schooling. In the final meeting, I asked Sarason to summarize his findings. He said: "Why did you bring me here? Your school system to me looks very close to what John Dewey had in mind and what I have been writing about teaching and schools for the last three decades."

Indeed, John Dewey dreamed of the teacher as a guide helping children formulate questions and devise solutions. Dewey saw the pupil's own experience, not information imparted by the teacher, as the critical path to understanding. Dewey also contended that democracy must be the main value in each school just as it is in any free society. The education system in Finland is, as Sarason pointed out, shaped by these ideas of Dewey and flavored with the Finnish principles of practicality, creativity, and common sense. What the world can learn from educational change in Finland is that accomplishing the dream of a good and equitable education system for all children is possible. But it takes the right mix of ingenuity, time, patience, and determination.

The Finnish Way of educational change should be encouraging to those who have found the path of competition, choice, test-based accountability, and performance-based pay to be a dead end. The future of Finnish education described above can moreover offer an alternative means to customized learning. For the Finns, personalization is not about having students work independently at computer terminals. The Finnish Way is to tailor the needs of each child with flexible arrangements and different learning paths. Technology is not a substitute but merely a tool to complement interaction with teachers and fellow students.

As a countervailing force against the global educational-reform movement driving school systems around the world, the Finnish Way reveals that creative curricula, autonomous teachers, courageous leadership and high performance go together. The Finnish Way furthermore makes plain that collaboration, not conflict, with teacher unions leads to better results. The evidence is clear and so should be the road ahead.

Notes

Introduction

1. The World Bank and OECD have used Finland as an example in Aho, Pitkänen, & Sahlberg (2006) and OECD (2010c). McKinsey Company refers to Finland as a global benchmark of good practice in Barber & Mourshed (2007) and Auguste, Kihn, & Miller (2010).

2. There was a public debate in the Finnish media soon after the first OECD PISA results were published. Several members of the Finnish academic community rejected the results by arguing that the tests didn't measure "pure" mathematics or physics, but rather some forms of common everyday knowledge that are irrelevant for further studies in these subjects.

3. Howard Gardner visited Finland in May, 2010, and his interview was published in Helsingin Sanomat on May 28, 2010 (p. B9).

Chapter 1

1. *Peruskoulu* is the Finnish term that refers to 9-year compulsory school consisting of six grades of lower-comprehensive school (primary school) and three grades upper-comprehensive school (lower-secondary school).

2. The Second Republic refers to the period of 1946–1994 in Finnish history in Ala-suutari (1996).

3. Tenth grade is a voluntary additional year following the completion of compulsory education. Students have personalized learning plans that are typically blended with academic and practical subjects or themes. One of the key purposes of 10th grade is to provide young people a second chance to improve their knowledge and skills so that they will be successfull in upper-secondary school. Tenth grade is arranged as part of normal *peruskoulu* and taught by their teachers.

4. Aquarium Project was the government-funded school improvement initiative to support the shift from a centrally steered system of management to local leadership and continuous improvement. A good description can be found (in Finnish) in the doctoral thesis of Hellström (2004).

Chapter 3

1. Bologna Process is an intergovernmental initiative that currently has 46 signatories. It aims at creating the European Higher Education Area with harmonized degree systems and

European Credit Transfer System (ECTS). Teacher education is described in Pechar (2007) and Jakku-Sihvonen & Niemi (2006).

2. Pan-European collaboration in teacher education has increased due to the Bologna Process and specific exchange programs in Europe, but strong and active research links have remained between Finnish and North American and Australian universities.

3. There has been a continuous debate about whether the matriculation examination negatively affects the way that teachers teach in upper-secondary schools. Some of the empirical research findings are reported in Häivälä (2009).

Chapter 4

1. These are two main academic journals that are dedicated to school improvement and educational change.

2. The initial idea of "a new educational orthodoxy" is from Andy Hargreaves. See Sahlberg (2011a).

3. I was leading a national project called Creative Problem-Solving in Schools that had close links to Finnish innovation enterprises such as Nokia, Kone, and Vaisala. It was administrated and funded by the National Board of General Education. Part of the inspiration to this project was the Creative Problem Solving initiative based in Buffalo, NY.

4. The World Economic Forum (WEF) is a Switzerland-based international organization that coordinates research on economics. Similar comparisons of national economic competitiveness are done by the International Institute for Management Development (IMD). In the European Union's internal ranking of its member states' economic competitiveness, Finland ranked at the top with Sweden in 2010.

5. This quote is from my personal notes, taken when I was leading the national curriculum Task Force for Science education from 1992 to 1994.

6. These issues were widely reported by *Helsingin Sanomat*, the major daily newspaper in Finland, in its monthly magazine, *Kuukausiliite*, in the September 2010 issue.

Chapter 5

1. A salient example of this accountabilty culture is the well-known and controversial "deliverology" approach, which relies on targets, measuring, and accountability to manage and monitor the implementation of education reform policies and strategies. For a pro-deliverology perspective, see Barber, Moffit, and Kihn's (2011) "field guide." For a critical perspective, see Seddon's (2008) critique.

2. For example, Hargreaves (2003), Schleicher (2007), and Grubb (2007) have underscored the importance of alternative education policies in transcending the conventional educational reforms.

3. Cultural factors have been discussed by external observers of Finnish education. See Hargreaves et al. (2008), Schleicher (2006), and Grubb (2007).

4. An archive of media coverage of Finnish education since the 2000 PISA survey can be found online at www.pasisahlberg.com.

5. To read about Pekka Himanen and his *School 2.0* see www.pekkahimanen.org/.

References

Adams, R. J. (2003). Response to "Cautions on OECD's recent educational survey (PISA)" *Oxford Review of Education, 29*(3), 377–389.

Aho, E. (1996). *Myrskyn silmässä* [In the eye of the storm]: *Kouluhallituksen pääjohtaja muistelee.* Helsinki: Edita.

Aho, E., Pitkänen, K., & Sahlberg, P. (2006). *Policy development and reform principles of basic and secondary education in Finland since 1968.* Washington, DC: World Bank.

Alasuutari, P. (1996). *Toinen tasavalta: Suomi 1946–1994.* Tampere, Finland: Vastapaino.

Allerup, P., & Mejding, J. (2003). Reading achievement in 1991 and 2000. In S. Lie, P. Linnakylä, & A. Roe (Eds.), *Northern lights on PISA: Unity and diversity in Nordic countries in PISA 2000.* Oslo: University of Oslo, Department of Teacher Education and School Development (pp. 133–146).

Alquézar Sabadie, J., & Johansen, J. (2010). How do national economic competitiveness indices view human capital? *European Journal of Education, 45*(2), 236–258.

Amrein, A. L., & Berliner, D. C. (2002). High-stakes testing, uncertainty, and student learning. *Education Policy Analysis Archives, 10*(18).

Asplund, R., & Maliranta, M. (2006). Productivity growth: The role of human capital and technology in the road to prosperity. In A. Ojala, J. Eloranta, & J. Jalava (Eds.), *The road to prosperity: An economic history of Finland* (pp. 263–283). Helsinki: SKS.

Atjonen, P., Halinen, I., Hämäläinen,S., Korkeakoski, E., Knubb-Manninen, G., Kupari, P. . . . Wikman, T. (2008). Tavoitteista vuorovaikutukseen. Perusopetuksen pedagogiikan arviointi [From objectives to interaction: Evaluation of the pedagogy of basic education]. *Koulutuksen arviointineuvoston julkaisuja, 30,* 197. Jyväskylä, Finland: Koulutuksen arviointineuvosto.

Au, W. (2009). *Unequal by design: High-stakes testing and the standardization of inequality.* New York: Routledge.

Auguste, B., Kihn, P., & Miller, M. (2010). *Closing the talent gap: Attracting and retaining top third graduates to a career in teaching.* London: McKinsey & Company.

Baker, E., Barton, P., Darling-Hammond, L., Haertel, E., Ladd, H., Linn, R. . . . Shepard, L. (2010). *Problems with the use of student test scores to evaluate teachers: Briefing paper 278.* Washington, DC: Education Policy Institute.

Barber, M., Moffit, A., & Kihn, P. (2011). *Deliverology 101: A field guide for educational leaders.* Thousand Oaks: Corwin.

Barber, M., & Mourshed, M. (2007). *The McKinsey report: How the world's best performing school systems come out on top.* London: McKinsey & Company.

Bautier, E., & Rayon, P. (2007). What PISA really evaluates: Literacy or students' universes of reference? *Journal of Educational Change, 8*(4), 359–364.

Berry, J., & Sahlberg, P. (2006). Accountability affects the use of small group learning in school mathematics. *Nordic Studies in Mathematics Education, 11*(1), 5–31.

Biddle, B. J., & Berliner, D. C. (2002). Research synthesis: Small class size and its effects, *Educational Leadership, 59*(5), 12–23.

Bracey, G. (2005). Research: Put out over PISA. *Phi Delta Kappan, 86*(10), 797.

Brophy, J. (2006). *Grade repetition. Education policy series 6.* Paris: International Institute for Educational Planning.

Carnoy, M. (with A. Gove, & J. Marshall). (2007). *Cuba's academic advantage. Why students in Cuba do better in school.* Stanford: Stanford University Press.

Castells, M., & Himanen, P. (2002). *The information society and the welfare state: The Finnish model.* Oxford: Oxford University Press.

Coleman, J., Campbell, E., Hobson, C., McPartland, J., Mood, A., Weinfeld, F., & York, R. (1966). *Equality of educational opportunity.* Washington, DC: Government Printing Office.

Committee Report. (2005). *Report of the committee on transition from basic to secondary education and training. Reports of Ministry of Education 33.* Helsinki: Ministry of Education.

Darling-Hammond, L. (2006). *Powerful teacher education: Lessons from exemplary programs.* San Francisco: Jossey-Bass.

Darling-Hammond, L. (2010). *The flat world and education. How America's commitment to equity will determine our future.* New York: Teachers College Press.

Department of Education. (2010). *The importance of teaching: The schools white paper.* London: Department of Education.

Dohn, N. B. (2007). Knowledge and skills for PISA. Assessing the assessment. *Journal of Philosophy of Education, 41*(1), 1–16.

Elley, W. B. (Ed.). (1992). *How in the world do students read?* Hamburg: Grindeldruck.

European Commission (2004). *Common European principles for teacher competences and qualifications.* Brussels: Directorate-General for Education and Culture. Retrieved from http://www.see-educoop.net/education_in/pdf/01-en_principles_en.pdf

Fullan, M. (2010). *All systems go: The change imperative for whole system reform.* Thousand Oaks, CA: Corwin.

Fullan, M. (2011). *Choosing wrong drivers for whole system reform* (Seminar series 204). Melbourne: Centre for Strategic Education.

Gameran, E. (2008, February 29). What makes Finnish kids so smart. *Wall Street Journal.* Retrieved from http://online.wsj.com/article/SB120425355065601997.html

Goldstein, H. (2004). International comparisons of student attainment: Some issues arising from the PISA study. *Assessment in Education: Principles, Policy and Practice, 11*(3), 319–330.

Grek, S. (2009). Governing by numbers: The PISA "effect" in Europe. *Journal of Education Policy, 24*(1), 23–37.

Grubb, N. (2007). Dynamic inequality and intervention: Lessons for a small country. *Phi Delta Kappan, 89*(2), 105–114.

Häivälä, K. (2009). *Voice of upper-secondary school teachers: Subject teachers´ perceptions of changes and visions in upper secondary schools.* Annales Universitatis Turkuensis C 283 (in Finnish). Turkey: University of Turkey.

Hargreaves, A. (2003). *Teaching in the knowledge society. Education in the age of insecurity.* New York: Teachers College Press.

Hargreaves, A., Crocker, R., Davis, B., McEwen, L., Sahlberg, P., Shirley, D., & Sumara, D. (2009). *The learning mosaic: A multiple perspectives review of the Alberta initiative for school improvement.* Edmonton: Alberta Education.

Hargreaves, A., Earl, L., Moore, S., & Manning, M. (2001). *Learning to change: Teaching beyond subjects and standards.* San Francisco: Jossey-Bass.

Hargreaves, A., & Fink, D. (2006). *Sustainable leadership.* San Francisco: Jossey-Bass.

Hargreaves, A., & Goodson, I. (2006). Educational change over time? The sustainability and nonsustainability of three decades of secondary school change and continuity. *Educational Administration Quarterly, 42*(1), 3–41.

Hargreaves, A., Halasz, G., & Pont, B. (2008). The Finnish approach to system leadership. In B. Pont, D. Nusche, & D. Hopkins (Eds.), *Improving school leadership, volume vol. 2: Case studies on system leadership* (pp. 69–109). Paris: OECD.

Hargreaves, A., & Shirley, D. (2009). *The Fourth Way: The inspiring future of educational change.* Thousand Oaks, CA: Corwin.

Hautamäki, J., Harjunen, E., Hautamäki, A., Karjalainen, T., Kupiainen, S., Laaksonen, S. . . . Jakku-Sihvonen, R. (2008). *PISA06 Finland: Analyses, reflections and explanations.* Helsinki: Ministry of Education.

Hellström, M. (2004). *Muutosote. Akvaarioprojektin pedagogisten kehittämishankkeiden toteutustapa ja onnistuminen* [The way of change—The implementation and success of pedagogical development projects at the experimental schools of the Aquarium-project]. Helsinki: University of Helsinki.

Itkonen, T., & Jahnukainen, M. (2007). An analysis of accountability policies in Finland and the United States. *International Journal of Disability, Development and Education, 54*(1), 5–23.

Kangasniemi, S. (2008, February 27). Millä ammatilla pääsee naimisiin? [With which profession to get married?] *Helsingin Sanomat Koulutusliite,* , pp. 4–6.

Jakku-Sihvonen, R., & Niemi, H. (Eds.) (2006). *Research-based teacher education in Finland: Reflections by Finnish teacher educators.* Turkey: Finnish Educational Research Association.

Jennings, J., & Stark Rentner, D. (2006). *Ten big effects of the No Child Left Behind Act on public schools.* Washington, DC: Center on Education Policy.

Jimerson, S. (2001). Meta-analysis of grade retention research: Implications for practice in the 21st century. *School Psychology Review, 30,* 420–437.

Jokinen, H., & Välijärvi, J. (2006). Making mentoring a tool for supporting teachers' professional development. In R. Jakku-Sihvonen, & H. Niemi (Eds.), *Research-based teacher education in Finland: Reflections by Finnish teacher educators* (pp. 89-101). Turku: Finnish Educational Research Association.

Joyce, B., & Weil, M. (1986). *Models of teaching* (3rd ed.). Englewood Cliffs: Prentice Hall.

Jussila, J., & Saari, S. (Eds.). (2000). *Teacher education as a future-moulding factor: International evaluation of teacher education in Finnish universities.* Helsinki: Higher Education Evaluation Council.

Kasvio, M. (Ed.). (2011) *The best school in the world: Seven Finnish examples from the 21st century.* Helsinki: Museum of Finnish Architecture.

Kauffman, S. (1995). *At home in the universe. The search for the laws of self-organization and complexity.* Oxford: Oxford University Press.

Kets De Vries, M. (2006). *The leader on the couch.* San Francisco: Jossey Bass.

Kiuasmaa, K. (1982). *Oppikoulu 1880–1980: Oppikoulu ja sen opettajat koulujärjestyksestä peruskouluun* [Grammar school 1880–1980: Grammar school and its teachers from school order to comprehensive school]. Oulu, Finland: Kustannusosakeyhtiö Pohjoinen.

Kivi, A. (2005). *Seven brothers* [*Seitsemän veljestä* R. Impola, Trans.]. Beaverton, ON: Aspasia Books, Inc. (Original work published 1870)

Koskenniemi, M. (1944). *Kansakoulun opetusoppi* [Didactics of primary school]. Helsinki: Otava.

Kumpulainen, T. (Ed.). (2008). *Opettajat Suomessa 2008* [Teachers in Finland 2008]. Helsinki: Opetushallitus.

Kupari, P., & Välijärvi, J. (Eds.). (2005). *Osaaminen kestävällä pohjalla. PISA 2003 Suomessa* [Competences on the solid ground. PISA 2003 in Finland]. Jyväskylä: Institute for Educational Research, University of Jyväskylä.

Kuusi, P. (1961). *60-luvun sosiaalipolitiikka* [Social politics of the 1960s]. Porvoo: WSOY.

Laukkanen, R. (1998). Accountability and evaluation: Decision-making structures and the utilization of evaluation in Finland. *Scandinavian Journal of Educational Research, 42*(2), 123–133.

Laukkanen, R. (2008). Finnish strategy for high-level education for all. In N. C. Sognel, & P. Jaccard (Eds.), *Governance and performance of education systems* (pp. 305–324). Dordrecht: Springer.

Lavonen, J., Krzywacki-Vainio, H., Aksela, M., Krokfors, L., Oikkonen, J., & Saarikko, H. (2007). Pre-service teacher education in chemistry, mathematics and physics. In E. Pehkonen, M. Ahtee, & J. Lavonen (Eds.), *How Finns learn mathematics and science* (pp. 49–68). Rotterdam: Sense Publishers.

Lehtinen, E. (2004). *Koulutusjärjestelmä suomalaisen yhteiskunnan muutoksessa* [Education system in the changing Finnish society]. Helsinki: Sitra.

Lehtinen, E., Kinnunen, R., Vauras, M., Salonen, P., Olkinuora, E., & Poskiparta, E. (1989). *Oppimiskäsitys* [Conception of knowledge], Helsinki: Valtion painatuskeskus.

Levin, B. (1998). An epidemic of education policy: (What) can we learn from each other? *Comparative Education, 34*(2), 131–141.

Lewis, R. (2005). Finland, cultural lone wolf. Yarmouth, ME: Intercultural Press.

Liiten, M. (2004, February 11). Ykkössuosikki: Opettajan ammatti [Top favorite: Teaching Profession]. *Helsingin Sanomat*. Retrieved from http://www.hs.fi/artikkeli/Ykk%C3%B6ssuosikki+opettajan+ammatti/1076151893860.

Linnakylä, P. (2004). Finland. In H. Döbert, E. Klieme, & W. Stroka (Eds.), *Conditions of school performance in seven countries. A quest for understanding the international variation of PISA results* (pp. 150–218). Munster: Waxmann.

Linnakylä, P., & Saari, H. (1993). *Oppiiko oppilas peruskoulussa? Peruskoulu arviointi 90 -tutkimuksen tuloksia* [Does pupil learn in peruskoulu? Findings of the Peruskoulu 90 reserach]. Jyväskylä: Jyväskylän yliopiston kasvatustieteiden tutkimuslaitos.

MacKinnon, N. (2011). The urgent need for new approaches in school evaluation to enable Scotland's Curriculum for Excellence. *Educational Assessment, Evaluation and Accountability, 23*(1), 89–106.

Martin, M. O., Mullis, I. V. S., Gonzales, E. J., Gregory, K. D., Smith, T. A., Chrostowski, S. J., Garden, R. A., & O'Connor, K. M. (2000). *TIMSS 1999 international science report: Findings from IEA's repeat of the third international mathematics and science study at the eighth grade*. Chestnut Hill, MA: Boston College.

Matti, T. (Ed.). (2009). *Northern lights on PISA 2006. Differences and similarities in the Nordic countries.* Copenhagen: Nordic Council of Ministers.

Miettinen, R. (1990). *Koulun muuttamisen mahdollisuudesta* [About the possibilities of school change]. Helsinki: Gaudeamus.

Ministry of Education. (2004*). Development plan for education and research 2003–2008.* Helsinki: Author.

Ministry of Education. (2007). *Opettajankoulutus 2020* [Teacher Education 2020]. Committee Report 44. Helsinki: Author.

Ministry of Education (2009). *Ensuring professional competence and improving opportunities for continuing education in education* (Committee report 16). Helsinki: Author.

Ministry of Foreign Affairs. (2010). *How Finland will demonstrate its strengths by solving the world's most intractable problems: Final report of the country brand delegation.* Helsinki: Author.

Mortimore, P. (2009). *Alternative models for analysing and representing countries' performance in PISA.* Paper commissioned by Education International Research Institute. Brussels: Education International.

Mourshed, M., Chijioke, C., & Barber, M. (2010*). How the world's most improved school systems keep getting better.* London: McKinsey.

Murgatroyd, S. (2007). Accountability project framework—Developing school based accountability. Unpublished Report. Edmonton: The Innovation Expedition Inc.

National Youth Survey. (2010). *KNT 2010.* Helsinki: 15/30 Research.

National Board of Education. (1999). *A framework for evaluating educational outcomes in Finland.* Helsinki: Author.

Newsweek. (1999, May 24). *The future is Finnish.* Retrieved from http://www.newsweek.com/1999/05/23/the-future-is-finnish.html

Newsweek. (2010, August 17). *The world's best countries.* Retrieved from http://www.newsweek.com/feature/2010/the-world-s-best-countries.html

Nichols, S. L., & Berliner, D. C. (2007). *Collateral damage: How high-stakes testing corrupts America's schools.* Cambridge, MA: Harvard Education Press.

Niemi, H. (2008). Research-based teacher education for teachers' lifelong learning. *Lifelong Learning in Europe, 13*(1), 61–69.

Nuikkinen, K. (2011). Learning spaces: How they meet evolving educational needs. In M. Kasvio(Ed.), *The best school in the world: Seven Finnish examples from the 21st century* (pp. 10–19). Helsinki: Museum of Finnish Architecture.

OECD. (2001). *Knowledge and skills for life: First results from PISA 2000.* Paris: Author.

OECD. (2004). *Learning for tomorrow's world. First results from PISA 2003.* Paris: Author

OECD. (2005a). *Equity in education. Thematic review of Finland.* Paris: Author.

OECD. (2005b). *Teachers matter: Attracting, developing and retaining effective teachers.* Paris: Author.

OECD. (2007). *PISA 2006. Science competencies for tomorrow's world* (Vol. 1). Paris: Author.

OECD. (2008). *Trends shaping education.* Paris: Author.

OECD. (2010a). *Education at a glance. Education indicators.* Paris: Author.

OECD. (2010b). *PISA 2009 results: What students know and can do. Student performance in reading, mathematics and science. Vol. 1.* Paris: Author.

OECD. (2010c). *Strong performers and successful reformers in education. Lessons from PISA for the United States.* Paris: Author.

Ofsted (Office for Standards in Education, Children's Services and Skills) (2010). *Finnish pupils' success in mathematics. Factors that contribute to Finnish pupils' success in mathematics.* Manchester: Author.

O'Neill, O. (2002). *A question of trust.* Cambridge: Cambridge University Press.

Pechar, H. (2007). "The Bologna Process": A European Response to Global Competition in Higher Education. *Canadian Journal of Higher Education, 37*(3), 109–125.

Piesanen, E., Kiviniemi, U., & Valkonen, S. (2007). *Opettajankoulutuksen kehittämisohjelman seuranta ja arviointi. Opettajien täydennyskoulutus 2005 ja seuranta 1998–2005 oppiaineittain ja oppialoittain eri oppilaitosmuodoissa* [Follow-up and evaluation of the teacher education development program: Continuing teacher education in 2005 and its follow-up 1998–2005 by fields and teaching subjects in different types of educational institutions]. Jyväskylä: University of Jyväskylä, Institute for Educational Research.

Popham, J. (2007). The no-win accountability game. In C. Glickman (Ed.), *Letters to the next president. What we can do about the real crisis in public education* (pp. 166–173). New York: Teachers College Press.

Prais, S. J. (2003). Cautions on OECD's recent educational survey (PISA). *Oxford Review of Education, 29*(2), 139–163.

Prais, S. J. (2004). Cautions on OECD's recent educational survey (PISA): Rejoinder to OECD's response. *Oxford Review of Education, 30*(4), 569–573.

Ravitch, D. (2010a, June 22). Obama's awful education plan. *Huffington Post.* Retreived from http://www.huffingtonpost.com/diane-ravitch/obamas-awful-education-pl_b_266412.html

Ravitch, D. (2010b, July 6). *Speech to the Representative Assembly of the National Education Association, New Orleans, LA.*

Ravitch, D. (2010c). *The death and life of the great American school system. How testing and choice are undermining education.* New York: Basic Books.

Riley, K., & Torrance, H. (2003). Big change question: As national policy-makers seek to find solutions to national education issues, do international comparisons such as TIMSS and PISA create a wider understanding, or do they serve to promote the orthodoxies of international agencies? *Journal of Educational Change, 4*(4), 419–425.

Rinne, R., Kivirauma, J., & Simola, H. (2002). Shoots of revisionist education policy or just slow readjustment? *Journal of Education Policy, 17*(6), 643-659.

Robinson, K. (with Aronica, L). (2009). *The Element: How finding your passion changes everything.* New York: Viking Books.

Robitaille, D. F., & Garden, R. A. (Eds.). (1989). *The IEA study of mathematics II: Context and outcomes of school mathematics.* Oxford: Pergamon Press.

Routti, J., & Ylä-Anttila, P. (2006). *Finland as a knowledge economy. Elements of success and lessons learned.* Washington, DC: World Bank.

Saari, J. (2006). Suomen mallin institutionaalinen rakenne [The institutional structure of the Finnish model]. In J. Saari (Ed.), *Suomen malli—Murroksesta menestykseen?* [The Finnish model—From reformation to success]. Helsinki: Yliopistopaino.

Saari, S., & Frimodig, M. (Eds.). (2009). Leadership and management of education. Evaluation of education at the University of Helsinki 2007–2008. *Administrative Publications 58.* Helsinki: University of Helsinki.

Sahlberg, P. (2006a). Education reform for raising economic competitiveness. *Journal of Educational Change, 7*(4), 259–287.

Sahlberg, P. (2006b). Raising the bar: How Finland responds to the twin challenge of secondary education? *Profesorado, 10*(1), 1–26.

Sahlberg, P. (2007). Education policies for raising student learning: The Finnish approach. *Journal of Education Policy, 22*(2), 173–197.

Sahlberg, P. (2009). Ideat, innovaatiot ja investoinnit koulun kehittämisessä [Ideas, innovation and investment in school improvement]. In M. Suortamo, H., Laaksola, & J. Välijärvi (Eds.), *Opettajan vuosi 2009–2010* (pp. 13–56). [Teacher's year 2009–2010]. Jyväskylä: PS-kustannus.

Sahlberg, P. (2010a). Rethinking accountability for a knowledge society. *Journal of Educational Change. 11*(1), 45–61.

Sahlberg, P. (2010b). Educational change in Finland. In A. Hargreaves, A. Lieberman, M. Fullan, & D. Hopkins (Eds.), *Second international handbook of educational change* (pp. 323–348). New York: Springer.

Sahlberg, P. (2011a) The fourth way of Finland. *Journal of Educational Change, 12*(2), 173–185.

Sahlberg, P. (2011b). Becoming a teacher in Finland: Traditions, reforms and policies. In A. Lieberman & L. Darling-Hammond (Eds.), *High quality teaching and learning: International perspectives on teacher.* New York: Routledge.

Sarason, S. (1996). *Revisiting "the culture of the school and the problem of change."* New York: Teachers College Press.

Schleicher, A. (2006). *The economics of knowledge: Why education is key for Europe's success.* Brussels: The Lisbon Council.

Schleicher, A. (2007). Can competencies assessed by PISA be considered the fundamental school knowledge 15-year-olds should possess? *Journal of Educational Change, 8*(4), 349–357.

Schulz, W., Ainley, J., Fraillon, J., Kerr, D., & Losito, B. (2010). *ICCS 2009 International Report: Civic knowledge, attitudes and engagement among lower secondary school students in thirty-eight countries.* Amsterdam: IEA.

Seddon, J. (2008). *Systems thinking in the public sector: The failure of the reform regime...and a manifesto for a better way.* Axminster, UK: Triarchy Press.

Simola, H. (2005). The Finnish miracle of PISA: Historical and sociological remarks on teaching and teacher education. *Comparative Education, 41*(4), 455–470.

Ståhle, P., & Wilenius, M. (2006). *Luova tietopääoma: Tulevaisuuden kestävä kilpailuetu* [Creative intellectual capital: Sustainable competitive advantage of the future], Helsinki: Edita.

Ståhle, P. (Ed.). (2007). *Five steps for Finland's future.* Helsinki: TEKES.

Statistics Finland. (n.d.a). *Education.* Retrieved from http://www.stat.fi/til/kou_en.html

Statistics Finland. (n.d.b). *Research and development.* Retrieved from http://www.stat.fi/til/tkke/index_en.html

Statistics Finland. (n.d.c). *Income and consumption.* Retrieved from http://www.stat.fi/til/tul_en.html

Statistics Finland. (2011). *Population structure.* Retrieved from http://www.stat.fi/til/vaerak/2010/vaerak_2010_2011-03-18_tie_001_en.html

Steinbock, D. (2010). *Winning across global markets: How Nokia creates advantage in a fast-changing world*. New York: Jossey-Bass.

Toom, A., Kynäslahti, H., Krokfors, L., Jyrhämä, R., Byman, R., Stenberg, K., Maaranen, K., & Kansanen, P. (2010). Experiences of research-based approach to teacher education: Suggestion for the future policies. *European Journal of Education, 45*(2), 331–344.

UNDP. (2007). *Human development report*. New York: Oxford University Press.

UNICEF. (2007). *Child poverty in perspective: An overview of child well-being in rich countries*. Florence: Innocenti Research Centre Report Card 2007.

Usher, A. & Medow, J. (2010). *Global higher education rankings 2010*. Affordability and accessibility in comparative perspective. Toronto: Higher Education Strategy Associates.

Välijärvi, J. (2004). Implications of the modular curriculum in the secondary school in Finland. In J. van den Akker, W. Kuiper, & U. Hameyer (Eds.), *Curriculum landscapes and trends* (pp. 101–116). Dordrecht: Kluwer.

Välijärvi, J. (2008). Miten hyvinvointi taataan tulevaisuudessakin? [How to guarantee welfare also in future?]. In M. Suortamo, H., Laaksola, & J. Välijärvi (Eds.), *Opettajan vuosi 2008–2009* [Teacher's year 2008–2009] (pp. 55–64). Jyväskylä: PS-kustannus.

Välijärvi, J., Kupari, P., Linnakylä, P., Reinikainen, P., Sulkunen, S., Törnroos, J., & Arffman, I. (2007). *Finnish success in PISA and some reasons behind it II*. Jyväskylä: University of Jyväskylä.

Välijärvi, J., Linnakylä, P., Kupari, P., Reinikainen, P., & Arffman, I. (2002). *Finnish success in PISA and some reasons behind it*. Jyväskylä: Institute for Educational Research, University of Jyväskylä.

Välijärvi, J., & Sahlberg, P. (2008). Should "failing" students repeat a grade? A retrospective response from Finland. *Journal of Educational Change, 9*(4), 385–389.

Voutilainen, T., Mehtäläinen, J., & Niiniluoto, I. (1989). *Tiedonkäsitys* [Conception of knowledge]. Helsinki: Kouluhallitus.

Westbury, I., Hansen, S-E., Kansanen, P., & Björkvist, O. (2005). Teacher education for research-based practice in expanded roles: Finland's experience. *Scandinavian Journal of Educational Research, 49*(5), 475–485.

Wilkinson, R., & Pickett, K. (2009). *The spirit level. Why more equal societies almost always do better*. New York: Allen Lane.

World Bank. (2011). Learning for All: Investing in people's knowledge and skills to promote development. Washington, DC: World Bank.

Zhao, Y. (2009). *Catching up or leading the way: American education in the age of globalization*. Alexandria, VA: ASCD.

Index

An *f* or *t* after a page number indicates a figure or table, respectively.

9-year compulsory school. *See Peruskoulu*

Ability grouping, 22
"About Possibilities of School Change," 34
Academic rigor of teacher education, 77
Accountability
   based on standardized tests, 65–66, 101, 103t
   and competition, 144
   focus on, 100
   in teaching and learning, 130
Achievement gap, historical, 45–46, 46f
Act of Basic Education, 117
Act on General Upper-Secondary Education, 25
Acts on Teacher Education, 78
Adams, R. J., 56
Adult educational attainment, 43–44, 44f
Agrarian Centre Party, 16
Agrarian Party, 24
Aho, Erkki, 15, 16, 21, 24, 29, 33, 122, 147
Ahtisaari, Martti, 1, 71
Ainley, J., 54, 54t
Aksela, M., 81, 83
Alasuutari, P., 147
Alberta Education Accountability Department, 67
Alberta Initiative for School Improvement (AISI), 36
Albertan Provincial Assembly, 67
Allerup, P., 42
Alquézar Sabadie, J., 107
Amrein, A. L., 39, 67
Aquarium Project, 36–37
Architecture of school buildings, 128

Arffman, I., 23, 51, 126, 128
Asplund, R., 107
Assessment
   in class, 66
   comprehensive evaluation of student progress, 66
   external, 67
   international rankings, 49–57, 50t
   methods of, 34, 130
   National Matriculation Examination, 25, 31–32, 89–90
   as responsibility of teacher, 89
   voluntary testing, 67
Association for Supervision and Curriculum Development (ASCD), 34
Atjonen, P., 35
Au, W., 67, 101
Auguste, B., 147
Aurora School (Espoo), 119
Automatic promotion, 60

Baker, E., 92
Barber, M., 9, 132, 147
Barton, P., 92
Bautier, E., 56
Berliner, D. C., 35, 39, 67, 128, 133
Berry, J., 26
Biddle, B. J., 128
Big Dream, 139–140
Björkvist, O., 79, 129
Bologna Process, 80, 93
Bracey, G., 56
Brophy, J., 58
Byman, R., 129

Campbell, E., 21
Capacity-building, xvii
Career guidance for students, 23
Carnoy, M., 112
Castells, M., 12, 105
Chijioke, C., 9
Chrostowski, S. J., 49
Civic education performance, 54
Civic knowledge, 54
Civic schools, 15
Classroom-based teaching, 141
Cohen, Elizabeth, 34
Coherence of economic and social reforms, 109, 110/111t
Coleman, J., 21
Coleman Report, 21
Collaboration for educational reform, 35–36
Commitment to basic school for all, 6
Committee Report (Ministry of Education), 30
Common educational goal, 6
Communist Party, 16
Complementarity principle, 98, 136
Completion of upper-secondary and higher education, 29–30, 30t
Comprehensive basic school. See Peruskoulu
Comprehensive evaluation of student progress, 66
Comprehensive School Curriculum Committee, 17
Comprehensive School Reform, 35–36
Conception of knowledge, 33, 35
"Conception of Knowledge," 34
Conception of learning, 33, 35
"Conception of Learning," 34
Conservative Party, 17
Core educational values, 19, 21
Core-subject focus, 100–101, 103t
Cost of education, 57–60
Country Brand Delegation, 10, 124
Creativity as criterion for success, 143
Credit system of teacher education programs, 80–81, 81t
Crocker, R., 36

Cultural and ethnic homogeneity, 8, 68
Cultural characteristics of Finns, 61
Culture of the School and the Problem of Change, The, 144
Curriculum for teacher education, 80–83, 81t, 82t
Curriculum for the comprehensive school frameworks, 22, 81, 88, 118, 128, 138
planning, 88–89
reform, 35
Customized learning plans, 141
Cygnaeus, Pastor Uno, 117

Darling-Hammond, L., 2, 35, 85, 92, 132
Davis, B., 36
Department of Education, 9
Development of public institutions, 109
Development of teaching profession, 7
Development Plan for Education and Research for 2007–2012, 134, 138
Dewey, John, 144
Differentiated syllabi, 22
Digital tools, 141–142
Diversification, 69
Diversification of society, 68–69, 68t
Dohn, N. B., 56
Dominant themes in national education policy after WWII, 16
"Drivers of change," 102
Dropout, 30

Earl, L., 99
Early childhood services, 48
Early intervention for special needs, 46–48, 48f
Early literacy, 128
Economic conditions following WWII, 15, 16
Economic progress, 114–115
Economic reform, contributing factors, 115–116
Educated labor force, 116
Educational attainment, 28–30, 28f, 30t, 43–44, 44f
Educational objectives focus, 17
Educational participation, 43–45, 44f

Educational policies that transcend culture, 6
Educational reform in Anglo-American
  cultures, xix–xx
Educational reform in Finland
  collaboration and networking, 35–36
  contributing factors, 115–116
  general, 24
  key elements, 103t
  phases of change, 32–33, 33f
  post-WWII, 17–21, 20
  principles since 1970, 110/111t
Education for all notion, 100
Education Reform Act of 1988 (England),
  65, 122
Education scheme in Finland, 40f
Education Sector Productivity Program for
  2006–2010, 138
Education spending relation to student
  performance, 57, 58f
Education System Committee, 17–18
Education system performance link to
  welfare state, 112–118
Efficiency in education, 38
Engagement as criterion for success,
  142–143
Engagement between Nokia and Finnish
  schooling, 118–121
Equal opportunity principle, 21, 23, 68,
  128–129
Equity in education, 45–49
Ethnic and cultural homogeneity, 8
European Commission, 86
European Credit Transfer and
  Accumulation System (ECTS), 80
European Higher Education Area, 80
European Union, 7, 106, 108, 109–112,
  110/111t
Expansion of upper-secondary education,
  25–27
External assessment, 67

Ferdinand, Reinhold, 117
Fink, D., 39, 98, 109
Finnish banking crisis, 106
Finnish Business and Policy Forum (EVA),
  121

Finnish Consensus, 24
Finnish Dream, 6
Finnish Folk School, 24, 117
Finnish Primary School Teachers'
  Association (FPSTA), 20
Finnish School Principals, 122
Finnish spirit, 108
Finnish Way, 7, 103t, 105–106, 109, 121,
  144
First International Mathematics Study
  (FIMS), 49, 50t
First International Science Study (FISS),
  50t
Flat World and Education, The, 2
Fourth Way, The, xviii, 2, 5, 102, 105–106
FPSTA, 20
Fraillon, J., 54, 54t
*Framework for Evaluating Educational
  Outcomes in Finland,* 126
Frimodig, M., 85
Fullan, M., xi, 8, 35, 102
"Future Is Finnish, The," 134
Future of Finnish education, 136, 138,
  140–145

Gameran, E., 65
Garden, R. A., 49
Gardner, Howard, 9
GERM. *See* Global Educational Reform
  Movement (GERM)
German model of education, 117
Global Competitiveness Index, 114
Global Educational Reform Movement
  (GERM), 99–106, 103t, 124
  versus Finnish approach, 102, 103t,
  104–105
Global Higher Education Rankings, 49
Globalization and education, 97–99
Global student learning and PISA, 49–57
Global system for mobile communications
  (GSM), 117
Goldstein, H., 56
Gonzales, E. J., 49
Good governance, 115
Goodson, I., 98
Grade repetition, 58–60

Grammar School Teachers' Union, 18
Gregory, K. D., 49
Grek, S., 9
Grubb, N., 46, 60, 132, 148

Haertel, E., 92
Häivälä, K., 148
Halasz, G., 92, 126, 131, 132, 148
Halinen, I., 35
Hämäläinen, S., 35
Hansen, S-E., 79, 129
Hargreaves, A., xviii, 2, 5, 34, 35, 36, 39, 65, 92, 98, 99, 100, 102, 105, 106, 109, 126, 131, 132, 148
Harjunen, E., 51, 69, 126
Hautamäki, A., 51, 69, 126
Hautamäki, J., 51, 69, 126
Hellström, M., 36, 119, 147
Hellström, Martti (school principal), 119
Helsinki and immigrant students, 68, 69
High academic requirement for teaching, 129
Higher Education Strategy Associates (Toronto), 49
High regard for teachers, 72–73
Himanen, P., 12, 105
Himanen, Pekka, 139
Hirvi, Vilho, 2, 130
Hobson, C., 21
Homework, 65
Homogeneity factor, 8
Human Development Index (HDI), 54

Immigration to Finland, 68t
Income gap, 139f
Income inequality and student learning, 113–114, 113f
Individualized learning plan, 141
Individual's potential for growth notion, 21
Induction of a new teacher, 86
Inequality in education, 138
Information society, 107–108
Instructional methods, 23
Instruction hours, Finland, 62–65, 63f, 64f, 76, 91f
Instruction hours, international, 90–91, 91f
Integration in policy development, 115

Interdependency among public sector policies, 109
International Civic and Citizenship Education Study (ICCS), 50t, 52, 54
International Educational Assessment (IEA), 49, 50t
International Mathematical Olympiad, 43t
International math rankings, 51, 65, 66f
International Olympiads, 42–43, 43t
International science rankings, 51
International spending on education, 57
Interpersonal skills, 141–142
Itkonen, T., 48

Jahnukainen, M., 48
Jakku-Sihvonen, R., 51, 69, 78, 148
Jennings, J., 101
Jimerson, S., 58
Johansen, J., 107
Johns Hopkins University, 34
Johnson, David, 34
Johnson, Peter, 137
Johnson, Peter (director of education), 137
Johnson, Roger, 34
Jokinen, H., 86
Journal of Educational Change, 98
Joyce, B., 35
Jussila, J., 85
Jyrhämä, R., 129
Jyväskylä, Finland, 117

Kangasniemi, S., 73
Kansanen, P., 79, 129
Karjalainen, T., 51, 69
Kasvio, M., 126
Kaufmann, S., 133
Kekkonen, Urho, 24
Kerr, D., 54, 54t
Ket De Vries, M., xvii
Kettunen, Pauli, 24
Kihn, P., 147, 148
Kinnunen, R., 34
Kiuasmaa, K., 15
Kivi, A., 13, 70
Kiviniemi, U., 87
Kivirauma, J., 131
Knowledge-based economy, 106–112

Knubb-Manninen, G., 35
Kokkola, City of, 137
Korkeakoski, E., 35
Koskenniemi, Matti, 16, 17, 74
Krokfors, L., 81, 83, 129
Krzywacki-Vainio, H., 81, 83
Kumpulainen, T., 87
Kupari, P., 23, 27, 35, 49, 51, 64, 126, 128, 130
Kupiainen, S., 51, 69
Kuusi, Pekka, 21
Kynäslahti, H., 129

Laaksonen, S., 51, 69
Ladd, H., 92
Languages of Finland, 8
Laukkanen, R., 125
Lavonen, J., 81, 83
Law on Education, 126
Learning results, 37
Legatum, 114
Lehtinen, Erno, 34, 35
Length of school day, 63–64
Levin, B., 101
Lewis, R., 61, 112, 130
Liiten, M., 72
Linn, R., 92
Linnakylä, P., 23, 51, 123, 126, 128
Long-term vision, 115
Losito, B., 54, 54t

Maaranen, K., 129
MacKinnon, N., 104
Maliranta, M., 107
Manning, M., 99
Market-oriented reform ideas, 101, 103t
Martin, M. O., 49
Master's degree requirement for teaching, 78, 129
Master's thesis, 80, 81
Mathematics Olympiad, 42–43, 43t
Mathematics performance of Finns on PISA study, 56f
Mathematics performance on PISA study, 51
Mathematics teaching, 51
Matriculation Examination, 25, 31–32, 89–90

Matti, T., 126
McEwen, L., 36
McKinsey and Company, 9
McKinsey report, 132
McPartland, J., 21
Medjing, J., 42
Medow, J., 49
Mehtäläinen, J., 34
Miettinen, R., 34
Miller, M., 147
Ministry of Education, 26, 30t, 31, 73, 79, 81, 86, 87, 118
Ministry of Education report on professional development, 87
Ministry of Foreign Affairs, 10, 124, 134, 136
Models from the corporate world, 101, 103t
Mood, A., 21
Moore, S., 99
Mortimore, P., 56, 134
Mother Tongue test, 31
Mourshed, M., 9, 132, 147
Mullis, I. V. S., 49
Municipal field school (MFS), 85
Municipal oversight of schools, 11t, 86–88, 93, 126
Murgatroyd, S., 36

National Board of Education, 126
National Board of Education (Finland), 2, 17, 24, 31, 67, 81, 126
National Board of General Education, 19, 34–35
National Curriculum for the Comprehensive School, 22
National Curriculum Framework, 128, 138
National Curriculum Reform of 1994, 35
National Framework Curricula, 88
National Framework Curriculum for Comprehensive School, 81
National Framework for Science Curriculum, 118
National Matriculation Examination, 25, 31–32, 89–90
National Youth Survey, 73
Networking for educational reform, 35–36
New Club of Paris, 134

New Comprehensive School, 21
New global partnership, 139
Newsweek, 113t, 135
Nichols, S. L., 67, 133
Niemi, H., 78
Niemi, Hannele (professor of education), 84
Niiniluoto, I., 34
No Child Left Behind (United States), xvi, 132
Nokia, 2, 106–107, 116–118
Nonclass organizational system, 25
Nontraditional "classroom," 141
Nuikkinen, K., 128

OAJ, 78, 127
Obama, President Barack, xv, xvi
O'Connor, K. M., 49
OECD, xiv, 5, 7, 9, 29, 37, 38t, 44, 45, 46, 51, 55, 56t, 57, 62, 63, 63t, 64, 64t, 65, 66t, 77, 86, 97, 107, 113, 113t, 120, 129, 131, 132, 138, 147
Office for Standards in Education (Ofsted), 51, 132
Ofsted. *See* Office for Standards in Education (Ofsted)
Oikkonen, J., 81, 83
Oittinen, Reino Henrik, 18
Olkinuora, E., 34
Ollila, Jorma, 10, 118
O'Neil, O., 127
Opposition to *peruskoulu,* 121–123

"Paradoxes" of Finnish education, 62–69
Paronen, S., 96
PATs (Alberta), 67
Pechar, H., 148
Pedagogical conservatism, 112
Pedagogical leadership, 92
Performance in international student assessments, 49–57, 50t
Permanent special education, 47
Personal road map for learning, 140–141
Peruskoulu
    9-year structure, 19
    central idea, 21–22, 22f
    and Comprehensive School

Curriculum Committee, 17
    and Comprehensive School Reform, 35–36
    defining a new school system, 20
    and educational attainment, 27–29, 28f, 30t, 43–44
    elements, 23
    and Finnish economy and society, 2
    as Finnish icons, 117–118
    and grade repetition, 59–60
    opposition, 121–123
    and student performance, 128–130
    and value of equity, 59
Pickett, K., 113, 138
Piesanen, E., 87
PISA
    competition and test-based accountability, 65
    and equal educational opportunity, 37
    and Finland performance, 50t, 51–52, 54, 55, 56f, 120
    and "Finnish miracle," 37
    as global measure of student achievement, 51, 100
    global performance in math, 65, 66f
    global performance in science, 53f (2), 58f
    and global student learning, 49–57
    and immigrant students, 69
    impact on global education, 55
    implications for Finland, 135, 138
    income and science learning, 113
    as indicator of quality of education, 56
    limitations, 134
    and school variance, 45–46, 46f
    and socioeconomic status, 38f
    and student anxiety, 26, 64
Pitkänen, K., 15, 16, 21, 29, 122, 147
Political stability of education system, 131
Pont, B., 92, 126, 131, 132, 148
Popham, J., 67, 100
Popularity of teaching as profession, 73
Poskiparta, E., 34
Post-WWII Finland, 14–17
Poverty and education, 69
Practicum experiences, 83–86
Prais, S. J., 56

Preschool services, 48
Prescribed curriculum, 101, 103t
Primary School Curriculum Committee, 17
Principles of improving learning, 126–127
Professional autonomy of teachers, 76
Professionalism in teaching, 76
Professional learning community (PLC), 76
Professional teacher development, 86–88
Programme for International Student
    Assessment (PISA). *See* PISA
Progress in International Reading Literacy
    Study (PIRLS), 9, 50t
Provincial achievement tests (PATs;
    Alberta), 67
Public financing of education, 44–45
Public institutions, central role of, 115–116
Public school system, origin of, 117
Public sector policies in Finland, 110/111t

Race to the Top, xv
Ravitch, D., xvi, 99, 132
Rayon, P., 56
Reading literacy performance, PISA scale,
    56f
Reading Literacy Study, 50t, 51
Reading performance and socioeconomic
    status, 38t
Reinikainen, P., 23, 51, 126, 128
Relevance of Finland as model for
    education, 8–9
Report cards, 66–67
Research-based teacher education, 78,
    83–85, 94
Responsibilities of teachers outside the
    classroom, 90
Retention. *See* Grade repetition
Riley, K., 56
Rinne, R., 131
Robinson, K., 140
Robitaille, D. F., 49
Routti, J., 12, 15, 105, 106, 107
Ruutu, Director General Yrjö, 17

Saari, H., 123
Saari, J., 12, 105
Saari, S., 85

Saarikko, H., 81, 83
Sahlberg, Carl Reinhold, 117
Sahlberg, P., xix, 15, 16, 21, 23, 26, 29, 30, 32,
    36, 37, 43, 49, 57, 58, 60, 71, 75, 76, 79t,
    91t, 99, 102, 107, 122, 126, 147, 148
Salonen, P., 34
Salonen, Veera (teacher-education
    student), 74
Sarason, S., 144
Schleicher, A., 7, 40, 56, 127, 148
School 2.0, 139
*School Effectiveness and School
    Improvement,* 98
School principal qualifications, 92–93
School Program Committee, 18–19
School-related stress, 64–65
Schools White Paper (England), 9
Schulz, W., 54, 54t
Science education, 52
Science performance, PISA scale, 56f
Second International Mathematics Study
    (SIMS), 49
Second International Science Study (SISS),
    50t, 51
Seddon, J., 148
Self-regulation of schools, 36
Seven Brothers, 13, 70, 132
Sharan, Shlomo, 34
Sharan, Yael, 34
Shepard, L., 92
Shifting focus of educational reform, 99
Shirley, D., xviii, 2, 5, 34, 36, 65, 99, 102,
    105, 106
Simola, H., 112, 126, 131
Sisu, 108
Size factor, 8–9
Slavin, Robert, 34
Smith, T. A., 49
Social Democratic Party, 16
Social inequality, 138
Social media, 141–142
Social policies link to education system
    performance, 112–116
Social values, 132
Soviet Union, peace treaty with, 14
Soviet Union collapse, 2, 106, 108

Special characteristics of Finland, 8, 10
Special education
　　as category of teaching, 71–72
　　as component of teacher education, 82t
　　and comprehensive school reform, 23
　　enrollment numbers, 47–48, 48f
　　and grade repetition, 60
　　pathways, 47
　　philosophy, 46–47
Spirit Level, The, 113
Ståhle, P., 136, 143
Standardization of teaching and learning,
　　100, 103t
Standardized testing, 65–66, 67
Stanford University, 34
Stark Rentner, D., 101
"State-generated social capital," 112
Statistics Finland, 8, 44, 107
Steinbock, D., 120
Stenberg, K., 129
Stora Enso, 107
Structure of education system, 20f, 21, 22f
Student assessment. *See* Assessment
Student learning and PISA rankings,
　　49–57
Student performance
　　academic domains, PISA results, 37
　　civic knowledge scores, 54, 54f
　　in core subjects (Finland), 56f
　　and education spending relationship,
　　　　57, 58f
　　and instruction hours relationship,
　　　　62–63, 63f, 64f
　　in mathematics, 42–43, 43t, 66f
　　ranking in international assessment
　　　　studies (Finland), 50t
　　in reading, 38f, 46f
　　in science, international, 53t (2), 113f
Study of Reading Comprehension, 50t
Sulkunen, S., 51, 126
Sumara, D., 36
Sustainable leadership policies and
　　practices, 39
Sustained educational leadership, 131
Sweden as model, 6

Teacher education
　　academic rigor, 78–80
　　annual application to programs, 75f
　　collaboration between subject faculties
　　　　and school of education, 94
　　competition for access to, 74–75, 75f
　　credit system of programs, 80–81, 81t
　　curriculum, 80–83, 81t, 82t
　　peculiarities of system, 93–95
　　primary-teacher programs, 81–82, 81t
　　programs, 51, 52
　　requirements by type of school, 79t
　　subject-teacher programs, 82–83, 82t
　　traditional teacher preparation, 71
　　training schools, 83–86
Teachers' roles
　　assess students, 66, 89
　　nonteaching responsibilities, 63–64
　　as researchers, 83–86
　　as transmitters of culture, 72
Teach First, 79
Teach for America, 79
Teaching hours. *See* Instruction hours,
　　Finland; Instruction hours,
　　international
Teaching profession
　　attraction of top talent, 76–77, 93–94
　　categories within teaching, 71–72
　　development of, 7
　　effectiveness of teacher, 90–92
　　reflection, 91
　　regard for, 72–73, 129
　　salaries, 77
Technology tools, 141–142
Tel Aviv University, 34
Test-based accountability, 65–66
Thesis requirement for teaching, 78
Third International Mathematics and
　　Science Study, 51
Third Sector, 63
"Third Way" of educational reform,
　　xvii–xviii, 105
TIMSS, 49, 50t
Toom, A., 129
Törnroos, J., 51, 126

Torrance, H., 56
Trade Union of Education in Finland
    (OAJ), 78, 127
Traditional model of education, 15–16, 112
Traditional teacher preparation, 71
Traditional views on education, 71
Transferability of Finnish model, 133
Transition from *peruskoulu* to upper-
    secondary education, 27–28, 28f
Trends in International Mathematics and
    Science Study (TIMSS), 49, 50t
Trilingual nature of Finland, 8
Trust in schools, 130–131

U2, 124
UNDP (United Nations Development
    Report), 113, 113t
UNICEF, 69
UNICEF Innocenti Research Centre, 69
United Nations 2006 Human Development
    Report, 113
University of Helsinki, 31, 74, 75, 75f, 81,
    82, 82t, 84
University of Jyväskylä, 81, 81t, 87
University of Minnesota, 34
University of Oulu, 85
Usher, A., 49

Välijärvi, J., 23, 24, 27, 30, 37, 49, 51, 58, 60,

    64, 86, 126, 127–128, 130
Valkonen, S., 87
Value-added modeling (VAM), 91–92
Vauras, M., 34
Vocational education, 25–26, 30, 31, 32
Voluntary testing, 67
Voutilainen, T., 34

Wall Street Journal, 65
Weil, M., 35
Weinfeld, F., 21
Welfare services, 48
Welfare state link to education system
    performance, 112–118
Westbury, I., 79, 129
Wikman, T., 35
Wilenius, M., 143
Wilkinson, R., 113, 138
Winning Across Global Markets, 120
World Bank, 9
World Bank Education Strategy 2020, 9
World Economic Forum (WEF), 107, 114
Written Composition Study, 50t
"Wrong drivers," 102

Ylä-Anttila, P., 12, 15, 105, 106, 107
York, R., 21

Zhao, Yong, xvi

About the Author

Pasi Sahlberg, PhD, is currently director general of CIMO (Centre for International Mobility and Cooperation) at the Finnish Ministry of Education and Culture and a member of the board of directors of the ASCD (Association for Supervision and Curriculum Development) in the United States. He has worked as a teacher, teacher educator, and policy maker in Finland and as an expert for several international organizations and consulting firms. During the last 2 decades he has analyzed education reforms around the world and worked with education leaders in the United States, Canada, Europe, the Middle East, Africa, and Asia. Dr. Sahlberg was a former staff member of the World Bank in Washington, DC, and the European Commission in Turin, Italy. He continues to train teachers and leaders and to coach schools in Finland and abroad. He is adjunct professor at the University of Helsinki and at the University of Oulu. For more information and updates on this book, please visit www.pasisahlberg.com.